ELEMENTARY DANCE EDUCATION

Nature-Themed Creative Movement and Collaborative Learning

JANICE POMER

LIBRARY OF
CONGRESS
SURPLUS
DUPLICATE

HUMAN KINETICS

Library of Congress Cataloging-in-Publication Data

Names: Pomer, Janice, 1955- author.
Title: Elementary dance education : nature-themed creative movement and
  collaborative learning / Janice Pomer.
Description: Champaign, IL : Human Kinetics, [2023]
Identifiers: LCCN 2022015671 (print) | LCCN 2022015672 (ebook) | ISBN
  9781718202955 (paperback) | ISBN 9781718202962 (epub) | ISBN
  9781718202979 (pdf)
Subjects: LCSH: Dance--Study and teaching (Elementary) | Movement,
  Psychology of. | Dance--Research. | Group work in education.
Classification: LCC GV1799 .P66 2023 (print) | LCC GV1799 (ebook) | DDC
  792.8083/4--dc23
LC record available at https://lccn.loc.gov/2022015671
LC ebook record available at https://lccn.loc.gov/2022015672

ISBN: 978-1-7182-0295-5 (print)

Copyright © 2023 by Janice Pomer

Human Kinetics supports copyright. Copyright fuels scientific and artistic endeavor, encourages authors to create new works, and promotes free speech. Thank you for buying an authorized edition of this work and for complying with copyright laws by not reproducing, scanning, or distributing any part of it in any form without written permission from the publisher. You are supporting authors and allowing Human Kinetics to continue to publish works that increase the knowledge, enhance the performance, and improve the lives of people all over the world.

Notwithstanding the above notice, permission to reproduce the following material is granted to persons and agencies who have purchased this work: table 0.1, figure 1.1, figure 1.2.

The online learning content that accompanies this product is delivered on HK*Propel*, HKPropel.HumanKinetics.com. You agree that you will not use HK*Propel* if you do not accept the site's Privacy Policy and Terms and Conditions, which detail approved uses of the online content.

To report suspected copyright infringement of content published by Human Kinetics, contact us at **permissions@hkusa.com**. To request permission to legally reuse content published by Human Kinetics, please refer to the information at **https://US.HumanKinetics.com/pages/permissions-information**.

The web addresses cited in this text were current as of May 2022, unless otherwise noted.

Acquisitions Editor: Bethany J. Bentley; **Managing Editor:** Anne E. Mrozek; **Copyeditor:** Michelle Horn; **Permissions Manager:** Laurel Mitchell; **Graphic Designer:** Denise Lowry; **Cover Designer:** Keri Evans; **Cover Design Specialist**: Susan Rothermel Allen; **Photograph (cover):** Barry Prophet; **Photographs (interior):** School photograph credit: Janice Pomer / Studio photograph credit: Barry Prophet, as noted.; **Photo Production Manager:** Jason Allen; **Senior Art Manager:** Kelly Hendren; **Illustrations:** © Human Kinetics; **Printer:** Versa Press

Printed in the United States of America   10 9 8 7 6 5 4 3 2 1

The paper in this book is certified under a sustainable forestry program.

Human Kinetics
1607 N. Market Street
Champaign, IL 61820
USA

United States and International
Website: **US.HumanKinetics.com**
Email: info@hkusa.com
Phone: 1-800-747-4457

Canada
Website: **Canada.HumanKinetics.com**
Email: info@hkcanada.com

E8278

Tell us what you think!
Human Kinetics would love to hear what we
can do to improve the customer experience.
Use this QR code to take our brief survey.

Contents

Preface   vii

Acknowledgments   xi

Getting Ready to Teach   xiii

Chapter 1   Basic Elements of Dance   1

The first chapter contains five foundation exercises that have a series of pedagogic variations to deepen students' understanding of the basic elements of dance. Because many of you are working with novice movers, it's important that you introduce these exercises to your students before moving on to the other exercises in this book. The sixth exercise, Collective Observation, reinforces the importance of discussion and shared observations introduced in the five fundamental exercises. This exercise expands students' observation skills and strengthens trust between fellow students. The process will support students throughout their artistic journey and can be applied to subjects across the curriculum.

Exercise 1.1 Exploring Shapes   4

Exercise 1.2 Exploring Motion   12

Exercise 1.3 Exploring Time   18

Exercise 1.4 Exploring Space   25

Exercise 1.5 Exploring Energy   35

Exercise 1.6 Collective Observation   39

Chapter 2   Plants   43

The second chapter explores a variety of growing things that have, or will have, roots. Differing shapes, textures, and environments played a part in the selection of this grouping. On-the-spot movement dynamics will be the common denominator for much of the choreography. Each plant (or seed) has unique characteristics that can inspire dynamic movement phrases and choreography.

Exercise 2.1 Trees   44

Exercise 2.2 Flowers   51

Exercise 2.3 Vines   57

Exercise 2.4 Tall Grasses   67

Exercise 2.5 The Three Sisters   72

Chapter 3   Animals   79

Each animal-inspired exercise begins with a simple 16-beat foundation dance based on actions associated with an animal in a specific animal grouping. The foundation dance is used to explore some of the animals' behavioral traits. Students are then encouraged to create their own dances inspired by other animals within the specific group. For example, the exercise Horns, Antlers, Hooves, and Herds presents a foundation dance inspired by caribou migration and later invites students to create dances inspired by buffalo and musk ox as well as gazelles and antelope.

Exercise 3.1 Birds of a Feather   82

Exercise 3.2 Wildcats   87

Exercise 3.3 Horns, Antlers, Hooves, and Herds   92

Exercise 3.4 Reptiles with Scales and Shells   97

Exercise 3.5 Spiders and Insects   103

Exercise 3.6 Rodents   108

Exercise 3.7 Animal Anthology
(Kindergarten Through Grade 3)   112

Exercise 3.8 Endangered Species (Grades 4 Through 6)   113

Chapter 4   Water   117

We are all bodies of water. When we are born, our bodies contain 75 percent water, which is almost the same percentage of water that covers the earth. Water is in the ground, in the air, and in the food we eat. The movement exercises in this chapter examine some of the many ways water moves and influences us: its cycles and currents and its life-giving and destructive forces. Each of the exercises in this chapter can be extended into in-depth choreographic pieces for novice and experienced movers.

Exercise 4.1 Water Words   118

Exercise 4.2 Waves   127

Exercise 4.3 Frost and Snow   134

Exercise 4.4 Rain   143

Exercise 4.5 Water Cycle   150

Exercise 4.6 Drought   155

Exercise 4.7 Water Pollution (Grades 4 Through 6)   159

Exercise 4.8 Wetland Habitats   164

Chapter 5   Earth   169

The exercises in this chapter are based on surface textures and shapes, and underground earth forces that can be felt and seen. These movement explorations will draw students' attention to the ways our planet supports us, the way they travel upon it, and the internal pressures that continue to reshape it.

Exercise 5.1 Earth Words 170

Exercise 5.2 Terrains 178

Exercise 5.3 Rocks and Sand 184

Exercise 5.4 Tectonic Plates 189

Exercise 5.5 Volcanoes 196

Exercise 5.6 Mapping the Land 201

Chapter 6　Sky　　207

Human beings have been studying the sky since the dawn of mankind; winds and weather impact our daily lives, and the stars and night skies continue to inspire us to dream of other worlds. In this chapter, students will look to the skies from multiple perspectives: personal observations, scientific knowledge, and traditional folktales or origin stories created to explain eclipses and the distant planets.

Exercise 6.1 Clouds 208

Exercise 6.2 Thunder and Lightning 216

Exercise 6.3 Painting the Sky 223

Exercise 6.4 Sun and Moon 229

Exercise 6.5 Eclipses 236

Exercise 6.6 Gravitational Forces 240

Exercise 6.7 The Planets 244

Chapter 7　People　　249

Humans are mammals, and like mammals and other living things, humans travel, have families, build communities, and communicate. In this chapter, students will revisit some of the previous exercises and examine how they relate to humans, specifically how the actions of their families, friends, and communities are closely linked to the patterns that govern plants, animals, water, earth, and sky. Unlike previous exercises, in this chapter, there is minimal instruction to guide you. The first two exercises provide direction, but after that you and your class decide how to explore, structure, and create the dances.

People and Plants　　250

Exercise 7.1 Revisiting Maple Keys 251

Exercise 7.2 Revisiting the Three Sisters 254

People and Animals　　255

Exercise 7.3 Revisiting Teamwork 256

Exercise 7.4 Revisiting Herd Migrations 257

People and Water   258

Exercise 7.5 Revisiting Snow   259

Exercise 7.6 Revisiting the Water Cycle,
              Droughts, and Floods   260

People and Earth   261

Exercise 7.7 Revisiting Tectonic Plates   262

Exercise 7.8 Revisiting Volcanoes   263

People and Sky   264

Exercise 7.9 Revisiting the Moon   265

Exercise 7.10 Revisiting Our Planet   266

Chapter 8   Other Wonders   269

The world is filled with wonders. The final chapter contains a list of fascinating natural wonders to explore.

Plants   271

Cacti and the Desert Environment, Carnivorous Plants, Ferns, Mushrooms and Fungi

Animals   271

Flightless Birds; The Platypus, Jellyfish, and Other Unique Animals; Animal Metamorphosis; Animal Architects

Water   272

Tsunamis, Subterranean Rivers, Hurricanes and Typhoons, Icebergs

Earth   273

The Carbon Cycle, Earth's Core, Gemstones, Fossil Sites and Tar Pits

Sky   274

Comets, Constellations, Supernovas, Our Galaxy

About the Author   277

PREFACE

We live in a world filled with movement: our planet spins; the earth quakes; volcanoes erupt; water erodes, recedes, and evaporates; and seedlings scatter, settle, and grow. Human beings are part of this ever-changing world that is constantly in motion. Nature has always been an important part of children's development, through personal observations and interactions, at school, and in dance and movement education. This book provides teachers with the skills they need to weave students' personal, academic, and physical learning styles together to transform their classroom nature studies into a multidimensional learning experience that stimulates students' minds and activates their bodies using embodied and experiential learning techniques initiated by creative movement explorations.

For those unfamiliar with embodied and experiential learning practices, *embodied learning* recognizes that the mind and the body can, and in many instances *should*, learn together. Students are physically involved in the learning process, which activates sensory awareness and gives form to ideas learned. *Experiential learning* actively engages students' curiosity, problem-solving skills, and creativity by posing questions, exploring ideas, seeking answers, and giving meaning to that which is discovered. Creative movement is one of the most effective tools to introduce and develop both of those methodologies in the classroom, especially when using a teaching template of "observe," "explore," "create," "share," and "reflect." Once this creative movement template is established, it can be applied to all areas of the curriculum. It's an invaluable tool for student engagement, satisfying children's capacity to watch, wonder, move, interact, discover, and share, as demonstrated in the following example.

When a child creates a dance where he moves like a comet shooting through the sky, he's demonstrating several things:

- Locomotor skills such as running and leaping
- Choreographic skills by the selection of timings, levels, shapes, and traveling patterns or pathways
- Scientific knowledge of comets and the solar system
- A personal interpretation of how it might feel to be a comet flying through the sky
- The ability to focus and commit himself to the activity

Creative movement activities develop important physical skills and artistic expression, help hone students' creative and critical-thinking skills, and provide visible evidence of students' knowledge and experiences: stars gazed at, rocks lifted, books read, and subjects studied.

The Process of Inquiry and the Creative Process

Throughout history, artistic disciplines evolved through the process of observe, explore, create, present, share, and reflect. This is how that process is applied to dance:

- **Observe** aspects of one's inner and outer world, including physical, emotional, and current or imaginary events.

- **Explore** how the body can interpret, illuminate, or symbolize what is studied by using the basic elements of dance: level and direction changes, tempo and rhythmic shifts, gestural and geometric shapes, spatial relationships with others, degrees of energy and attack.

- **Create** and choreograph a dance or movement phrase to communicate, celebrate, or commemorate that which has been observed.

- **Present** the dance or movement creation to others in workshop settings, in theatrical presentations, or through film or video.

- **Reflect** upon the comments of those who viewed the presentation and evaluate the process; identify areas of success as well as aspects of the dance that may require revision.

This process is not unique to dance or the arts. Indeed, it has much in common with the scientific process of inquiry, which uses these steps:

- **Observe** a specific environment, object, or event (including macro- and microscopic realms).

- **Explore** and study what happens in that (or to that) environment, object, or event using numerical data, written accounts, and visual observations while it's in its natural state and when other stimuli are introduced.

- **Create** a theory or theories based on one's understanding of what has been observed and explored.

- **Present** the theory to others through a variety of mediums: spoken word (lectures, debates), written word (thesis papers, books, articles), visual tools (drawings, film, graphs maps, models, and reenactments), and more recently through movement. The number of doctoral science students entering the Dance Your PhD competition has more than tripled in past years. Founded in 2008 by John Bohannon and sponsored by the American Association of Science and *Science Magazine*, this annual international competition covers four fields of science—biology, chemistry, physics, and social sciences—and is open to all PhD candidates ready to take on the challenge of explaining their thesis through movement.

- **Reflect** upon the process, taking into account feedback from peers who listened to, read, or viewed the work; evaluate areas of success and areas where data or arguments may need to be revised or strengthened.

The creative and scientific processes of inquiry described above are presented side by side in table 0.1 for the sake of comparison.

Creative movement and embodied and experiential learning practices bring an increased level of engagement to the classroom. Students are actively involved in fact finding and research, and much of the learning is done collaboratively and produces multiple perspectives on ways they might interpret ideas and information, thereby strengthening students' communication and social skills. Creative movement develops students' kinesthetic learning skills; supports students who have difficulty sitting, listening, and processing spoken information; and builds self-confidence in students who are timid or have limited language skills.

Table 0.1   The Creative and Scientific Processes of Inquiry

CREATIVE PROCESS OF INQUIRY	SCIENTIFIC PROCESS OF INQUIRY
Observe aspects of one's inner and outer world, including physical, emotional, and current or imaginary events.	**Observe** a specific environment, object, or event (including macro- and microscopic realms).
Explore how the body can interpret, illuminate, or symbolize what is studied by using the basic elements of dance: level and direction changes, tempo and rhythmic shifts, gestural and geometric shapes, spatial relationships with others, degrees of energy, and attack.	**Explore** and study what happens in that (or to that) environment, object, or event using numerical data, written accounts, and visual observations while it's in its natural state and when other stimuli are introduced.
Create and choreograph a dance or movement phrase to communicate, celebrate, or commemorate that which has been observed.	**Create** a theory or theories based on one's understanding of what has been observed and explored.
Present the dance or movement creation to others in workshop settings, in theatrical presentations, or through film or video.	**Present** the theory to others through a variety of mediums: spoken word (lectures, debates), written word (thesis papers, books, articles), visual tools (drawings, film, graphs maps, models, and reenactments), and through movement.
Reflect upon the comments of those who viewed the presentation and evaluate the process; identify areas of success as well as aspects of the dance that may require revision.	**Reflect** upon the process, taking into account feedback from peers who listened to, read, or viewed the work; evaluate areas of success and areas where data or arguments may need to be revised or strengthened.

From J. Pomer, *Elementary Dance Education: Nature-Themed Creative Movement and Collaborative Learning* (Champaign, IL: Human Kinetics, 2023).

In a traditional classroom setting, when a question is asked, students raise their hands and answer one at a time. By incorporating movement exploration into the classroom, teachers create opportunities for the entire class to respond simultaneously. Learn is a verb. It's an activity our *entire* being can and *should* be involved in.

How to Use This Book

The first chapter of the book contains the **foundation exercises** to introduce and develop students' understanding of the basic elements of dance. If you are working with students who fully grasp these concepts, then the foundation exercises can be used as quick warm-ups before moving on to the deeper movement exploration assignments in chapters 2 through 8. If your class is unfamiliar with movement fundamentals, use these exercises as building blocks from which their creative work will grow. Once students develop confidence manipulating the basic elements of dance, they'll have the skills they need to succeed in their nature-inspired dance creations.

The first chapter concludes with an exercise to introduce students to the concept and practice of *collaborative observation*. This exercise helps students understand that their classroom is an inclusive space where everyone's perspective is respected. The exercise highlights the importance of listening to and working with those who may not always see things the same way you do. Together, the foundation exercises provide the scaffolding to support your students throughout their artistic journey.

The book next presents seven chapters of movement exercises focusing on specific areas of study: plants, animals, water, earth, sky, people, and other wonders. These chapters contain exploration exercises and multitiered choreographic projects that can be used to excite and challenge students in primary and junior grades. The exercises, like all things in nature, are not static; they evolve in multiple directions, contain suggestions for simplifying or increasing the level of difficulty, and offer strategies for developing awareness and growth in specific skills.

Each chapter refers to videos highlighting topics your students will be exploring. A list of video links that correspond to the exercises is provided online in HK*Propel* along with access to the recommended music tracks mentioned throughout the book. Some of the videos are of dancers, some are science-based, and others contain breathtaking images of the natural world. Your class will watch, learn, and be inspired to translate their ideas and observations of the natural world into dance and share their dances with others.

The exercises in this book are designed to promote creativity and curiosity, to engage and challenge students' minds and bodies, and to help children learn to appreciate and support each other as they work together exploring, creating, and sharing their ideas and insights about the natural world through dance.

See the card at the front of the print book for your unique HK*Propel* access code. Ebook users can refer to the HK*Propel* access code instructions on the page immediately following the cover.

ACKNOWLEDGMENTS

A warm thank you to the many students and teachers who've participated in my Dance the Moving World and Way of Water creative movement programs and dance projects over the years. Your keen interest and heartfelt enthusiasm inspired me to record and collate my nature-based movement exercises for others to use and enjoy.

Special thanks to the schools, studio, and students whose photographs and journal entries appear in the book: Keele St. P.S., Churchill Heights P.S., Bedford Park P.S., and Queen Victoria P.S. Special thanks also to the Ontario Arts Council and Toronto District School Board for funding many of my school-based projects and to my students at Pegasus Dance Studio (Jane Davis Munro, artistic director).

Two of the exercises in this book were created for earlier dance study guides. The first exercise is Sun and Moon, originally created for the *CanAsian International Dance Festival Study Guide 2008* (Denise Fujiwara, artistic director). The second is Water Words, originally created for *Dusk Dances Digital Study Guide 2020* (Sylvie Bouchard, artistic director). Both of these exercises have been modified for this book to accommodate younger grades. Some of the material found in the introductory section of this book appears in my article entitled "Dance the Moving World" published by the *Journal of Dance and Somatic Practices*, in their "Somatics and Eco-Consciousness" issue, volume 13, published 2021 by Intellect Ltd.

Thanks to Barry Prophet for contributing an evocative array of musical compositions to inspire and support students' dance creations.

This is my third book with Human Kinetics. Each one has been a journey of discovery and reflection. Thank you to the entire HK team and special thanks to Bethany Bentley and Anne Mrozek for their guidance and support.

Getting Ready to Teach

Every class is different, and no single teaching strategy works for everyone. It's handy to have a variety of teaching and class management tools to help you and your students navigate your learning time together. This section contains successful strategies for implementing creative movement in classroom settings and outdoors and provides explanations about how to use the lesson plan suggestions that accompany each exercise, as well as the music tracks and video links.

Creating a Safe Learning Environment

The focus on the first day of all my school programs is to create an inclusive learning environment where the students feel safe and protected. Dance is a visual art form where you *are* the art, and that can be terrifying if you're not a confident mover.

I let the students know that I'm not there to teach them a set dance routine. I tell them that instead we'll be exploring environmental movement patterns; like scientists, we'll investigate how and why these movement patterns exist, and like painters and musicians, we'll discover ways to express what we see and how we feel about what we've observed without words.

The exercises in this book use a template for movement discovery where your students will observe, explore, create, and share. After each step, there will be opportunities to reflect through journaling and discussions.

Journals

I like to incorporate journaling in all my school dance programs. For kindergarten and grade 1, the journal assignments can be painted or drawn. Prep the materials before the movement class, and you'll find that journal art is a great way for your students to individually reflect on the fun they had in dance and transition to a quieter learning period. You can make the journals for older grades by stapling blank or lined paper together. I use a combination of artwork and text for grades 2 and 3, while older grades focus predominately on written entries, though there are times when I'll ask for a visual component.

I let the students know that over the course of the program I'll be looking at the journals, and they're invited to include personal notes to me, including things about the class they like and things they don't like. After reading the journals, I try to respond to their comments, never naming names but thanking the class for articulating their ideas and feelings.

As the students realize that I'm truly interested in what they think and feel, they reflect more deeply about the activities; there is less resistance and greater personal commitment, learning, and enjoyment.

> *I constantly find myself worrying about what other people think. When I create poses, I'm afraid I'll embarrass myself. I love how fun the class is and hope it will help me overcome my fears.*
>
> Grade 6 student

I like how we're connecting our dances with nature. You can be anything—soft and billowy like clouds or crushing and destructive like earthquakes. And all those feelings are in people too.

Grade 6 student

Through their journals, your students will let you know if you're communicating effectively, if the movement work is resonating with them, and how deeply they're engaged.

Discussions

Dance creation stimulates thoughtfulness. Make sure there is time for your students to share their ideas and observations. Inviting students to share their knowledge and taking the time to discuss differing interpretations and points of view build fertile ground for learning. Shy students feel safe asking questions, creating, exploring, and sharing, and novice movers are more comfortable going out of their comfort zones once they realize that dance isn't only for those who are flexible and know how to perform complicated moves in perfect unison.

It's fun hearing what other people have to say. A lot of them say things I would never have thought of. It makes me think harder to come up with something creative to add to the conversation.

Grade 5 student

Some of the most impressive choreographic pieces I've seen in school settings have been created by students with no previous dance training, students who fully embraced the idea of translating what they've observed and studied into movement. After a grade 5 class presented their Fire and Water dances to their grade 1 reading buddies, a grade 1 student asked the dancers, "How hard was it to do?" The first grade 5 student to reply said, "The most challenging thing was that I had to stop being me and become the thing I was dancing." Many of his classmates nodded their heads in agreement; they'd come to understand that dance creation required mental, physical, and emotional commitment.

Preparing Your Classroom for Movement

Some elementary schools have a dedicated drama or dance room and a specialist teacher who works with students once or twice a week or a physical education teacher who dedicates a portion of their classes to dance every year, but in many elementary schools, the classroom teacher is expected to provide all the arts programming, including dance, drama, visual arts, and music.

That can be challenging, especially for teachers without an arts background, but it's a huge benefit for students who are active learners. Integrating the arts into students' daily routine engages active learners, and when the themes for art exploration intersect with areas of the curriculum, students who may not excel at written or oral assignments have an opportunity to shine. Teachers regularly tell me how pleased and surprised they are when they see students who struggle academically thrive in dance and other active learning situations.

Integrating dance and creative movement into the daily curriculum means teachers must find ways to transform their classroom space or find an alternative venue where their students can move safely. Kindergarten and grade 1 classrooms are designed with open areas and can be easily reoriented to provide greater space as needed, but for teachers working with older grades (and larger students), providing a safe, open space to work in is an issue.

As a guest artist visiting schools for over four decades, I've observed dozens of teacher strategies for transforming classroom spaces for dance and drama lessons. I've been in classrooms where the first 10 minutes of my 45 to 60 minute session has been spent with the teacher and students chaotically moving desks, chairs, boxes of books, and other accumulated stuff, while in other classrooms, the desks are moved and the floor is swept in two minutes. The teachers whose classes are in the latter group know the key to transforming crowded classrooms into open space is planning and teamwork.

Each teacher does it differently, but here's the basic template for grades 2 through 6:

- In the first week of school, practice transforming the room into an open space and engage students with simple dance and drama exercises.
- By transforming the classroom during the first week of school, you're letting students know that dance, drama, and embodied learning activities will be a regular occurrence.
- If desks are in rows, assign each row a color and a specific side of the room to move their desks and chairs to.
- If desks are in pods or small clusters, two pods can have the same color and area to move to.
- By using colors, and not numbers or letters, there's no assigned order. Red can move first, second, or last. When designations aren't sequential, everyone has to pay attention—no one knows when it's their turn to move.
- If the classroom is on the second or third floor, highlight the importance of lifting the desks so as not to disturb the class below.

© Janice Pomer

A classroom can be transformed into an open space.

- Lifting means teamwork; two people lift a desk, they each lift their own chair, together they lift the second desk, and they're done.
- The desks should be placed as close together as possible and create straight lines along the perimeters of the room.
- Chairs should be placed under the desks, not on top, as chairs can fall from the vibrations of jumping and other vigorous movements.
- Have a broom and dustpan available (some teachers have two brooms) for volunteers to sweep the floor so students feel comfortable working at low levels.

Dancing Outdoors

Another option is working outdoors. Schools with lots of property and year-round access to the outdoors regularly hold classes outdoors, while communities with inclement weather tend to use the outdoors less. (There are inspiring exceptions, including a physical education teacher in Toronto, Canada, who takes his primary classes outdoors for their lessons all year long. The school community makes sure every child has a snowsuit and boots if families are unable to provide them.)

What you need when working outdoors:

- Cell phones and small, lightweight portable speakers make teaching dance outdoors easy. You can carry your sound system in your pockets or small bag.
- If you're working on asphalt, you'll need sticks of sidewalk chalk (the chalk for classroom use is too thin and fragile). Designate the work space with chalk. Use the same area each lesson, and in time your class will stay within the work space without needing it drawn out.
- If you're working on a grassy field, you'll want to use props to clearly delineate the working space. Use the same area for each lesson.
- Establish a system for getting your students' attention. Use a whistle, flag, or obvious position (standing with both arms reaching overhead) to let your students know it's time to stop and listen.
- Bring a marker and a few sheets of flip chart paper to record students' ideas.
- If you're working on asphalt, you can use the chalk to write student ideas and word lists on the ground, photograph the lists, and download or project the photo for future reference. I prefer paper because you can post it on the wall once everyone's back in the classroom where it's easy for students to add their ideas between lessons.
- Your students can do their journal entries outdoors; put pencils and all the journals in a basket so they aren't lying on the ground or being blown away, or do them after you've returned to the classroom. I prefer returning to the classroom and giving students five minutes of quiet time to notate their dances or respond to the journal entry questions.
- If your school doesn't have schedule for outdoor classes, start one. Post it in the staff room. You may inspire other teachers to start taking their classes outdoors.

Every learning situation is different; what works in one school may not be feasible in another, and what works with one group of students may not resonate with another.

Lesson Plan Suggestions

Lesson plan suggestions are included at the top of every exercise; most of the exercises contain a number of steps and variations, and often an exercise will take two classes to complete. Classroom teachers have more flexibility over class length than specialist teachers who move from class to class, so you may wish to complete the exercise in an extended or double period. The class plan suggestions in this book are based on class lengths of

- 30 to 45 minutes for kindergarten through grade 2 and
- 45 to 60 minutes for grades 3 through 6.

With grades 4 through 6, I'll often work with the class for 45 minutes before recess and 45 minutes after recess to complete all the steps in an exercise in one visit. You don't need to follow the plan, but it provides a framework to follow. The plan also lets you know if there is a video component to the exercise and which track(s) of music to use.

The Music

With this book comes a treasury of instrumental compositions in HK*Propel* created and performed by Barry Prophet to support and inspire your students' movement explorations. Each composition conveys a range of images and emotions; unlike songs, they have no text to confine your students' movement choices. A single composition will inspire a multiplicity of responses; let the joyful rhythms, mysterious textures, driving beats, and gentle atmospheres invite your students to imagine, move, and create.

Online Resources

Access the music, charts, and links to suggested videos through HK*Propel*. See the card at the front of the print book for your unique HK*Propel* access code. Ebook users can reference the HK*Propel* access code instructions on the page immediately following the book cover.

Note to Teachers With Little or No Movement Experience

If you have little or no experience teaching dance and feel uncertain about your ability to facilitate a creative movement program, consider this: Dance is language, and classroom teachers excel in language arts. Every day, you immerse your class in a language-rich environment where your students listen, converse, read, and write and are introduced to new vocabulary. You devise creative ways for your students to develop and demonstrate their understanding of language, inviting them to write poems, tell stories, solve word puzzles, and perform skits. You develop your students' fine motor skills in the areas of printing, writing, and keyboarding so they're able to preserve their work and share their text-based creations with others. Every day, you follow a similar template to the one proposed in this book; the only difference is the medium we're inviting children to use to communicate.

© Janice Pomer

CHAPTER 1

Basic Elements of Dance

Foundation Exercises

The foundation exercises are designed to strengthen your students' movement awareness and confidence and introduce them to successful creative structures and protocols before they venture on to the nature-inspired exercises in the body of this book. If you have little experience teaching movement, the foundation exercises will provide the information you need to facilitate safe and dynamic creative movement lessons. Many of the structures introduced in these exercises appear throughout the book in more complex forms. The foundation exercises are arranged pedagogically; each exercise builds on the previous one as they guide your students through a variety of physical and reflective experiences. If you are an experienced movement teacher, you'll appreciate having a new series of exercises to strengthen students' physical and choreographic skills and help develop their internal focus, external awareness, problem-solving and critical-thinking skills, teamwork, and group dynamics.

Basic Elements of Dance

The exercises in this section introduce students to the basic elements of dance (shape, motion, time, space, and energy) as shown in figure 1.1. (You can download the chart from HK*Propel*, print it, and post it in your classroom.)

The basic elements of dance are intricately linked; no one element can be performed without the others. For example, you can't make a shape without moving, and no movement can be made without time.

Each exercise in this chapter highlights one element and invites you and your students to explore that specific element in a variety of ways. As the exercise progresses, other dance elements are introduced to enhance the primary one. For example, exercise 1.1 focuses on shapes. In the penultimate step, students are asked to make shapes while they jump and turn. The culminating step has students choreographing short duets in which they alternate jumps and turns with "freeze frame" shapes.

Use the class discussions to stimulate student collaboration and reflection. Each exercise is followed by a short discussion, which will help you and your students identify areas of interest, celebrate successes, and address difficulties. The discussions help strengthen students' communication skills as they articulate their ideas and listen to their classmates, and they learn to appreciate that each person has a personal perspective. When we interpret an idea or imagine it into movement, there is no absolute answer. The magic of the creative movement process is in the endless possibilities.

Each discussion section contains two or three questions for your class to answer. Sometimes your students will be asked if there was an aspect of the exercise they found challenging. When your students identify a challenge, let them know that they have understood one of the reasons the exercise was taught. For example, step 1 of exercise 1.1 asks your students to create a variety of different shapes, hold each shape for different duration, and then return to parallel position. Here are some of the challenges students will identify:

- Coming up with new ideas for shapes
- Moving quickly and quietly in and out of shapes
- Holding difficult shapes in stillness

Once your students have identified these challenges, you can ask them to share how they were able to accomplish the tasks. Their answers may be similar to these:

- "I saw a picture in my mind and made that shape."
- "I saw someone else's shape and was inspired by it."
- "When I was balancing, I didn't look around. I stared straight ahead at the wall."

Remind students that there's no right or wrong answer to the questions or how they experienced the exercise. By inviting students to reflect on individual aspects of an exercise, you are encouraging them to be introspective, acknowledge their feelings, and become more observant of their thought process—important tools not just for movement creation but for all aspects of life.

Basic Elements of Dance

Shape

Definition: the form the individual dancer or group of dancers create in stillness or in motion

Explore a wide range of shapes employing different levels, directions, qualities, and textures, including curves, angles, open, closed, symmetrical, asymmetrical, rough, smooth, and dramatic.

Motion

Definition: the traveling patterns used across the floor, on-the-spot, or the movement isolation of a section of the body

Explore foot patterns and level changes in different directions and with different timings while traveling across the floor or moving on-the-spot. Isolate the hands, arms, feet, legs, and torso to explore the movement potential of each area.

Spatial Relationships

Definition: the space within an individual's shape (when arms are akimbo or legs apart), the space between individual dancers, the space the space between the dancers and their performance area, or the performance area itself

Explore ways to vary the distance between dancers, paint the space around you by drawing in the air, and follow curved and angular pathways while traveling across the performance area.

Timing and Rhythm

Definition: the duration of a single motion or the rhythmic pattern framing a series of movements

Explore by moving at a moderate tempo, using extremes of slow and fast and combining them in specific orders, slowly moving from one shape to another followed by quick jumps and runs, and moving to time signatures other than 4/4.

Energy

Definition: dynamic and dramatic range injected into every shape, spatial relationship, motion, and rhythm dancers inhabit

Explore how simple actions are transformed through intent and imagination by the conscious use of emotions and dynamic qualities.

The elements of dance are connected; every shape fills a space, and every space has a shape. No shape can be made without motion, and no movement can be made without time. Energy is everywhere—visible, invisible, in action and rest.

Figure 1.1

From J. Pomer, *Elementary Dance Education: Nature-Themed Creative Movement and Collaborative Learning* (Champaign, IL: Human Kinetics, 2023).

EXERCISE 1.1   EXPLORING SHAPES

Lesson Plan Suggestions

Kindergarten Through Grade 3

First lesson: Steps 1, 2, 3, and 4

Second lesson: Quickly review steps 1, 2, 3, and 4, and do step 5 (follow the grade-appropriate variation); create journal cover

Grades 4 Through 6

First lesson: Steps 1, 2, 3, and 4

Second lesson: Quickly review steps 1, 2, 3, and 4, and do step 5 (follow the grade-appropriate variation); create journal cover

Before you begin this exercise, introduce students to *parallel position* as shown in the accompanying photograph: Feet are hip-width apart, legs are straight, spine is long and tall, and the arms hang by the sides of the torso.

In drama, this position is often called *neutral position.* Whether you use the term *neutral position* or *parallel position,* the concept is to demonstrate stillness in body and mind. The dancer or actor becomes a blank sheet of paper ready to embrace any action, image, or idea that is presented to them. Many exercises in this book start with students in parallel position. When your class is standing in parallel position, you know they are focused and ready to begin.

The students in the photograph created a new name for the position, calling it *still water* because still water is calm but alive with possibilities. I loved how they embraced the concept of the position and connected it with nature. Since then, I've

Parallel position.

© Janice Pomer

shared that term with other classes, and for some students *still water position* resonates more strongly than *parallel position* or *neutral position*. In these exercises, we'll use the technical the term *parallel position*, but feel free to share the still water story. Your students may be inspired to create their own name for the position.

Step 1: Simple Shape Exploration

Instructions

1. With your class, compile a list of large structures and small objects and write their suggestions on a flip chart. Your class list should include large structures such as the Eiffel Tower, the Egyptian pyramids, the Golden Gate Bridge, and the Statue of Liberty. It should include small everyday objects such as forks and spoons, umbrellas, chairs, scissors, or rings.

2. If you haven't already, move the chairs and desks to the side (see Preparing Your Classroom for Movement suggestions in the Getting Ready to Teach section at the front of the book).

3. Ask your students to stand in parallel position throughout the room, arm's-length apart and facing the front.

4. Tell the class that you'll be calling out some of the objects they suggested, and all they have to do is create a shape inspired by the object.

5. Let them know that even though they'll all be creating shapes based on the same object, not all of their shapes will be the same. For example, some shapes inspired by the word *chair* could have armrests and some might not, some of the chair shapes may be wide and others narrow, or some could be thrones and others old and broken.

6. Everyone should work quietly and move into their shapes as quickly as possible.

7. Once your students are in their shapes, they should hold them until you ask everyone to return to parallel position.

8. Wait until everyone is standing in silence and stillness and then call out another object they suggested.

9. Keep everyone frozen in that shape for several breaths, then ask them to return to parallel position.

10. Here's an example for calling out the objects the students suggested:
    - Umbrella
    - Pyramid
    - Fork
    - Chair
    - Bridge

11. Call out other shape ideas.
    - Letters:
      - M
      - E
      - K

© Barry Prophet

Chair.

12. If everyone has performed the on-the-spot shapes quietly, invite the class to walk around the room (without talking) instead of returning to parallel position between each shape.

• Abstract shapes:
  - A twisted shape
  - A shape with one foot off the ground
  - A symmetrical shape
• Dramatic shapes:
  - Surprise
  - Frustration
  - Fear
• Animal shapes:
  - Eagle
  - Lion
  - Horse

13. After the final shape, let your students relax and sit down where they are for a brief discussion.

Angular shapes and balances.

© Janice Pomer

Discussion

• "Did you make some shapes you've never made before?" If many students say yes, ask your class to show you one of their newly found shapes.

• "Was there anything difficult or challenging about the exercise?" If yes, ask students to identify the challenge (*Some shapes were difficult to hold, couldn't think of what to do*) and to share how they worked to accomplish the task (*Stared at the wall to help keep balance, looked at others' shapes for inspiration and ideas*).

After a student has contributed an idea, ask students to raise their hands if they had the same or similar experience. This allows more students to participate in a shorter period of time.

Step 2: Add an Action

Recommended Music

Track 1

Instructions

1. Play the music; identify the downbeat; and call out the beats, emphasizing beat 1: **1**, 2, 3, 4; **1**, 2, 3, 4.

2. Ask your students to lift their heels and rise up on their toes while reaching their arms up on beats 1 and 2 and gently lower their arms and heels on beats 3 and 4. Repeat 3 or 4 times.

3. Now ask students to do the following:

- Jump up and reach their arms up on beat 1
- Land quietly through the feet and bring the arms down on beat 2
- Gently straighten their knees on beat 3
- Stand in parallel position on beat 4

4. Practice the jumps in unison 4 or 5 times.

5. Ask your class if they noticed that they have to bend their knees before jumping up and bend them again in order to land quietly.

6. Point out that basketball players and dancers land jumps the same way: first through the toes, then the ball of the foot, and lastly the heels. Land with the knees bent, gently straighten the knees, and then bend them again to jump.

7. Landing a jump should be quiet.

8. Observe students to see who is landing quietly and safely. If some students are having difficulty, ask those who are more skilled to demonstrate.

9. Once everyone is landing carefully through the feet, return to parallel position.

Variations

- Invite your class to try this variation:
  - Jump up high on beat 1.
  - Land in a dynamic shape (other than parallel position) on beat 2.
  - Hold the shape for beats 3 and 4.

- Practice jump and freeze 4 or 5 times. Encourage students to create new shapes every time they land. If necessary, call out prompts like "Land in a low shape," "Land in a dramatic shape," or "Land on one foot."

- After they have performed a simple jump and freeze several times in unison, rest for a moment, and then ask your class to consider changing the shape they jump in.

Step 3: Maintaining Shapes While Moving

Recommended Music

Track 1

Instructions

- Some of these jumps will be wide, so if you're working in a small room, you may want to ask that half of your students stand in parallel position as the other half jump.

- If you've divided your class into two groups, let the first group try a new jump 2 times (use the jump 1, 2, freeze 3, 4 structure), then ask the second group to try it. Here are a few suggestions:
  - Jump with your arms and legs extended out, making a big X.
  - Jump in a twisted shape (students can twist their torso to one side or try crossing their arms or legs in the air).
  - Jump with your legs in a diamond (bring the feet together in the air).
  - Make up your own jump (give students time to work on their own).

- Let everyone show their original jumps, then they can sit where they are and discuss their jump shapes.

Discussion

- "Did you try doing a jump you'd never done before? If yes, what was it? How did it feel? Scary? Exciting? Fun?"

- "Were all the jumps easy to land, or were some more difficult?" If some were more difficult, discuss why.

- If some students created unique jumps, invite them to teach the jumps to the class.

Step 4: Discover Different Shapes for Turning or Spinning On-the-Spot

Recommended Music

Track 1

Instructions

- Invite students to explore turning on-the-spot in different shapes. For this exploration, the turns should stay on the ground (no 360° jumps in the air).

- Ask your class to spread throughout the room, arm's-length apart. Remind everyone that the turns are on-the-spot. No one should travel into another person's space.

- Older students can work on their own to explore different ways of turning while younger students will benefit from the teacher calling out ideas to explore. All grades should explore doing a variety of turns:
  · On both feet
  · On one foot
  · With arms open or closed
  · With straight or bent legs
  · On their bottoms or their backs *but not on their heads*

- To prevent dizziness, tell your class to rest every 15 to 20 seconds.

Safety Note: Cartwheels, handstands, headstands, head spinning, and other upside-down movements should not be performed in school classrooms even if students have the skills and training to perform them.

- After students have explored turns on their own, invite everyone to stand in a large circle, arm's-length apart, in parallel position.
  1. Tell your class that you'd like to see students perform a turn and freeze in a shape other than parallel position.
  2. Let your class try turning and freezing together 2 or 3 times.
  3. Now invite your students to present their turns and freezes one at a time around the circle.
  4. Ask for a volunteer to go first. The person standing to the right of the volunteer will be second, the next will be third, and so on around the circle.

5. When people are waiting to turn, they should stand in parallel. After turning, they should stay frozen in the finishing shape.

6. Try to present the turn-shape-freeze phrase without pauses between individuals.

7. Go around the circle 2 or 3 times so everyone can show a variety of turns and shapes.

Discussion

- "Was it easy to come up with new ways of turning?"

- "Was it hard to hold your frozen shape after turning?" If yes, have the students explain what strategies they used to maintain their shapes after turning.

Step 5: Creating a Duet With Contrasting Shapes and Actions

Kindergarten and Grade 1 Variation

Kindergarten and grade 1 classes will benefit from working on this assignment without partners and their teachers leading.

- Teachers can create a phrase combining shapes, jumps, and turns with the entire class. Here are two suggestions:

  1. Jump in a big X and land in a big X.

  2. Turn on-the-spot and finish in a closed shape.

- Repeat the pattern 2 or 3 times, then try the following:

  1. Jump and land in a dramatic shape (someone surprised).

  2. Turn and finish in an animal shape (a lion snarling).

  3. Jump and land in a dramatic shape (someone brave).

  4. Turn and finish in an animal shape (a lion fearful).

Grades 2 and 3 Variation

- Before your class begins to create, review the protocol for collaborative dance creation in figure 1.2.

- Ask your students to work with a partner and follow this simple structure to create a short duet:

  1. Both dancers jump at the same time and in the same shape, then make the same low shape and freeze.

  2. Both turn at the same time and in the same shape, then make the same high shape and freeze.

  3. One jumps while the other turns, then each dancer makes a different shape at a contrasting level (high or low) and freezes for 4 beats.

Grades 4 Through 6 Variation

Instructions

- Before your class begins to create, review the protocol for collaborative dance creation in figure 1.2.

- The jumps and turns can be different from the ones used in the previous exercises. Required elements for the duets are the following:
    1. Jump in the same shape at the same time, then freeze in the same low shape.
    2. Turn in the same shape at the same time, then freeze in the same high shape.
    3. One jumps, the other turns, and each dancer freezes in a contrasting (different) high or low shape.
    4. Perform four quickly changing shapes in unison.
    5. Finish with a jump or turn and final shape to freeze (jump and turn and shapes can be the same or different from their partner)

Class Management and Presentation Suggestions

- Play the music at a low volume while your class is working so they create and practice while hearing the tempo they'll be presenting with.
- Allow 7 to 10 minutes of creation and practice time (experienced movers will need less), then ask students to present.
- If time is an issue, invite two duets to present at the same time. Place one duet to the right of center and the other duet to the left.
- When groups present at the same time, remind everyone that all the duets will start at the same time, but because their creations may be different lengths, everyone should stay frozen in their final shape until the music stops.
- Play the music and count the presenters in.
- After all the duets have presented, begin the discussion.

Discussion

- "What was the biggest challenge you faced when you were creating your duet?" (*Agreeing on what to do, practicing the fast shape changes.*) Use students' answers to highlight the importance of not giving up when faced with obstacles.
- "What do you feel was the most eye-catching shape or action of your dance?"
- "Identify one of the eye-catching shapes or actions you saw in other people's duets."

Journal Entry For All Grades

"Use the letters *D*, *A*, *N*, *C*, and *E* to create a cover or front page for your dance journal. Make the letters big or small, with twists, with curves and angular lines, and with arrows. Place some letters higher (they're jumping) and some overlapping or melting downward." Show the class figure 1.3 for ideas.

Protocol for Collaborative Dance Creation

- No one person is in charge. Collaborative dance creation is a shared experience.
- Listen to each other's ideas. New ideas are opportunities for learning.
- Contribute ideas and support other people's ideas.
- Understand that choreographic restrictions mean there will be times when not everyone's ideas will be used.
- Be positive and work constructively.
- Solve problems together.
- Create a dance that contains all the exercise requirements.
- Sometimes, everyone must do a required element in unison. At those times, select something that everyone can perform with confidence.
- Other times, the requirements ask group members to perform different actions. In those situations, students can highlight individual abilities.
- Cartwheels, handstands, and headstands are not appropriate due to safety concerns.
- If your group has a problem or disagreement that can't be solved through cooperation, don't let it escalate. Ask your teacher for assistance.

Figure 1.2

From J. Pomer, *Elementary Dance Education: Nature-Themed Creative Movement and Collaborative Learning* (Champaign, IL: Human Kinetics, 2023).

Figure 1.3   Examples of journal cover ideas.

EXERCISE 1.2   EXPLORING MOTION

In the previous exercise, your students explored shapes and used jumps and turns to intensify their frozen shapes. In this exercise, they will explore on-the-spot and traveling actions.

Lesson Plan Suggestions

Kindergarten Through Grade 3

First lesson: Steps 1, 2, 3, and 4 (follow grade-appropriate variations); journal entry

Grades 4 Through 6

First lesson: Steps 1, 2, and 3 (follow grade-appropriate variations); if time allows, introduce step 4

Second lesson: Warm up with step 2 and one of the variations in step 3; use step 4 to create, practice, and present students' choreography; journal entry

Step 1: On-the-Spot Action Words

Recommended Music

Track 2

Instructions

With your class, compile a list of on-the-spot action words.

- Feet can step, stomp, tap, hop, point and flex, and circle at the ankle.
- Legs can kick, bend, jump, swing, lunge (keep one foot on-the-spot), and turn in and out.
- Arms and hands can clap, reach, swing, twist, bend, and open and close.
- Spines can twist, arch, flatten, circle, curve, roll, and pulse.

© Janice Pomer

Forward lunges.

Step 2: Exploring On-the-Spot Actions

Kindergarten Through Grade 3 Variation

- Use the list of on-the-spot actions to help you lead a creative exploration.
  - Ask your students to stand arm's-length apart.
  - Let the class know that you'll be calling out different actions and body parts for them to explore.
  - For example, if you ask students to swing their arms, they can swing forward and back, in large and small circles, with their arms close to the floor or over their heads. But while swinging their arms, they shouldn't be swinging their legs or jumping up and down.
  - One of the challenges is to stay focused on the individual body part (arms) and required action (swing).
  - While exploring, they should stay on-the-spot and work quietly so they can hear your instructions that will tell them the next action to explore.
- After reviewing those rules, ask everyone to start in parallel position.
  - Put the music on, call out the first body part and action, and invite your students to move.
  - After 15 to 20 seconds, call out another body part and action.
  - Offer six to eight different actions for your students to explore using a variety of body parts, such as:
    - Legs swing front, back, and side to side
    - Elbows circle together and separately
    - Feet tap quickly and slowly
    - The spine sways from side to side
    - Fingers wiggle up overhead and down near the floor
  - Finish with 20 to 30 seconds of open improvisation, letting your class create their own on-the-spot dance.
- Allow several moments of stillness after their improvisation to let students calm down after all that work, then sit down for a brief talk.
  - Ask your students to put their hands up if they liked exploring the different action and body isolations.
  - Ask each student to show a movement they enjoyed doing, and if they wish, they can say why they liked doing it.
- Create a simple 8-beat on-the-spot phrase with your class based on your students' favorite isolation actions. Practice and memorize the phrase (it will be used in step 3).

Grades 4 Through 6 Variation

Recommended Music

Track 2

Create Your Own On-the-Spot Warm-Up

- You can create your own class warm-up with suggestions from your students, or you can follow the warm-up suggestion that follows.

- Start with students standing in parallel position arm's-length apart, facing front.
- Listen to the music for a moment then count everyone in.

  1. Extend arms out wide at shoulder height and reach right, left, right, left for 4 beats.
  2. Reach arms up overhead, alternating right, left, right, left for 4 beats.
  3. Reach both arms down, drop the head, and roll down through the spine for 4 beats.
  4. Roll up through the spine for 3 beats and clap on beat 4.
  5. Make four small parallel jumps from side to side (right, left, right, left) for 4 beats.
  6. Lift and drop the shoulders 4 times (looks like shrugs) for 4 beats.
  7. Swing the right leg forward, back, forward, and put it down on beat 4.
  8. Swing the left leg forward, back, forward, and put it down on beat 4.
  9. Twist to the right: Turn your head, look behind, and wrap the arms around the torso for 2 beats.
  10. Twist to the left: Turn your head, look behind, and wrap the arms around the torso for 2 beats.
  11. Create a left-right rainbow with the arms: Reach from the left, create an arc as the arms travel overhead, and bring arms down to the right for 4 beats.
  12. Create a right-left rainbow with the arms: Reach from the right, create an arc as the arms travel overhead, and bring arms down to the left for 4 beats.

- If students find the combination difficult, review the problem areas. If everyone is comfortable with the combination, do it 2 more times without pausing.

Step 3: Combine a Simple Traveling Action With On-the-Spot Actions

Kindergarten through grade 3 should use the 8-beat phrase created at the end of step 2. Grades 4 through 6 can create a new 8-beat on-the-spot phrase or select an 8-beat phrase from the warm-up. Take the time to make sure everyone is confident performing the phrase.

All Grade Variation 1

1. Start with everyone standing in parallel position, arm's-length apart and facing the same direction.
2. Make sure there is enough room in front of students so they can take 4 steps forward.
3. When the music begins, ask your students to walk forward for 4 beats.
4. Have them walk backward for 4 beats. (Tell students to keep looking forward as they travel back.)
5. Have them perform their 8-beat on-the-spot phrase.
6. Repeat the sequence of walking forward for 4, backward for 4, and the 8-beat on-the-spot phrase 3 or 4 times.

Kindergarten Through Grade 3 Variation

Divide your class into groups and watch each other perform.

Grades 4 Through 6 Variation 1

1. Ask half the class to move to the right side of the room and the other half to move to the left.

2. Both groups should stand in parallel position facing the center of the room.

3. Make sure there is enough open space in the center of the room for students to walk into.

4. Both groups will move at the same time, but one group will perform their 8-beat on-the-spot phrase while the other group walks forward and back.

5. Ask students on the right side to walk forward for 4 beats and backward for 4 beats and then perform their 8-beat phrases on-the-spot.

6. Ask students on the left to perform their 8-beat phrases on-the-spot and then walk forward for 4 beats and back for 4 beats.

7. Put the music on and count everyone in.

8. Stop after the first 16 beats. If both sides were able to perform their part without issue, repeat 2 more times, then move on to the next variation. If there was difficulty, review the phrases and instructions and try again.

Grades 4 Through 6 Variation 2

Change the 4 forward walks to 2 forward runs, a jump, and freeze.

- The forward phrase will now start with 2 runs for beats 1 and 2. Then jump straight up, land quietly, and freeze in a shape for beats 3 and 4.

- Describe the new traveling combination to your class and ask for volunteers to demonstrate.

- To travel backward, they can walk calmly for 4 beats as they had done in the original phrase.

Allow time for everyone to practice the new phrase, then ask everyone to stand in their lines at either side of the room. When the music begins:

1. Students on the right side will run forward for 2 beats, jump on beat 3, freeze on beat 4, walk backward for 4 beats, and then perform their 8-beat phrases on-the-spot.

2. Students on the left side will perform their 8-beat phrases on-the-spot, run forward for 2 beats, jump on beat 3, freeze on beat 4, and walk backward for 4 beats.

3. Repeat 3 times.

Discussion for Grades 4 Through 6

- "Was it easy to stay focused on your actions even when the people across from you were doing different actions?"

- "Can you think of another way to travel backward after the leap-jump-freeze?" If yes, let them know there'll be an opportunity to use their ideas in step 4.

Step 4: Explore Other Traveling Actions

- Compile a list of traveling actions other than walking and running, including leap, hop, roll, skip, gallop, swoop, creep, glide, drag, and float.

• Remind students that cartwheels, flips, somersaults, and other gymnastic or acrobatic skills are not appropriate due to limited room and safety issues.

Kindergarten Through Grade 3 Variation

• If space is limited, explore the traveling actions using the following structure:

1. To avoid students bumping into each other, create lines of five or six students.

2. Ask the first line to skip across the room and wait quietly at the far end of the room while each of the other lines skip across.

3. Repeat working line by line, exploring a new traveling action each time.

• After your class has explored all the traveling actions they listed, create forward and back traveling patterns that your class can perform together, for example:

· Swoop forward like an eagle and hop back like a rabbit.

· Roll forward for 4 beats and float backward for 4 beats.

· Stomp forward and tiptoe backward.

Grades 4 Through 6 Variation

• Invite your students to work in groups of four or five and choreograph a piece containing on-the-spot and traveling actions with the following requirements:

· An original 8-beat on-the-spot phrase

· Two contrasting 4-beat traveling motions (running backward contrasted with lunging steps with outreached arms)

· Four freezes in different shapes (use different levels)

· Not everyone should be doing the same thing at the same time

• Before they begin to work, remind your class of the following:

· Everyone in the group should contribute ideas to the choreography.

· No one is the leader.

· No one can just sit back while others do all the work.

· Students should support each other.

· If someone suggests a shape or actions that only half of the group is able to do, the other half can perform another action—constant unison is not a requirement in this assignment.

1. Allow students 15 minutes to create and memorize their new choreography.

2. Visit the groups throughout the creative process, listen in, and watch as they work. If a group is having trouble, join them and ask to see what they've created. Even if they only have one or two ideas, encourage them to show you their work. Offer positive feedback and help them brainstorm ideas for what happens next.

3. At the 7-minute mark, stop the class and ask how everyone is doing. If a number of groups are struggling, spend extra time with them. Depending on your students' age and level of experience, your class may need more time.

Presentation

• If time allows, have students present one group at a time. If that's not possible, have two groups present together.

- The groups will start at the same time. Everyone should hold their final pose until the music has been turned off. That way, if a group has finished early, they won't be a distraction while the other group is still performing.
- Make sure performers are focused on their starting positions (some groups may have chosen to start in an original shape other than parallel position), play the music, and count students in to begin.
- After everyone in the class has presented, congratulate them on their work. Come together and reflect upon the process.

Discussion

- "What was the biggest challenge your group faced? How was it solved?"
- Did all the groups create pieces that fulfilled all the requirements?
- Did some groups do more than what was required? If yes, what additional elements did they add, and how did they affect the choreography?

Journal Entry for All Grades

"Write a short paragraph or poem describing your favorite way to travel (such as bike, walk, skate, swim, run, ski, or paddle)." Younger grades may draw their favorite way to travel.

EXERCISE 1.3   EXPLORING TIME

Lesson Plan Suggestions

Kindergarten Through Grades 6

First lesson: Steps 1, 2, and 3 (follow grade-appropriate variations)

Second lesson: Steps 4 (video: Tarambé Percusión Corporal ensemble from Costa Rica, 4:27) and 5 (follow grade-appropriate variations) to create and present; journal entry

Step 1: Fast and Slow

Recommended Music

Tracks 13, 14, and 15. The track suggestions are specific: Track 14 is fast, 13 is slow, and 15 mixes the fast and slow compositions together.

Kindergarten Through Grade 3 Variation

Warm your students up with this structured improvisation.

1. Ask your students to find a space in the room and create their own bubble.
2. Give them a moment to stretch their arms up high and then to the sides, front, behind, and down to their feet. Everyone stays in their own bubble on their own spot.
3. Before you begin moving, ask your students what on-the-spot movements can be performed quickly. Their suggestions may include to jump, shake, run on-the-spot, hop on-the-spot, wiggle, and swing their arms. Explore those on-the-spot actions for 1 minute with track 14.
4. Now ask your students what type of on-the-spot movements would work best when performed slowly. Their suggestions may include reaching, melting, floating, swaying, or balancing. Explore those on-the-spot movements using track 13.
5. Let your class know that the last piece of music they'll be moving to will shift from fast and rhythmic to slow and atmospheric. Their job is to change their movements to fit the speed of the music using the fast and slow actions they've already explored.
6. Play track 15. Keep your class moving for the entire composition.

Grades 4 Through 6 Variation

1. Use track 14 to run through the warm-up your class learned in exercise 1.2 to loosen everyone up.
2. Play track 13. The music is slow. Invite your class to perform the warm-up as slowly as they can.
3. Play the first 30 seconds of track 15. The music changes from fast to slow, and the changes aren't fixed. They happen randomly. When moving to this composition, your students will have to shift speeds.
4. Brainstorm images of things that melt and move slowly (wax dripping down a candle, icicles and snow melting in the sun) and images of things that accelerate quickly (racehorses, the wind, squirrels darting about).

5. Invite your class to try performing the warm-up using track 15. Or if they prefer, they can make up their own actions to match the music.

Discussion

- "Was it easier to stay focused on the actions when the music was fast? Did you feel a deeper stretch when you worked slowly?"
- "When you worked with the final composition, did you listen to the music more intensely? Were you able to shift speeds easily? Was slowing down easier than speeding up?"

Remember, there's no right answer. Everyone's experience is unique.

Step 2: How Slow Can You Go?

Recommended Music

Track 13

For All Grades

Ask students to imagine themselves in a slow-motion film. Lead the class with the following activities performed in slow motion with music playing softly in the background.

1. Eating an apple:
   - Slowly reach for an apple.
   - Slowly bring the apple toward your mouth.
   - Open your mouth wide.
   - Take the first bite.
   - Chew slowly using all your face muscles.
   - Swallow slowly.
   - Take another bite.

2. For running on-the-spot, imagine running the last portion of a race in slow motion:
   - Slowly pump the arms forward and back.
   - Slowly lifting one foot and then the other.
   - Arrive at the finish line.
   - You won! Celebrate in slow motion! Make a big smile and put your fists in the air.

© Janice Pomer

Celebrate after the race.

3. Ask students for suggestions of actions to explore in slow motion. Try two or three more and save other suggestions for another day.

   • This type of slow-motion exercise can be performed in the aisles or at one's desk. Use it as a fun and effective way to quietly stretch and refocus your class when they need a quick break during the school day.

Discussion

   • "Was working in slow motion hard work, calming, or a little of both?" Ask students to explain what was challenging and what was calming.

   • "Slow motion is used in movies to magnify or stretch out actions. Are there other reasons film directors use slow motion in their films?" (*To intensify emotions, to increase the suspense.*)

Step 3: Body Beats

Creating rhythmic patterns with your body.

Kindergarten Through Grade 3 Variation

Use this call-and-response exercise to develop your students' listening skills and coordination.

   • Sit in a circle.

   • Create simple rhythmic clapping patterns for your class to repeat back to you. You can clap your hands or tap your thighs, shoulders, and head.

   • When you're presenting the patterns for your students, do it without speaking. You want your students to be solely focused on the sounds of the body beats and actions.

   • Before you begin, let them know that you'll be sending them a pattern and will signal them when it's time for them to echo it back to you.

   • If everyone in the class echoes the pattern back correctly, send out another pattern. If the sonic elements aren't clearly echoed back, send the same pattern out again until everyone is able to replicate it. Start simply and slowly increase in difficulty. For example:

   1. Simple 4-beat phrase: clap hands twice, then slap your thighs and hold.

   2. Building on first example, slap both thighs at the same time, clap your hands, tap your right shoulder, and then tap your left shoulder.

   3. Building on the second example, an 8-beat phrase would be to slap your thighs, clap your hands, slap your thighs, clap your hands, tap both shoulders 3 times, and clap once.

   4. Add new actions and greater levels of difficulty for new 8-beat phrases. Tap your stomach twice with both hands, rub your hands together for 2 beats, clap your hands together twice, clap your right hand on your right thigh, then clap your left hand on your left thigh.

   • After leading several patterns, ask student volunteers to create a pattern for the class to echo.

If your class found rhythmic hand patterns easy, try this challenge. Work standing up so that foot actions and sounds can be added to the rhythmic patterns. Start simply and develop a level of difficulty, for example:

- Step on-the-spot with the right foot on beat 1, clap on beat 2, step on-the-spot with the left foot on beat 3, and clap on beat 4. Repeat 3 or 4 times.
- Change the first clap to 2 quick claps. Step on-the-spot right on beat 1, make 2 quick claps on beat 2, step on-the-spot left on beat 3, and clap on beat 4. Repeat 3 to 4 times.
- Try traveling forward with each step.

Grades 4 Through 6 Variation 1

Instructions

- Review the list of on-the-spot actions from exercise 1.2, with a particular focus on actions that create sounds, including:
  - Hands can clap, rub, and flap, and fingers can snap.
  - Feet can step, stomp, tap, and hop, and feet can clap together in the air when a student jumps.
  - Legs can be lifted (clap hands under lifted leg or bend the knee, bring foot to opposite hand, and clap the foot) or when legs rotate inward and outward, try clapping the inner and outer thighs.
- Ask two volunteers to demonstrate this simple exercise, where each mover creates their own original 4-beat rhythmic phrases.
  1. Stand in parallel position facing each other.
  2. Student A creates a 4-beat sound or action phrase.
  3. Student B creates a different 4-beat sound or action phrase.
  4. Student A creates another phrase, and student B creates another phrase.
- While working, let your class know they should try to:
  1. Maintain a steady beat—both phrases should be at the same tempo without long pauses in between.
  2. Find new combinations of actions and sounds with each turn they take.
  3. Work without talking—the only sounds they can make are body beats.
  4. Use some silences within the phrase, such as jump on beat 1, extend arms wide on beat 2 (silent action), clap on beat 3, and extend arms wide on beat 4 (silent action).
  5. Count the beats internally (silently) so if student A finishes her phrase with a silent action, student B knows when it's his turn to start.
  6. Make sure each duet knows who will be starting first.
  7. The exercise is performed without musical accompaniment.
  8. Everyone should follow the tempo you establish.
  9. Establish a beat the class should try to follow. Call out a moderate tempo: 1, 2, 3, 4, 5, 6, 7, 8.
- Let your class work for 2 or 3 minutes, then ask everyone to sit down and discuss the challenges.

Discussion

- "Was everyone able to maintain a steady beat? Were you counting internally and able to stay focused on your partner and not get distracted?"

- "Was everyone able to find new body-beat combinations for every turn? If yes, how? If no, what actions did you regularly repeat?"
- "Was everyone able to do the exercise without talking?"

Grades 4 Through 6 Variation 2

Instructions

1. Instead of working in equal sections of fours, try working with sevens. Introduce working in sevens with two volunteers demonstrating this pattern:
   - Student A claps on beats 1, 2, 3.
   - Student B claps on beats 4, 5.
   - Student A claps on beats 6, 7.
   - Student B claps on beats 1, 2, 3.
   - Student A claps on beats 4, 5.
   - Student B claps on beats 6, 7.

2. Working with uneven numbers means that student A and B alternate clapping the first 3 beats.

3. Practice the phrase with your entire class.

4. Now divide the class in half. Group A starts first with clapping on beats 1, 2, 3. Group B claps on beats 4 and 5 Group A claps on beats 6 and 7. Then Group B claps on beats 1, 2, 3. Group A claps on beats 4 and 5, and group B claps on beats 6 and 7.

5. After the class practices together, ask everyone to find a new partner to explore sevens using a wide range of body-beat actions.

6. Count them in so everyone is working with the same moderate tempo.

7. When you count, try emphasizing the first, fourth, and sixth beat: **1**, 2, 3, **4**, 5, **6**, 7.

8. After 2 or 3 minutes of working with 7-beat phrases, sit down and discuss.

Body beats.

© Barry Prophet

Discussion

- "Was it challenging to work with an uneven phrase? If yes, what did you and your partner do to maintain the phrase?"
- Ask your class to think about the music they normally listen to. Most Western pop music is in 4/4 timing, though 3/4 and 6/8 is used as well. Many world music traditions use 5/4, 7/4, and other more complex timings to create beautiful polyrhythmic compositions using multiple layers of rhythmic patterns.

Grades 5 and 6 Variation

1. Try combining fours and sevens to work in 15-beat phrases. Ask for volunteers to demonstrate clapping the following:
   - Student A claps on beats 1, 2, 3, 4.
   - Student B claps on beats 1, 2, 3, 4.

- Student A claps on beats 1, 2, 3.
- Student B claps on beats 4, 5.
- Student A claps on beats 6, 7.
- Student B claps on beats 1, 2, 3, 4.
- Student A claps on beats 1, 2, 3, 4.
- Student B claps on beats 1, 2, 3.
- Student A claps on beats 4, 5.
- Student B claps on beats 6, 7.

2. Ask students to find new partners and to practice the new clapping phrase for a minute.

3. When everyone has the hang of doing the 15-beat phrase, they can apply their full body-beat vocabulary.

4. After 2 minutes of working with 15-beat phrases, sit down and discuss.

Discussion

"Was the 15-beat phrase harder or easier than the 7-beat phrase? Remember, there's no correct answer, but it's important to share the reason for your response. For example, some people find that having 2 sets of 4 helps them prepare for the uneven section."

Step 4: Video—All Grades

- Watch the video of the Tarambé Percusión Corporal ensemble from Costa Rica (4:27) from the list of video links in *HKPropel*. This body-beat performance will inspire your students to expand their body-beat repertoire and create complex choreography.

- After watching the video, work with your students to compile a list of the choreographic elements featured in the video with special focus on rhythm and tempo. Your list should include these elements:
  - Unison rhythmic work
  - Call and response
  - Rhythmic duets
  - Smooth transitions between different tempos and rhythm changes
  - Moments of silence (and of stillness)
  - Level changes (volume of sound and bodies)
  - Changes in spatial relationships
  - Maintaining rhythm work while traveling

Step 5: Creating Body-Beat Choreography

Kindergarten Through Grade 3 Variation

- Using students' observations from the video, work with your class to create an on-the-spot body-beat phrase.
  1. Ask your students to spread throughout the room, arm's-length apart.
  2. Invite them to explore some of the moves they saw in the video but ask them to stay on-the-spot as they work while you call out prompts.

3. After about 2 minutes of students working on their own, tell them to stop and rest.

4. Ask them for their help creating a Body-Beat dance the class can perform together.

5. Ask students if they have a favorite move and if so, demonstrate it.

6. Keep it simple, 8 to 16 beats to start.

7. Body-beat choreography helps develop coordination, fine and gross motor control, focus, and self-control.

8. Keep the choreography on-the-spot. That way, you can use the dance phrase throughout the day whenever your class needs to release some energy. They can stand up beside their chairs, stretch for a moment, and then perform their dance.

9. Many classes like to practice their body-beat phrase daily. Once everyone is confident with the choreography, add another 8 to 16 beats to the phrase (ask your students to contribute ideas.)

10. You can build their Body-Beat dances for months. Some students do their dances during recess, and students from other classes join in.

11. Besides performing their phrases in unison, you can divide the class into groups A and B to create call-and-response sections.

Grades 4 Through 6 Variation

Instructions

Invite your class to work in groups of four or five students and create a 16- to 24-beat piece of body-beat choreography that contains these required elements:

- Unison rhythm work
- Call-and-response rhythm work
- Level changes (of bodies and sound)
- One formation to start and another to finish—for example a straight line into a V or a square into a semicircle

Clarity and focus are required for rhythm work, and that takes practice. Provide students with enough time to create, practice, and present their work one at a time.

Discussion

- Did all the groups include all the required elements in their dance?
- Did some groups change tempos or use a variety of rhythmic patterns?
- Did some groups include additional elements? If yes, what were they?

Journal Entry For all Grades

- Have students write a short paragraph about time dragging or whizzing by. Prompt them by saying, "When does time pass slowly? When does it fly by?" Younger students can create a picture showing two activities: one that makes time fly and the other where time seems to never end.

EXERCISE 1.4   EXPLORING SPACE

In this exercise, your class will be exploring the space between shapes, animating the space around them, and traveling in and out of spatial relationships.

Lesson Plan Suggestions

Kindergarten Through Grade 3

First lesson: Steps 1 (follow the grade-appropriate variation), 2, and 3

Second lesson: Steps 4 (video: Bhangra Empire, 8:19) and 5 (follow the grade-appropriate variation)

Grades 4 Through 6

First lesson: Steps 1 (follow the grade-appropriate variation), 2, and 3

Second lesson: Steps 4 (video: Bhangra Empire, 8:19) and 5 (follow the grade-appropriate variation)

Third lesson: Practice and present dances from step 5 (follow the grade-appropriate variation); step 6 introduces students to stage blocking and explains how to use it in future choreography

Recommended Music: Tracks 18 and 14

Step 1: Warm Up by Exploring Spaces Between High and Low

Review of some of the dynamic shapes students made in exercise 1.1 (twisted, angular, arched, tilted, dramatic, opened, closed).

In this warm-up, your class will be exploring the space between high and low shapes in the following manner:

1. Ask your students to make the highest shape they can. Tell them that the height of that shape is level 10.

2. Ask your students to make the lowest shape they can. The lowest shape is at level 1.

3. Ask students to make a mid-level shape halfway between their highest and lowest.

4. Their mid-level shape is level 5.

5. Ask your students to make a new shape at level 6. Everyone's shape should be a little higher than their shape at level 5.

6. Return to the level 5 shape, then ask your students to make a different shape at level 4. Everyone should move a little lower.

7. Tell your class that you will be calling out numbers from 1 to 10, and their job is to create new shapes at each level and to hold their shape until you call out the next level.

8. Make sure you allow several beats (or breaths because you'll be doing the exercise in silence) for students to hold their shapes in total stillness.

Kindergarten Through Grade 3 Variation

Use this exercise to support students' understanding of sequential numbers. Practice going from level 1 through 10 and back again at equal intervals. Repeat the sequence 2 or 3 times.

Grades 4 Through 6 Variation

- Call out the numbers from 1 to 10 and back from 10 to 1, then call the numbers out of sequence—for example, 1, 3, 5, 10, 2, 7, 9, 4, 6, 8.
- If students' shapes become repetitive, call out specific shape requirements:
  - A symmetrical shape at level 5
  - A shape with one hand on your ankle at level 7
  - A closed, twisted shape at level 2
- After 1 to 2 minutes, stop and take a moment to reflect.

Discussion

- "Did the exercise make you more aware of the range of the space between high (10) and low (1)?"
- "Did you have to be more thoughtful about your shapes in order to properly define each level and use equal intervals? If yes, explain how." (*I had to consider the distance between each movement, I used my spine more than before, I imagined I was a thermometer going up and down.*)

Step 2: The Space Between Shapes (Negative and Positive Space)

Apply students' new appreciation for space between high and low in the next step.

Instructions

Divide your class into three groups and ask one group to stand in a horizontal line across the performance area while the other two groups sit and watch.

1. The students in the line should be arm's-length apart in parallel position.
2. Ask the students who are watching to observe the line with special attention to the space between the students.
3. At present, the space between the students is neutral. All the spaces are equal distance apart and have straight edges, thanks to the parallel position of students' arms and legs.
4. The only spatial difference is vertically, where people standing beside each other are different heights, like city skylines or mountain ranges.
5. Let the student standing at the right end of the line know that he's number 1, the next person is number 2, then 3, 4, and so on.
6. Students can make shapes at any level they wish as long at their shape is at a different level from those beside them.
7. Student 1 will make a shape and freeze, number 2 will make a shape and freeze, and so on through the line until everyone has created a shape.
8. The last person should hold her shape for a moment or two, then create a new shape at a different level to reverse the sequence going back through the line.

9. Student 1 will be the last person to make a new shape.

10. After he has held it for a moment, he should return to parallel position. Then student 2 will go into parallel position until everyone is in parallel position.

11. Ask those who were watching to notice how the space between the students changed when their shapes changed.

12. Invite group 2 to go into the performance area and the first group to join the viewing area.

13. Ask the new group to follow the same sequential pattern, creating shapes at different levels that enter the space between the people beside them without touching.

14. After group 2 has finished, invite group 3 to the performance area.

15. Ask group 3 to make shapes that emphasize the space and different shapes their arms and legs can create (circles, diamonds, triangles).

High and low shapes.

Discussion

- Visual artists call the space between shapes *negative space* and the object that defines the space *positive space*. Look around your classroom and out the window to bring students' attention to examples of negative and positive space; the space between chairs and their desks is a good example. ("If there was no space, where would your legs go?") Lead a discussion on the importance of the space in between. ("Is the space between things important?")

- Make a list of objects students encounter daily. The list will include lockers, notebooks, bowls, and forks. Ask them the following:

  - "What do you do when there's no space left in your knapsack or locker?"

  - "Would a fork work if there were no spaces between the tines?"

  - "How useful would a bowl be if its center space were the size of a spoon?"

  - "If there were no space between written words, how would you know when a word ended and another began?"

  - "Would music sound the same without space between notes?"

Step 3: Paint the Air With Movement—All Grades

Imagine you're a painter standing in front of a huge blank canvas. You reach for your paintbrush and begin to fill the empty canvas with lines and color. That's the inspiration for this next exercise, but instead of using paintbrushes, students will use their hands and feet to paint the air in front of them.

Instructions

1. Ask your students to stand arm's-length apart throughout the room and to imagine that they are standing in front of a huge blank canvas.
2. Each student has their own canvas; the bottom of the canvas rests on the floor, the top is higher than their hands can reach, and their canvas is twice as wide as their side reach.
3. On the floor in front of each canvas are buckets of paint, but there are no paintbrushes. Instead, students will have to use their hands and feet to bring the paint to the canvas.
4. Their job is to create an abstract painting. The painting will contain angles, curves, swirls, splashes, geometric shapes, and bold lines from bottom to top and from side to side.
5. They'll need to jump to reach the top of the canvas, bend low or use their feet to paint the bottom, and make dots and smudges with their elbows and nose.
6. Every line and shape they make on the canvas will be generated from body movements.
7. Start by calling out different elements for your class to paint, then after a bit invite them to improvise.
8. Remind students to be aware of others when they move from side to side so they do not interfere with people working nearby.
9. You want to see everyone using full-body movements and to keep working on the image you've called out until the next is called.
10. Play track 18.
11. Invite everyone to dip their hands and feet in the paint, then stand in parallel position.
12. Call out these and other images for your class to paint:
    - A giant swirling circle in the center of the canvas
    - Long rippling waves all along the bottom
    - Footprints as high as your feet can reach above the waves
    - Zigzag lightning bolts high up in the upper right corner
    - A cluster of splashes in the upper left corner
    - Use your elbows to paint triangles inside the big circle
    - Flick the paint with your fingers across the very top
    - Use your nose to place tiny dabs of paint below the zigzags
13. After they have followed your directions for a minute or two, invite students to improvise.

Discussion

- Ask students to raise their hands if they were able to see the painting they were creating in front of them. Of those who said yes, did they see colors as well as shapes?

- Regardless of whether students visualized their paintings externally or worked through a different process, did they feel that their actions filled the space? If yes, ask if there were specific actions that worked exceptionally well. If no, ask what else they can do to help their actions fill the space.

Step 4: Choreographing Using Multiple Spatial Relationships

In steps 1, 2, and 3, your class explored the space between their highest and lowest shapes, identified negative and positive space between moves, and painted the space around them. In previous exercises, they explored traveling through space and the space between sounds and silence.

Bhangra is a dance that originated in the 15th century in India and was created by Punjabi farmers to celebrate the harvest. Over the centuries, the popularity of bhangra grew, and the dance was widely performed at weddings and festivals. This high-energy, joyful dance form became modernized in the 1960s and is now enjoyed around the world.

Instructions

Watch the Bhangra Empire video (8:19) from the list of video links in HK*Propel* to see choreography packed with constantly evolving spatial relationships and level changes. The camera angle lets viewers fully appreciate the complexity of the choreography and the dancers' perfect spacing. If time is limited, watch until 5:20 and leave the final movement for another day.

Post-Video Discussion

- "The choreography utilized more than a dozen geometric formations. How many do you remember?" Compile a list with your class.
- "While moving from shape to shape, the dancers never bumped into each other and always kept equal distance apart. How do you think they managed to do that?" Answers may include *practice, teamwork, using peripheral vision, clearly communicating the choreography beforehand*, and *drawing or mapping out ideas*.

Step 5: Create a Dance Inspired by the Video

Kindergarten Through Grade 1 Variation

1. Tell your class that they're going to learn how to move in and out of different geometric shapes, just like the dancers in the video.
2. Draw a horizontal line on the chalkboard or chart paper, or if you're working outdoors, use sidewalk chalk on the asphalt.
3. Ask students how they can turn a line into a circle. There may be a number of interesting suggestions. Ask students what the simplest way to do it is. When someone suggests that the ends could curve and meet, agree to try it.
   - Go the board where you've drawn the flat horizontal line: ___ .
   - Draw a *U* beside it, the ends curving and moving out of the line.
   - Beside the *U* draw an *O*. The ends have come together to create an *O*.
4. Ask your class to stand in a line, then ask the students at either end of the line to walk into a U shape then turn inward and walk toward each other to create the *O*.

5. The people at the center of the line won't be traveling. They are the anchors and will need to hold their position to keep the integrity of the shape.

6. Return to the horizontal line by reversing the process: *O* to *U* to __.

7. Now try the process with some sound and motion.

8. Once they are in a straight line, ask your class to clap for 8 beats, then create a high shape and hold for 8 beats.

9. Walk into the *U* while clapping for 8 beats—anchor students will walk on-the-spot.

10. Create and hold mid-level shapes for 8 beats.

11. Walk into the *O* while clapping for 8 beats—anchor students will walk on-the-spot.

12. Create a high shape for beats 1 and 2, a mid-level shape for beats 3 and 4, jump up on beat 5, land in a new shape on beat 6, and hold on beats 7 and 8.

13. Repeat the sequence, increasing the level of difficulty by asking students to suggest more complex traveling actions.

14. Or ask your class how they can move from a horizontal line into a V and then into a diamond. If they're up for the challenge, brainstorm ideas, draw out the plan, and describe it again. Then try it out.

Grades 2 and 3 Variation

Instructions

Invite your class to work in groups of four or five to create a dance accompanied by music from track 14 with the following requirements:

- Start in a spatial relationship (circle, diamond, diagonal line).
- Perform an 8-beat, on-the-spot phrase in unison (try using arm movements from the Paint the Air exploration).
- Travel for 8 beats into a new spatial relationship.
- Repeat the 8-beat on-the-spot phrase in unison.
- Travel for 8 beats into a third spatial relationship and freeze.

Discussion

- "Did everyone move in and out the spatial relationships smoothly?"
- "How many different spatial relationships did the class create?"

Journal Entry for Kindergarten Through Grade 3

"Create a picture using only a single shape: *X*, *O*, a rippling line, a zigzag, or an image like a flower, cat face, umbrella, or tree. Draw it in different sizes and place the shapes or images in different spatial relationships: in a circle, diagonally across the page, in clusters of twos and threes." Show the class figure 1.4 for ideas.

Grades 4 Through 6 Variation

Instructions

- Ask students to work in groups of five or six to create original choreography inspired by the video. The required elements are:

  1. Use an opening position that isn't a straight line.

Figure 1.4 Exploring spatial relationships.

2. Begin the dance with 8 beats of on-the-spot movement (use level changes).

3. Travel for 8 beats into a second spatial relationship (other than a straight line) using a traveling pattern other than walking (leaps, rolls, complex footwork).

4. Perform a different 8-beat on-the-spot movement phrase while in the second spatial relationship (use level, direction, and rhythmic changes).

5. Travel into the third and final spatial relationship using a new traveling step. Don't forget to incorporate arm movements while traveling.

6. Perform a different 8 beat on-the-spot movement phrase.

7. Create a final position where half the dancers are at one level and direction, and the other half are at another.

8. Freeze and hold for 8 beats.

- Remind students that even though they don't have the full performance area to practice in, they will have the full area to present their work. On-the-spot choreography should paint the space with jumps, reaching arms, and upper-body actions, and the traveling patterns should be high energy and dynamic. Use track 14 to accompany the choreography.

- This is the most complex choreographic assignment yet, and because much of the focus is on spatial relationships, groups should share their pieces one at a time.

- Your class may need to create, practice, and record their choreography in their journals at the end of lesson 2 and review, practice, and present one group at a time during lesson 3.

Discussion Grades 4 Through 6

- "What strategies did you use to stay equal distance apart?"

- "Did any group start in a small shape and move their spatial relationship farther apart?" Ask each group how they selected their three spatial formations and their reason for selecting them.

Step 6: Learning Technical Terms for the Space of the Stage

Grades 4 Through 6

Understanding stage directions is the final spatial exploration in this exercise. Stage directions help make planning, remembering, performing, and writing out choreography less complicated. (Younger grades need not worry about stage directions because the teacher facilitates most of the collaborative choreography.)

Most stages are rectangular. Imagine dividing the stage into nine different areas, and each of the nine areas has its own name. First divide the length of the stage into three sections by drawing two imaginary and equally spaced lines horizontally across the length of the stage. The length of the stage closest to the viewing area is called downstage, the middle length of the stage is called center stage, and the area farthest from the viewing area is called upstage, as seen in figure 1.5a.

Now place two more imaginary lines vertically for stage depth. The area to the audience's left is called stage right, the area to the audience's right is called stage left, and the area in the center in is called center stage, as seen in figure 1.5b. When combined, the 2 sets of lines look like a large tic-tac-toe grid with each of the nine areas having their own specific name (upstage right, downstage left, center stage), as seen in figure 1.5c. This exercise helps students learn the stage areas and practice how to use the terms when giving instructions.

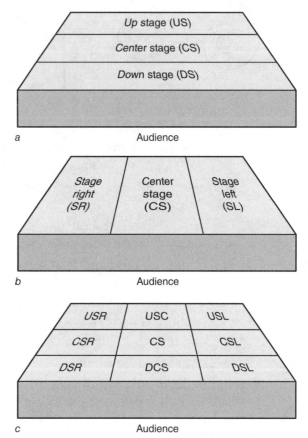

Figure 1.5   Areas of the stage.

Instructions

- Introduce students to the stage areas by drawing them on the flip chart. If you're working outdoors, you can draw a huge grid on the asphalt. Invite your class to sit facing the performance area.
- Ask for four volunteers to demonstrate how to follow stage directions with this simple example:
  1. Direct two of the volunteers to stand in upstage right.
  2. Direct the other two to stand in downstage left.
  3. Direct those in upstage right to walk to upstage left.

    4. Direct those in downstage left to walk to downstage right.

    5. Direct everyone to walk to center stage, hold for 2 beats, then walk back to their original positions.

- Divide your class into four groups and try these more complex staging examples:

  · Example for Group 1

    1. Invite group 1 to stand at upstage center.
    2. Direct them to run to downstage center for 2 beats, freeze for 2 beats, then slowly walk backward to upstage center (keep facing the audience).
    3. Once at upstage center, direct them to slowly melt into low-level shapes and freeze.

  · Example for Groups 2 and 3

    1. Invite group 2 to stand in upstage left.
    2. Invite group 3 to stand in upstage right.
    3. Direct group 2 to walk to downstage right.
    4. Direct group 3 to walk to downstage left.
    5. Direct the group in downstage right to spread out and create a line from downstage right to upstage right.
    6. Direct the group in downstage left to spread out and create a line from downstage left to upstage left.
    7. Ask both lines to take 2 leaps toward center stage and freeze for two beats.

  · Example for Group 4

    1. Invite group 4 to stand in center stage left.
    2. Direct them to slowly creep (moving at low levels) to center stage.
    3. Direct them to look up, then stand up and reach up as high as they can.
    4. Direct them to cover their heads and run to center stage right.

  · Let students direct each other.

    1. Keep working in the same four groups.
    2. Invite volunteers to give stage directions to a group.
    3. Volunteers should use the appropriate stage terms when giving their instructions.
    4. Don't make the directions complicated; keep them short and clear.
    5. Allow two or three students to give directions to each group, then change groups.
    6. Invite the first group to return to the performance area, select the first volunteer director from that group, and let the student director begin.

- After all the groups have been directed by students, sit down to discuss.

Discussion

- "When you were in the stage area, were you able to follow the stage directions without much trouble? If no, explain what was difficult so others can help clarify."

- "When you were directing, did you always remember that your right was the performers' left?"

Writing each stage direction can take time, which is why directors and choreographers use short forms: *upstage center* is USC, and *downstage right* is DSR.

Journal Entry for Grades 4 Through 6

For a quick journal entry, ask students to write three movement directions using abbreviations (see figure 1.5). For example, "Start in DSC, slowly walk backward to USC, melt to a low level, and half of the group rolls to USL and half rolls to USR." Use some of your students' suggestions in future lessons when you need to review stage directions.

EXERCISE 1.5   EXPLORING ENERGY

Energy often refers to the amount of focus or effort invested in a movement. Energy for dancers isn't just a matter of intensity or speed; it's also the ability to express one's ideas, imagination, and emotions through an action.

Lesson Plan Suggestions

Kindergarten Through Grade 3

First lesson: Steps 1, 2, and 3 (follow grade-appropriate variations); journal entry

Grades 4 Through 6

First lesson: Steps 1, 2, and 3 (follow grade-appropriate variations); journal entry

Second lesson: This is only needed if students didn't have enough time to present their dances; do a quick warm-up, then work in their groups to review and practice their dances before presenting them

Step 1: What's at the End of the Rope?

Instructions

1. Ask your students to stand arm's-length apart in parallel position.
2. Invite them to imagine that it's a beautiful summer day with a clear sky and gentle breeze. They're in a park, and someone has given them a kite to fly.
3. The kite is already airborne. All they have to do is take hold of the kite string and watch it fly.
4. Support them with prompts: "Can you pull the kite toward you?" "Give it more string and watch it soar." "Follow the breeze." "Can it swoop around and around?"
5. After 15 to 20 seconds, tell the class that instead of flying kites in the park, they now have 2 big dogs to walk.
6. The dogs are strong. They want to run and keep wanting to go in different directions.
7. Support your students with prompts: "Don't let the dogs pull you; you have to be in charge." "Try to get the dogs to walk together." "They're strong, but you can do it."
8. Let students work with the dogs for 15 to 20 seconds, then tell them the dog leashes have turned into a kite string, and they can fly the kite again.
9. After 10 to 15 seconds, the kite string turns into the leash. The dogs are pulling in opposite directions—control the dogs!
10. Go back and forth from kites to dogs, changing the length of the intervals.
11. After 2 to 3 minutes of controlling dogs and flying kites, bring the exploration to a close.

Discussion

Ask your students how they are feeling (the most common answer is that their arms are tired). If they say their arms are tired, ask them why. They'll say they're tired because they've been pulling. My response is, "What have you been pulling?" to which the entire class will scream "Dogs!" I look around and say, "Dogs? I don't see any dogs."

This simple exercise is a great way to illustrate the importance of intent and imagination in the performing arts. When performers stay focused on their task, they create images and feelings so intense that their intensity and commitment grabs the audience's attention.

Other questions to ask in discussion include the following:

- "Did the kite string feel different from the dog leashes? If yes, explain how."
- "Did you have vivid images of your kite and your dogs?"

Step 2: Just Passing Though

Kindergarten Through Grade 3 Variation

1. Moving quietly throughout the room, invite your class to explore ways to do the following. Before each exploration, tell your class the environment they'll be traveling through and quickly brainstorm ideas.
   - Creep through a jungle (there's no path, just lots of vines and distant animal sounds)
   - Wander through a haunted house (look out for spider webs and ghosts!)
   - Float in space (there's no gravity in space; you can't move quickly)
   - Walk in a snowstorm against a strong, cold wind (don't lose your hat!)
2. While your class is moving, call out prompts to support their work.
3. After each environment, highlight some of their movements.

After the four environments have been explored, ask for student suggestions and explore 2 or 3 additional environments.

Grades 4 Through 6 Variation

1. Ask students to line up horizontally at one side of the room.
2. Have six to eight students in the first line, another line behind them, and so on.
3. Tell students you will be calling out different environments for them to move through (use the environments listed in the Kindergarten to Grade 3 Variation or create your own).
4. Their job is to travel to the far side of the room while they move through that environment.
5. When the first line gets halfway across the room, the second line will begin.
6. When a line gets to the far side, they should walk quietly along the perimeter of the room so they don't interfere with the students who are still working.
7. When all the lines have returned to the starting area, give them a new environment to explore.
8. Afterward, ask students for additional environments to travel through.

Discussion for All Grades

- "Which environment was the easiest to imagine or travel through?"
- "Which environment was the most challenging to imagine or travel through?"
- "Which environment did you most enjoy exploring? Why?"

Step 3: Infusing Dance With Dramatic Expression

Recommended Music

Tracks 13 and 14

Kindergarten Through Grade 3 Variation

- Compile a list of emotions, such as happy, sad, confident, shy, surprised, frustrated, and nervous.
- In exercise 1.1, some of the shapes your class made were inspired by emotions. Now instead of freezing, your class will explore movements inspired by emotions.

1. Play track 13 for 20 seconds. Your class will remember it as the slow composition from exercise 1.3.
2. Make a list of the emotions that would work best with this composition.
3. Play track 14 for 20 seconds. This was the fast composition from previous exercises.
4. Make a list of the emotions that would work best with this composition.
5. Play 2 minutes of each composition while your students explore ways to move that communicate different emotions.
6. Use prompts to support their work: "What are your hands and feet excited about?" "Can you show nervousness with your entire body?" "What levels should you move in to show that you're tired?"

- After improvising, work with your class to create two dance phrases, one for each composition communicating contrasting emotions.

7. Include elements introduced in the previous exercises: shapes, traveling steps, level, direction, and tempo changes.
8. Kindergarten and grade 1 can start with Sad and Happy dances.
9. Sad might use closed, low- to mid-level shapes and slow actions.
10. Happy might use high, open shapes and bouncy, quick actions.
11. Practice the dance phrases together several times.

- Once your students are confident with their happy or sad phrases, create other contrasting phrases. Besides being a great way to develop your students' dramatic expression, these dances help students understand that emotions can transform: Anger becomes calm, shy becomes friendly, and fearful becomes courageous.

Journal Entry for Kindergarten Through Grade 3

"Draw a picture where half of the page communicates one emotion and the other half communicates a different emotion."

Grades 4 Through 6 Variation

Instructions

1. Ask your class to go into groups of four or five and create a 16-beat unison dance phrase that utilizes the elements introduced in the previous exercises, including shapes, traveling steps, level and direction changes, and rhythmic patterns.

2. Create these dances in silence.

3. Once they have created their dance phrase, ask each group to select an environment they traveled through in step 2 and modify their dance so it communicates the specific qualities of the place and the emotions of the characters they imagine would be there.

4. Use either track 13 or 14 to support the dances. For example, students could modify their dances and become:
   - Ghosts or zombies dancing in a haunted house
   - Splashing cool water
   - Astronauts floating outside the space station
   - Dancing while being blown away by the cold, stormy, north wind

5. Their dance phrase will need to be modified, but students shouldn't add additional vocabulary, for example:
   - A simple 1-beat action, such as reaching up, will take longer if the group is floating in space.
   - An action might be repeated multiple times if students are waves.
   - The spatial relationship may fluctuate from an open to a tight grouping as students dance against the north wind and keep getting blown apart.

6. Give students 10 to 15 minutes to rework their dances and review the original dance phrase. When presenting, ask each group to perform their original dance phrase first, followed by the modified re-imagined version.

Discussion

- Ask each group to identify two challenges they had when modifying their original movement phrase into their re-imagined version.
- Did all the re-imagined dances succeed in communicating their chosen environment? Identify some of the most successful adaptations and discuss why they worked so well.

Journal Entry for Grades 4 to 6

"What makes you feel energized: a sunny day, good food, playing sports, helping others, time for yourself, or riding your bike? Write a short paragraph about how it feels to be recharged with energy (think of superheroes who need to recharge their powers). If you like graphic novels, use that format to describe how you recharge."

EXERCISE 1.6   COLLECTIVE OBSERVATION

The foundation exercises in chapter 1 were designed to help your students develop the confidence to express themselves through creative movement exploration while speaking and listening to each other in group discussions. Every exercise had opportunities for students to make their own movement discoveries and contribute personal reflections for the class to consider, explore, and build upon. In the upcoming chapters, the process of observe, explore, create, share, and reflect will continue to be used. The template provides a foundation to ensure that regardless of your students' physical abilities, everyone will feel appreciated and included.

Before you move on to the nature-based exercises in chapters 2 through 7, use this final exercise to reinforce the importance of providing a safe and inclusive space in your class where everyone's perspective is respected. Use this final foundation exercise to highlight the importance of listening to and working with those who may not always see things the same way you do.

1. Ask your class to sit in a large circle.

2. Invite five or six volunteers from different areas in the circle to enter the circle and come together in the center.

3. Tell the volunteers that you'd like them to create a tableau with the following instructions:

   • Everyone should face different directions.

   • Be close enough that people overlap but not touch.

   • Individuals should create a shape they can hold for least a minute.

   • Use a different level and different quality from those next to you.

   • Hold your shape in stillness until you get further instructions.

Once the tableau is set, let those on the outside know that their job will be seeing and sharing.

1. Ask students in the large circle to quietly observe the tableau.

2. Ask for a volunteer to share one or two details of the tableau they can see.

3. Using a clock face analogy, the person who speaks first is at 12.

4. Those sitting at 11 and 1 will be able to see most of what 12 sees, but the information 12 shares may be completely invisible from 5, 6, or 7.

5. Ask a student sitting at 5, 6, or 7 to share something they see.

6. Ask more students to share what they see, and ask them to focus on small details: a closed hand, a pointed foot, a bent knee, or the focus of someone's eyes.

7. As students share these finer details, the class' understanding of the composition deepens because each person's perspective broadens the group's knowledge base.

8. After a minute or so, invite the volunteers in the center to relax and join the outer circle.

9. Invite another group of volunteers to create a new tableau and repeat the process of observation and sharing.

10. Invite your class to contribute ideas for the tableau: a specific theme, adding a movement, using music, or having those in the tableau enter one by one.

11. Ask those sitting on the outside to change their spots so their perspective of the room changes.

12. Over the course of two or three tableaus, make sure every student has had an opportunity to share what they see.

The exercise also works well using classroom objects.

1. Assemble a still life on the floor during recess.

2. When the students return, invite them to sit in a circle around the assemblage of books, rulers, makers, a plant, and water bottle.

3. Give them 10 to 20 seconds to study the still life.

4. One by one, ask students to give a detail of what they see.

5. Challenge the class to find enough details so that no one repeats what another has contributed. It's a great way to help students settle down and refocus their recess energy.

Whether your class observes each other in tableau or classroom objects, the concept of the exercise is to develop their observation skills and to learn to listen and learn from each other. What was invisible becomes visible by the simple act of sharing, listening, and *accepting* that each person has a different point of view and that everyone's point of view has *value*. What was hidden is illuminated, or as a student once exclaimed, "It's like seeing the dark side of the moon!" There's nothing wrong with being drawn to people who like the same things as you do, but there is a problem when we don't extend ourselves beyond what we know. One student wrote this in her journal regarding working with people she wasn't friends with:

> *I really enjoyed working in this group because I got to work with people I usually don't work with. I feel the reason kids tend to gravitate to their friends is because they are safe in the knowledge that they will cooperate. I was worried about working with some of the people in my group, but to my surprise the entire group participated and offered up ideas. We had great chemistry and ultimately choreographed a very strong piece that displayed the Earth forces of push and pull.*

I still remember the dance those students created. The entire class thought it was great, and it inspired everyone to step out of their comfort zones and work with people other than their friends, which led to a more inclusive class dynamic.

In another journal entry from another program, someone noticed how working with people you normally chat with can mean that less works gets done.

> *Natalie's group got a lot of work done within the time we were given. We all got the same about of time, but their group members worked very well together.*

Those two journal excerpts show how journaling can be an effective tool to help students reflect on how they and their classmates work and approach new challenges.

SUMMARY

You and your students are now familiar with the basic elements of dance and are ready to explore the exercises in the upcoming chapters. Chapters 2 through 6 present exercises pedagogically, and each chapter's culminating exercise provides your students with the opportunity to combine all the skills they've gained in that chapter into a large piece of choreography. All the exercises begin with brainstorming sessions. Use flip charts to write down your students' responses and refer to the lists through the exercise. Some of your students will have responses similar to yours, while others will respond with ideas you may never have considered. When teachers listen and appreciate everyone's responses, students learn to listen and appreciate each other; they'll express their ideas more often, learn to value contrasting opinions and aesthetic sensibilities, and discover commonalities among students outside of their social circle.

Go to HK*Propel* to find audio files, reproducible forms, and a list of video links corresponding to chapter exercises.

© Janice Pomer

CHAPTER 2

Plants

In the upcoming nature-inspired exercises, the movement explorations and dance creations will evolve as you and your students collectively gather and share knowledge and ideas. The simplest method for collective gathering has students build vocabulary that describes or relates to the subject they'll be studying. Some lexical sets can be built easily; it's not uncommon for primary students to come up with dozens of action words for water without teacher prompts, but building a lexicon for plants can at first be more challenging.

While working with one grade 2 class, I noticed they started off strong, with a list that included *grow*, *sprout*, *sway*, *reach*, *climb*, *bend*, *open*, *close*, and *die*, but after that they were stuck. I offered the prompt, "What happens when a blossom has opened to its fullest?" Their answers included *fade*, *wilt*, *drop*, *droop*, *wrinkle*, *smell*, and *rot*.

I offered another prompt: "How do plants interact with other living things?" Their answers included *shelter*, *feed*, *shade*, *protect*, *hide*, *heal*, and *poison*. Those two prompts helped students access words that more fully demonstrated their understanding of the cycles and activities of plants and expanded the depth of their movement compositions.

Word lists help your students:

- Demonstrate personal understanding of a subject
- Expand their vocabulary
- Strengthen the knowledge base of the class
- Stimulate discussion
- Provide an array of ideas and images to investigate through movement

EXERCISE 2.1   TREES

This exercise helps build physical skills, including core strength and balancing. It provides opportunities for students to work alone and with others, to move to a prescribed number of beats, and to improvise shapes and traveling patterns.

Lesson Plan Suggestions

Kindergarten Through Grade 3

First lesson: Teach steps 1, 2, and 3 (follow the grade-appropriate variation)

Second lesson: Review steps 2 and 3; learn the simplest form of step 4; do step 5; journal entry

Grades 4 Through 6

First lesson: Teach steps 1, 2, and 3 and introduce step 4 (follow the grade-appropriate variation)

Second lesson: Review step 4, and do step 5; journal entry

Step 1: What We Know About Trees

Recommended Music

Track 3

Instructions

- Set aside 2 to 3 minutes for students to share their knowledge of trees.
- With your class, compile a list of words and phrases about trees. The words might relate to shapes (fan, conical, triangular), benefits (shelter, food, clean air), types of trees (flowering, fruit-bearing, deciduous, evergreen), names of tree species (maple, oak, cedar, spruce), the way to determine the age of a tree, the relationship between the crown and the roots, or local areas of concern or interest (old-growth conservation, clear cutting).
- Ask students to apply the information they have shared in the following introductory movement exercise.
- Using track 3, introduce the movement pattern to students. Model the pattern yourself or ask for a volunteer.
  1. Stand in parallel position as described and practiced in exercise 1.1 and other foundation exercises.
  2. On beat 1, create a tree shape.
  3. Hold the tree shape and maintain the shape for 4 beats.
  4. Return to parallel position and hold for 4 beats.
  5. Create a new tree shape and hold for 4 beats.
  6. Return to parallel position and hold for 4 beats.
- Prepare the class.
  1. Ask students to spread throughout the room, standing arm's-length apart in parallel position.

2. Students work on-the-spot as they create a variety of tree shapes inspired by their brainstorming session.

3. Play the music and clearly count 4 beats to introduce the tempo.

4. When doing the pattern for the first time, call out "Tree shape 1, 2, 3, 4; parallel for 4 beats; tree 1, 2, 3, 4; parallel for 4 beats."

5. Primary teachers may want to continue counting aloud throughout the exercise.

6. Call out prompts to help your students explore new tree shapes. "Can you bend your torso like a willow tree?" "How wide can you make your tree trunk?" "Are your arms covered in leaves or pine needles?"

- Repeat the pattern 5 or 6 cycles, creating new tree shapes each time.

- Afterward, sit down and discuss the experience.

Discussion

- "Was it easy to make different tree shapes each time?" If yes, ask students how they made each of their shapes unique. (*Balancing on one foot, twisting the torso, asymmetrical arms, bending the torso to make mid-level tree shapes.*)

- "Did thinking of specific trees help you find new shapes?" (*Willow trees bend, elms are fan shaped, pines have needles.*)

- "What similarities did most of the shapes have?" (*Torso tall, in upright position, arms reaching.*)

- Some of your students may be familiar with the yoga tree pose (as shown in figure 2.1). The Sanskrit name for tree pose is *Vriksasana*. *Vriksa* means tree and *asana* means pose.

  · Did anyone use this pose when they were making their tree shapes? Ask those who did to demonstrate. Then ask everyone to stand up and try it.

  · Did anyone make a shape similar to this one? Ask those who created a similar shape to demonstrate theirs. Then invite everyone to stand up and try those variations.

Figure 2.1 Tree pose with hands at heart center.

Step 2: Tree Poses

Instructions

Learn and practice the reaching tree and bending tree pose variations as shown in the two photos. The position of the lifted foot does not need to be high up on the inner thigh. It can be placed at mid-calf or just above the ankle. The primary focus of the tree pose is balance and to feel rooted and calm. The height of the lifted foot and openness of the hips are secondary.

1. *Reaching tree pose.* The lifted foot can be placed wherever students feel most stable (above the ankle, mid-calf, or mid-thigh). The arms are diagonally up-

ward in a wide V. The wider arms help with balance and create a fan or elm tree silhouette. For an extra challenge, try looking up.

2. *Bending tree pose.* Place the left foot on the right leg (at ankle, mid-calf, or mid-thigh). Instead of maintaining a straight spine, gently curve the spine to the left as the right arm curves overhead, reaching toward the left wall. Keep the left arm low and curving, reaching across the hips toward the right. Repeat on the second side.

Try these poses with a partner and small groups.

1. *Reaching tree pose with partner.* Stand beside your partner, shoulder to shoulder (without touching). Lift the outside leg, extend the outside arm diagonally, and reach the inside arm straight up. With your partner, your outside arms create a wide V. Repeat on the second side.

2. *Bending tree pose with partner.* Stand back-to-back, beside, or slightly behind your partner (without touching) as shown in the accompanying photograph. Lift one leg and place that foot on the standing leg at a comfortable position. Reach the arms and bend the torso over the bent leg. Try back-to-back and side-to-side variations. Repeat them on both sides.

3. *Reaching tree pose with three or more students.* Stand in a small circle, facing outward (without touching). Reach both arms up and diagonally.

4. *Bending tree pose with three or more students.* Stand in a small circle with the right shoulder inward. Everyone will face the back of the person in front of them. Lift the outside (left) leg to a comfortable height, bend the torso outward to the left, and reach the inside (right) arm overhead, curving outward. Repeat on the second side.

Solo reaching tree.

Bending tree with partner.

Discussion

After the class has completed exploring the tree pose variations, take a moment to discuss the challenges and strategies students discovered.

- "Which solo pose was the most challenging?" Identify the reasons it was difficult. (*It's hard to hold the balance while bending the torso, losing balance when looking up.*) Ask students to suggest solutions.
- "Which group pose was the most challenging?" Identify the reasons it was difficult. (*Getting distracted when working near others, confused with directions when standing in a circle.*) Ask students to suggest solutions.

Step 3: Combining Stillness and Motion

All Grades

Instructions

Use the music to signal when to move and freeze. You should use a mixture of short and long intervals between traveling actions and tree shapes.

1. Ask your class to spread out throughout the room, arm's-width apart and standing in parallel position.
2. Start the music and invite your students to travel silently throughout the room.
3. Younger students enjoy pretending they are walking through a forest (creeping carefully, stepping over rocks and roots, watching birds and other wildlife). Older students may prefer to walk in neutral.
4. Turn off the music. Students freeze and listen for instruction.
5. Call out which pose you want students to make. It can be any of the following:
   - Reaching pose
   - Bending pose
   - Their own original tree shapes
6. Students freeze in the tree pose or shape until the music resumes.
7. Increase the length of the freeze as students become stronger and more confident.
8. After working on solo shapes 2 or 3 times, ask your students to do poses with a partner or in groups of three, four, or more. When you turn off the music, call out a number and which type of tree shape they should do.
9. Forming the group tree shapes should be done as quickly and quietly as possible.
10. Original trees are improvised. There's no time for students to talk.
11. Students should work with the people nearest them and not run across the room to be with a friend.
12. If there is an extra person (when the class cannot be evenly divided by two or three), the teacher can join in.
13. Play the music for different lengths of time so students can't anticipate when the freeze will come.
14. Try large groupings of seven, eight, or nine to create huge, old-growth trees.
15. If the class is very large, have half the class perform the exercise while the others watch. Then switch.

Afterward, discuss the exercise.

Discussion

- "What was challenging about the exercise?" (*Holding the poses, creating original tree shapes, finding the right number of people to work without talking.*)
- "When going into the yoga poses, were you always lifting the same leg and standing on the same foot?" It's common for people to have a dominant side. Encourage students to use this exercise to help them strengthen their weaker side.
- "Was it challenging to create original tree shapes when you were working in groups? How did you manage without talking?"
- "Did you try to convey the idea that you were walking through a forest?" If yes, what actions did they use? (*Looking up at trees, being nervous or lost.*)

Kindergarten Through Grade 3 Variation

Instructions

Ask half the class to be trees and half to travel through the forest without talking or touching the trees.

1. Assign roles: Group A will be trees, and group B will be travelers.
2. Let group A randomly space themselves throughout the room.
3. Group B stands spread out along the perimeter.
4. Before the music starts, ask group A to create their tree shapes. (The shapes can be any of the solo yoga poses or original tree poses.)
5. Start the music and signal group B to enter the forest and move through the trees without touching them.
6. Call out prompts to support those who are traveling ("Are you lost, frightened, or confident walking through the forest?" "Do you hear animal sounds?" "Are you looking for something? Do you find it?")
7. After 12 to 16 beats, call out, "Change."
8. Those who were traveling become trees, and those who were trees become travelers.
9. After 12 to 16 beats, call out, "Change." Group A becomes trees, and group B returns to traveling.
10. Let students cycle through the changes 4 or 5 times, then sit down and discuss.

Discussion

- How did they feel when they were traveling through the forest?
- How did they feel when they were trees watching people wander through the forest while they stayed rooted on-the-spot?

Step 4: Creating a Choreographic Phrase—All Grades

This choreographic phrase is inspired by maple trees and their seedling keys (see figure 2.2) that flutter like little helicopters off the mother tree in search of a place where they can take root and grow.

Instructions

Take a moment for students to share what they know about maple keys: what the maple key is, its shape, its flight pattern, and what happens to the key once it's on the ground.

This choreographic phrase combines tree shapes with improvised on-the-spot motion and traveling phrases. Use the same music as the previous exercise to support the following choreographic exploration:

1. Create a tree pose or original tree shape and hold (8 beats).
2. Slowly move your hands and arms to illustrate the action of maple keys falling to the ground. This is an on-the-spot improvisational section. Hands and arms can twist and turn, moving from high to low. Students in yoga poses can put the lifted foot down to maintain balance as they move their arms around and down (8 beats).
3. Now the wind is blowing the maple keys throughout the room. Students gently turn, swirl, roll, and glide to a new spot (8 beats).

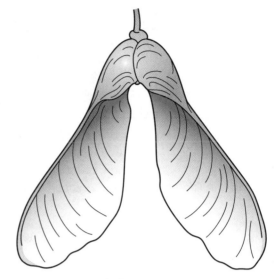

Figure 2.2   Maple keys.

4. Create a new tree pose or shape to start the choreographic phrase again.
5. Repeat the choreographic phrase 3 or 4 times without stopping. Encourage students to try different ways to represent maple keys falling and the wind blowing them with each repetition.
6. Divide your class into two groups. Invite one group to watch while the other performs the choreography twice, then ask those who were presenting to watch while the others perform.

Discussion

- "The phrase contained specific timings and transitions: from still tree to falling maple keys and from being blown by the wind to becoming a still tree. Which was the hardest? Which was the easiest?"

- "The phrase was repeated several times. Did you find ways to make each repetition unique?" If yes, ask your students to explain how. (*Worked fingers, wrists, and elbows differently at every falling maple key section; used the tree pose variations and created original tree shapes; used different tempo, direction, and level changes when moving with the wind.*)

Grades 4 Through 6 Variation

Instead of asking everyone to perform the same actions at the same time, try the choreographic phrase in three groups, with each group performing a different action.

- Group 1 starts the phrase as originally practiced: tree, maple keys, and wind.
- Group 2 starts the phrase with the maple key section, then does wind and tree.
- Group 3 starts the phrase with the wind section, then does the tree and maple keys.

Instructions

1. Divide the class into three groups. Name them Trees, Maple Keys, and Wind to identify which section of the dance they do first.

2. Let the class practice in their groups 3 or 4 times with the music, then ask half of each of the groups to stay in the performance area while the others sit and watch.

3. Invite those presenting to perform the sequence 2 or 3 times. Then ask those students to sit down and invite those who were watching to perform.

After everyone has seen and performed the choreography, discuss and reflect.

Discussion

- "Was the choreography more interesting to watch in this format than when everyone was moving in unison?" If yes, ask students to explain why. (*The choreography had multiple levels and movement qualities, like a real forest where leaves and maple keys fall at different times.*)

- "Does the choreography show what happens to trees and how tree seeds spread and grow?"

Step 5: Original Tree Dances

Kindergarten Through Grade 3 Variation

Ask your class if they have additional ideas to add to the Maple Key dance or if they have ideas for a new tree dance. Compile a list of student ideas, collectively explore the ideas, and create an order for the actions to be performed in. Practice the new Tree dance.

Grades 4 Through 6 Variation

Ask students if they have additional ideas to add to the Maple Key dance or if they have ideas for new choreography inspired by trees (boreal forests, rain forests, evergreens, what trees have witnessed over the centuries, historical or mythical trees).

1. Compile a list of student suggestions for new tree choreography.
2. Divide the class into working groups of four or five.
3. Ask groups to create an original 16- or 24-beat Tree dance or devise a new variation of the Maple Key dance.
4. Bring the groups together for presentation and discussion.

Discussion

Ask each group to briefly explain what aspect of trees inspired the dance or variation.

Journal Entry

Kindergarten Through Grade 3

"What would it be like to be a tree?" Invite your class to draw or write a response.

Grades 4 Through 6

Ask your class to write from the perspective of a maple key (or pinecone or acorn) after you have shared these questions:

- "How would you feel if you were hanging from your parent tree then suddenly fell to the ground? Would you be frightened? Excited? Surprised?"

- "What happens after you land? Are you looking up at your siblings, who are still hanging from the tree? Does the wind blow you away? Does a squirrel carry you off to its nest?"

- "What happens next? Will you be one of the lucky ones and become a tree?"

EXERCISE 2.2   FLOWERS

Exercise 2.1 focused on creating and holding a variety of tree shapes and added arm and hand improvisation in step 4 inspired by falling maple keys. This exercise develops students' hand and arm dexterity even further as they create individual flowers and group gardens.

Lesson Plan Suggestions

Kindergarten Through Grade 3

First lesson: Steps 1, 2, 3, and 4

Second lesson: Warm up with step 2; step 5 (video: Shiva Shambho Bharatanatyam Dance, 3:55; follow the grade-appropriate variation); journal entry

Grades 4 Through 6

First lesson: Steps 1, 2, 3, and 4

Second Lesson: Warm up with step 2; step 5 (video: Shiva Shambho Bharatanatyam Dance, 3:55; follow the grade-appropriate variation); journal entry

Recommended Music: Tracks 2 and 15 (for step 4 only)

Step 1: What Do We Know About Flowers?

Work with your class to compile a list of words and phrases about flowers, including the names of flowers (lilies, daffodils, daisies, tulips), parts of flowers (petals, stems, thorns, stamen, pollen, bulbs, roots), different uses (gifts, oils for perfume, flavor for cooking including saffron, paper making, decorative art), and the different life cycles (reseeding, bulbs and rhizomes, blossoms to fruit).

Step 2: Warm-Up for Arms and Hands

Ask your class to sit arm's-length apart and start with this warm-up exercise to awaken hand articulation. It can be performed in silence or with the music. Start with straight arms reaching forward, palms facing the ceiling

1. Rotate the arms down and around so the palms face away from each other on beats 1 and 2.
2. Rotate the arms so that the palms face the ceiling on beats 3 and 4.
3. Rotate the arms again so the palms face away from each other on beats 5 and 6.
4. Rotate the arms so the palms face the ceiling on beats 7 and 8.
5. Make a fist on beats 1 and 2.
6. Stretch the fingers wide on beats 3 and 4.
7. Make a fist on beats 5 and 6.
8. Stretch the fingers wide on beats 7 and 8. Try to keep the fingers extended as you bring the fingers back in one at a time, starting with the pinkie finger 1, the ring finger 2, middle finger 3, index finger 4, and thumb 5, hold in fist for 6, 7, 8.
9. Then reverse and extend the thumb 1, index finger 2, middle finger 3, ring finger 4, and pinkie finger 5, hold fingers in outstretched position for 6, 7, 8.

10. Repeat curling and uncurling the fingers a second time.

11. Rub the hands together for 4 beats.

12. Shake the arms and hands for 4 beats.

13. Repeat rubbing and shaking a second time.

14. Reach the arms up and press the palms up to the ceiling for 4 beats.

15. Stretch the arms out to the sides and press the palms to the wall for 4 beats.

16. Repeat stretching up and out a second time.

17. Press the palms together in front of the chest, with the elbows lifted and hold for 4 beats.

Repeat the warm-up a second time.

Step 3: Creating Flowers

The warm-up finishes with the palms together in front of the chest, the forearms parallel to the floor, and the elbows pointed to the sides. That's the second shape of the flower phrase they'll be performing together.

Roots, shoot, bud, and flower.

© Barry Prophet

Instructions

Introduce the four-part flower phrase to your class and practice it while sitting in a circle.

- Shape 1

    1. Press the backs of your hands together with the fingers downward; they represent the roots.

    2. The forearms stay parallel to the floor; they represent the top of the soil.

    3. After establishing the starting position, slowly begin the movement.

- Shape 2

    1. Move the wrists away from each other but keep the knuckles together. The arms will open a little wider.

    2. Slowly curl the fingers up out of the soil and bring the palms together. This represents the tiny shoot rising up from the soil.

- Shape 3

    · Let the hands rise (keep the palms together; they represent the closed flower bud) while bringing the elbows together. The line of earth disappears, and the elbows become a long stem.

- Shape 4

    1. Keep the forearms and elbows together and slowly open the fingers (petals) to create a beautiful open flower.

    2. Hold the flower shape for several beats.

    3. If students are able, they can raise their arms higher as long as their elbows stay together.

    4. Then slowly the flower begins to wilt. Our petals can't fall off; instead let them wither and curl inward. The wrists open slightly to receive the fingers as the entire sequence is reversed until everyone has returned to the starting position with the backs of their hands touching and the fingers reaching into the earth.

    5. Repeat the sequence 2 or 3 times with music; use your own timing for the growing and opening sections and the same amount of time for the wilting, decaying section.

    6. Encourage students to find new flower shapes each time they open their fingers.

    7. If they need inspiration for new shapes, remind them that daffodils have center trumpets, pansies have large and small petals, and irises have beards.

Take a moment to shake out the arms and hands and discuss.

Discussion

- "Was it difficult coming up with new flower shapes?" Ask everyone to show one of the flower shapes they made, and ask those with unique flower shapes to teach them with the class.

- "Were you able to get your fingers to do what you wanted them to do?" Students often discover that they have limited control over individual fingers. This is a great exercise to do on a regular basis because it helps develop fine motor skills.

Step 4: Petals and Thorns

Recommended Music

Track 15

Instructions

- Compile a list of flowering plants that have thorns. Roses and cacti immediately come to mind. Other prickly flowering bushes and trees include quince, holly, hawthorn, blackberry, and raspberry.

- Ask your class why some plants have thorns. The most common answer will be protection. Follow the idea further, asking what the thorns are protecting and who or what the predators are.

- Invite your class to stand up in the open area arm's-length apart.

- As you'll remember from chapter 1, this composition alternates between fast and slow tempos. In this exploration, the contrast between sharp and smooth textures is as important as the tempo changes.

  1. Let the fast, sharp music inspire students to explore thorns. Thorns are warriors in armor repelling predators. Students can move in and out of angular shapes, make sharp freezes and short cutting actions, and have watchful and alert facial expressions.

  2. When the music is smooth and soft, invite your class to be inspired by petals slowly opening. Students can create huge, majestic flowers using their arms and full-bodied actions at low and high levels.

  3. Slow motions can also explore the soft membrane that's under the prickly hard surface of a cactus. Cacti flesh contains life-saving moisture that desert animals would feast on if not for the spiky exterior.

- The composition changes speed and texture randomly; there are no set counts. Keep your students moving until the end, then invite the class to sit and discuss.

Discussion

- "When the music was prickly, what images helped you come up with ideas? (*A samurai warrior, porcupine, electrical sparks.*)

- "When the music was smooth, did you think of anything besides flowers to inspire your movement? If yes, describe them."

- "Can people be prickly? Does being prickly on the outside mean that a person is prickly inside, too, or are they like cacti wearing armor to protect their feelings?"

Step 5: Create a Garden

Bharatanatyam is one of the classical dance forms of India and has been performed for over 2,000 years. Bharatanatyam dancers exquisitely combine intricate hand positions (mudras), full-bodied shapes, and actions with complex, rhythmic footwork. Before watching this performance, ask your class to look for moments when the dancers create living pictures of flowers, trees, and flowing streams.

Watch the Shiva Shambho Bharatanatyam Dance video (3:55) from the list of video links in HK*Propel*. After watching the video, invite your students to share their impression of the dance, with a focus on the variety of dancers' hand shapes (mudras) and how the dancers smoothly transitioned from one shape to another.

Kindergarten Through Grade 3 Variation

- Invite your students to work on their own and create the following:
  - Two different flower shapes using just their hands at low and mid-levels
  - Two different full-bodied flower shapes at mid- and high levels (a lifted leg can become a low petal or leaf)
  - Kindergarten students can create just one of each type of flower
- If necessary, use prompts to help your students find variety in their flower shapes, such as: Can you make one flower with open fingers and another with some of your fingers rounded? Do both sides of the flower have to be the same, or can the sides be different? Does your flower's stem have thorns? Can you balance on one foot in your high-level flower?
- Divide the class in half and invite students to share their shapes with each other.
- Ask your class to work in pairs.
- With partners, students can create a low-level flower shape and a high-level flower shape. These shapes should be different from their individual flowers.
- Explore your students' low, high, and group flowers using the following format:
  - Start in one of the flowers students created with a partner and hold for 8 beats.
  - Then have students go into one of their low solo flowers and hold for 8 beats.
  - Follow this with one of their high solo flowers and hold for 8 beats.
  - Finally, students go into the second flower shape with a partner and hold for 8 beats.
- Repeat the pattern twice, then invite students to add an improvised traveling phrase between each flower freeze. Students should:
  - Start beside the partner to perform the first flower for 8 beats.
  - Travel away from the partner for 8 beats.
  - Create the first solo high or low flower shape for 8 beats.
  - Travel throughout the room for 8 beats.
  - Create the second solo high or low flower shape for 8 beats.
  - Travel back to the partners for 8 beats.
  - Create the final flower shape with your partner and hold for 8 beats.
- Can they find different ways to move for each traveling section? If students had difficulty coming up with ideas for traveling, use prompts: "Could you be walking through a garden picking flowers or running through a meadow? Are you the wind, a bee, a bird?"
- Practice this variation twice, then divide your class into two groups so they may perform it for each other.

Grades 2 and 3 Variation

Instructions

- Suggest that the class create a garden where flowers bloom at different times. A simple way to do this is to assign students a number between 1 and 4. The 1s move first, the 2s second, and so on. But instead of staying in their number groups, ask them to position themselves randomly. Brainstorm other ideas: Should the flowers wilt after blooming? Should anyone be traveling through the garden? If yes, who and why?

- Does the garden have a theme? Are they magical flowers, carnivorous flowers, tropical flowers, or night flowers?

- Explore and create together.

Discussion

"What was the most challenging aspect of creating the last garden exploration?"

Grades 4 Through 6 Variation

Instructions

1. Invite students to work in small groups of four or five to create a 16- or 24-beat garden with the following requirements:

   - Each dancer creates at least two individual flower shapes.
   - The flowers should vary in height (work levels from 1 to 10).
   - Flowers may grow and fade at different times, and some flowers may remain upright through much of the dance.
   - Create two group flowers formed by three or more people.
   - Flowers have roots, so everyone is rooted on their spots with at least one foot never leaving its starting point (students may lunge toward and away from each other when creating group flowers).
   - Ask students this question: "Can you create at least two different spatial relationships (line, zigzag, curve) while everyone keeps at least one foot rooted to the spot?"

2. Allow your class 10 to 15 minutes to create and practice their pieces, then present them.

Discussion

- Every group had to create two flowers made by more than one person. Did any group create a flower using all of its members? If yes, how did they all manage to stay rooted?

- Were the level and timing changes inspired by specific plants or seasonal changes?

Journal Entry for All Grades

"Some people evaluate their day using petals and thorns. Petals represent the good things that happened, and thorns represent things that didn't go well. Draw or write about an experience you had that started thorny but finished with petals."

EXERCISE 2.3   VINES

Every summer, my backyard fence is transformed into a living wall of purple and white morning glories. I planted some seeds 16 years ago in front of a small section of fence, and now hundreds of seedlings rise up every spring. As they grow, the seedlings reach to each other (and to other plants) and twist themselves together, creating a living rope. When the shoots are tall enough, they latch on to the bottom of the fence and weave through the lattice, traveling high and wide. By midsummer, the fence is a wall of leaves and blossoms that last until autumn.

The intricate growing patterns of vines has inspired painters, weavers, jewelers, and dancers for centuries. Artists and craftspeople portray vines in paint, fabric, silver, and gold, and dancers use foot patterns and traveling pathways.

Lesson Plan Suggestions

Kindergarten Through Grade 3

First lesson: Steps 1 and 2 (videos: Traditional Greek Grapevine Step, 2:11, and Lil Buck Performs Memphis Jookin, 3:02); for step 3, follow grade-appropriate variations

Second Lesson: Do a quick review of step 3 and then follow grade-appropriate variations for step 4; journal entry

Grades 4 Through 6

First lesson: Steps 1 and 2 (videos: Traditional Greek Grapevine Step, 2:11, and Lil Buck Performs Memphis Jookin, 3:02); for step 3, follow grade-appropriate variations.

Second Lesson: Do a quick review of step 3 and then follow grade-appropriate variations for step 4; journal entry

Recommended Music: Track 9

Step 1: What Do We Know About Vines?

With your class, compile a list of words and phrases about vines, including types of flowering vines (morning glory, honeysuckle, wisteria, and trumpet creeper); nonflowering vines (Virginia creeper, English ivy, and poison ivy); fruit-bearing vines (grape, tomato, beans, and peas); low-lying vines (pumpkin, squash, melons, and cucumbers); and vines in rainforests and jungles, where woody vines called lianas can grow up to 3,000 feet long!

Step 2: Explore Two Great Vine-Inspired Dance Styles

In dance, the term *grapevine* refers to repeatable footwork combinations that twist from side to side and forward and back on itself. Grapevine dance steps have been used for thousands of years and can be found in many traditional dances from around the world. The following two videos juxtapose traditional Greek folkdance to "Memphis Jookin."

Instructions

- Watch the video of the traditional Greek Grapevine Step (2:11) from the list of video links in HK*Propel*. Consider this video a tutorial on the sirtaki, a popular Greek folkdance performed at festivals and community events and, more recently, by flash mobs.
- Watch the video Lil Buck Performs Memphis Jookin at the Kennedy Center (3:02) from the list of video links in HK*Propel*. Unlike the sirtaki, Memphis Jookin is a dance style that was started in the 1980s and became popular in the early 2000s. It uses fluid, intertwining footwork, and those smooth moves twist and twine upward through the torso and arms.

Post-Video Discussion

Take a moment to identify the similarities and differences between the two styles.

Step 3: Learn a Simple Grapevine Step

All Grades

Warm up with twisting vine-inspired shapes

1. Ask your students to stand in parallel position, arm's-length apart.
2. Then create a twisted shape and freeze for 4 beats.
3. Ask everyone to untwist their shape and return to parallel 4 beats.
4. Create another twisted shape to hold for 4 beats.
5. Repeat 4 more times, encouraging your class to work at different levels as they twist their arms, legs, and torso in new ways.

Vine exploration.

© Janice Pomer

Warm up with a vine-inspired footwork improvisation.

1. Remind your students to work in their personal bubbles.
2. They can travel a few steps forward, back, and side to side.
3. Let your class know they will be creating their own twisting and turning footwork inspired by the footwork they saw in the videos and explore their own ideas of how vines twist and twine.
4. Play the music for a minute or two and call out prompts if needed. Prompts include: Have you traveled in all directions? Are you lifting your feet and bending your knees? How many ways can you twist your legs? Can you twist your arms as you move your feet? Can you lift your heels high, and can you bend down low?

At the conclusion of the improvisation, ask your students to return to parallel position and take a moment to rest and refocus.

Kindergarten Through Grade 3 Variation 1

Teach a simplified form of the grapevine step. Start by introducing this simple step-together combination:

1. Step to the right with the right foot.
2. Move the left foot next to the right foot.
3. Step to the right with the right foot.
4. Move the left foot next to the right foot.

Repeat 3 or 4 times to the right, then practice to the left:

1. Step to the left with the left foot.
2. Move the right foot next to the left foot.
3. Step to the left with the left foot.
4. Move the right foot next to the left foot.

Once your class is comfortable doing the step-together pattern, try crossing behind:

1. Step to the right with the right foot.
2. Move the left foot behind the right foot.
3. Step to the right with the right foot.
4. Move the left foot next to the right foot.

And go to the other side:

1. Step to the left with the left foot.
2. Move the right foot behind the left foot.
3. Step to the left with the left foot.
4. Move the right foot next to the left foot.

Practice on both sides to make sure everyone is confident, then invite your students to create an original twisted shape at the end of the phrase. Add a twisted shape:

1. Step to the right with the right foot.
2. Move the left foot behind the right foot.
3. Step to the right with the right foot.

4. Move the left foot behind the right foot.

5. Make a twisted shape and hold for 3 beats.

6. On beat 4, go into parallel position.

7. Repeat the entire sequence, this time going to the left.

Practice the combination on both sides 2 or 3 times.

Kindergarten Through Grade 3 Variation 2

Travel vertically with crossover steps. Start with the grapevine version students already know.

1. Step to the right with the right foot.

2. Move the left foot behind the right foot.

3. Step to the right with the right foot.

4. Move the left foot next to the right foot.

After the left foot is placed beside the right, travel forward:

1. Move the right foot to the front and a little across from the left foot.

2. Step forward with the left foot a little across from the right foot.

3. Step forward with the right foot a little across from the left.

4. Move the left foot next to the right.

Repeat the grapevine step to the left:

1. Step to the left side with the left foot.

2. Move the right foot behind the left foot.

3. Step to the left with the left foot.

4. Move the right foot next to the left foot.

After the right foot is placed beside the left, travel backward:

1. Step to the back, with the left foot behind and a little across from the right foot.

2. Step the right foot behind and a little across from the left foot.

3. Step the left foot behind, a little across from the right.

4. Move the right foot next to the left foot.

Practice slowly and repeat several times until students feel confident.

Kindergarten Through Grade 3 Variation 3

Instructions

Put it all together:

1. Perform the grapevine step to the right for 4 beats.

2. Perform the crossover step forward for 4 beats.

3. Improvise on-the-spot grapevine-inspired footwork and arm ideas for 8 beats.

4. Freeze in the last shape for 4 beats.

5. Come to parallel position for 4 beats.

6. Perform the grapevine step to the left for 4 beats.

7. Perform the crossover step backward for 4 beats.

8. Improvise on-the-spot grapevine-inspired footwork and arm ideas for 8 beats.

9. Freeze in the last shape for 4 beats.

10. Come to parallel position for 4 beats.

Discussion

"Which was more challenging: remembering where to put your feet while doing the unison grapevine step or improvising your own twisting footwork and arms?"

Grades 4 Through 6 Variation 1

There are many different grapevine steps in traditional folk, square, and line dancing. This simple grapevine sequence is prevalent in North American square and line dancing, ballroom dancing, tap, and jazz styles:

1. Step to the right with the right foot.

2. Step the left foot behind the right foot.

3. Step to the right with the right foot.

4. Step the left foot in front of the right foot.

5. Repeat 2 or 3 times without stopping and traveling to the right.

6. Stop by placing the left foot beside the right in parallel position.

And reverse the pattern to go to the left:

1. Step to the left with the left foot.

2. Step the right foot behind the left foot.

3. Step to the left with the left foot.

4. Step the right foot in front of the left foot.

5. Repeat 2 or 3 times, traveling to the left.

6. Stop by placing the right foot beside the left in parallel position.

Add crossover steps to travel vertically. First start with the grapevine step:

1. Step to the right with the right foot.

2. Step the left foot behind the right foot.

3. Step to the right with the right foot.

4. Step the left foot in front of the right foot.

After the left foot is in front of the right foot:

1. Step to the front with the right foot a little across from the left.

2. Step the left foot in front and a little across from the right.

3. Step to the front with the right foot a little across from the left.

4. Step the left foot beside the right and come to parallel position.

Repeat the grapevine step to the left:

1. Step to the left side with the left foot.

2. Step the right foot behind the left foot.

3. Step to the left with the left foot.

4. Step the right foot in front of the left foot.

After the right foot steps in front of the left:

1. Step to the back with the left foot a little across from the right.
2. Step the right foot back and a little across from the left.
3. Step to the back with the left foot a little across from the right.
4. Step the right foot beside the left and come to parallel position.

Practice 2 times in each direction.

Grades 4 Through 6 Variation 2

Try the following:

1. Grapevine to the right for 4 beats.
2. Crossover step forward for 4 beats.
3. Improvise twisting footwork, arm patterns, and turns on-the-spot for 8 beats.
4. Grapevine to the left and do the crossover steps backward.
5. Improvise twisting footwork, arm patterns, and turns on-the-spot for 8 beats.

Practice the pattern in both directions 2 or 3 times and encourage everyone to try new vine-inspired moves at each improvisational section.

Grades 4 Through 6 Variation 3

Instructions

Invite your class to work in groups of three or four and choreograph their own vine-inspired sequence. The sequence should contain the following:

- The grapevine and vertical crossover steps, which should be performed in unison
- Original vine-inspired footwork on-the-spot or traveling, which does not need to be performed in unison
- A twisting arm phrase in unison—combine it with a traveling step in unison or perform it on-the-spot.
- A final grapevine-inspired shape to finish in

Allow 5 to 10 minutes for students to create and practice, then invite two groups to present at the same time. Remind performers to stay frozen in their final shapes until the music has stopped.

Discussion

- "Did you find yourself looking down at your feet while you were doing the footwork? If yes, why?"
- Did groups come up with a variety of rippling, twisting arm movements? Were some of them similar? Which ones were unique? Ask the groups that created unique arm movements to teach them to the class.

Step 4: Winding Pathways

Kindergarten to Grade 3 Variation 1: Vine-Inspired Pathways

Draw two parallel undulating lines on the board or flip chart as shown in figure 2.3. If you're working outdoors, draw the lines on the asphalt for your students to run on.

1. Ask all your students to go to one side of the room and form two lines, with the leader of each line standing at the corners.

2. The other students should line up one behind the other so that only the two leaders are at the start position. The others will be standing along the perimeter to the right or left of the line leaders.

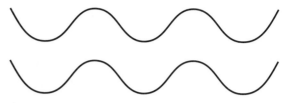

Figure 2.3   Two parallel ripples.

3. Ask the leaders of each line to take a few steps toward center so they're away from the sides and have enough room to ripple-run to the left and right without coming too close each other or the students who are waiting in line along the sides of the room.

4. The leaders will start running in ripple formation to right, left, right, left across to the far side of the room.

5. When the leaders get to the end of the room, they'll walk along the sides of the performing area to line up at the back of their respective line.

6. The waiting students will start rippling every 8 beats until everyone has rippled across the room and walked back to the end of their line.

Let everyone have two turns before moving on to the next variation.

Kindergarten to Grade 3 Variation 2: Twisting and Twining Arms

- Draw two intertwining lines on the board or asphalt as shown in figure 2.4.

- Invite your students to explore the following intertwining arm patterns:

  · Try intertwining the arms up and down and forward and back while staying on-the-spot.

  · Try intertwining the arms while they travel on the rippling pathway (K to 1 students can do simple arm ripples while they do their ripple runs).

- Once your students have successfully performed rippling arms while ripple-running, try this on-the-spot grapevine-inspired arm phrase with your students:

  1. Start in parallel position with bent knees and torso hanging downward. Use intertwining arms to straighten up vertically for 4 beats (imagine a vine is growing up a pole).

  2. Arms are open wide and stay at shoulder height (imagine large buds on the vine blossoming) for 4 beats.

Figure 2.4   Two lines intertwining.

  3. Bend the right elbow and let the right forearm hang downward (the fruit on the vine is getting heavy) for 2 beats.

  4. Bend the left elbow and let the right forearm hang downward (the fruit on the vine is getting heavy) for 2 beats.

  5. Drop the head and upper torso, bend the knees slightly, and let the arms drop down (the fruit is ready to be harvested) for 4 beats.

- Repeat the pattern 2 or 3 more times.

Kindergarten to Grade 3 Variation 3: Combine All the Elements

- Add all the grapevine-inspired elements together and try the following:
  - Grapevine step to the right for 4 beats.
  - Crossover step forward for 4 beats.
  - Ripple intertwined arms vertically upward for 4 beats.
  - Open the arms wide for 4 beats.
  - Bend the right elbow and let the forearm hang down for beats 1 and 2.
  - Bend the left elbow and let the forearm hang down for beats 3 and 4.
  - Drop the head, torso, through the spine, bend the knees, touch the floor for 4 beats.
  - Improvise on-the-spot rippling and twisting actions to rise up for 8 beats.
- Repeat the combination to the left.
- Try to perform the combination to the right and the left without stopping in between.
- Ask your class if they have any vine-inspired movement ideas to add to the movement phrase.
- Explore those ideas collectively or let your class work in small groups.
- Allow 5 to 10 minutes of creation and practice time, then ask the groups to share their new vine-inspired movement phrases with each other.

Grades 4 Through 6 Variation 1: Twists and Turns

Ask the class if they have ever tried to separate twisted vines. When they're tightly intertwined, vines can appear to have no beginning or end. When drawn on its side, the figure eight is the symbol for infinity, as shown in figure 2.5.

1. Draw the image and ask your class to make large figure eights in the air with each arm several times.

2. Invite your class to find a spot in the room and try walking in a figure eight. The figure eight should be approximately 2 yards (2 m) in length.

Figure 2.5   Infinity symbol.

3. Let everyone practice walking the figure eight pattern for 20 to 30 seconds so they are confident enough that they can perform it without looking down at the ground.

4. Invite two volunteers to demonstrate how two people can travel on the same figure eight.

5. Ask the volunteers to stand back-to-back at center stage.

6. Their job will be to walk the figure eight, overlapping at the center, and continue looping and overlapping without ever bumping into each other.

7. No person should walk faster than the other. Use the following beats to stay equal distance apart.

8. The person facing stage left will begin by walking downstage on beats 1 and 2, and then curve upward on beats 3 and 4. He will then travel along upstage on beats 5 and 6 and then move toward center on beats 7 and 8 (where he'll meet his partner). Next, create the second loop by walking downstage (1, 2), curving upward (3, 4), traveling along upstage (5, 6) and veering up to center to complete the figure eight (7, 8).

9. The person facing stage right will begin by walking upstage on beats 1 and 2, then curve downward on beats 3 and 4, travel along downstage on beats 5 and 6, walk toward up to center on beat 7, and meet the partner at center on beat 8. She then creates the second loop of the 8 by walking upstage (1, 2), curving downward (3, 4), travel along downstage (5, 6), and coming to center (7, 8).

10. The pattern is more difficult to write than it is to do. Refer to figure 2.6 and draw it out for your class if needed.

11. Once your class has watched the demonstration, invite everyone to work in pairs to practice it.

12. Once everyone is comfortable, add figure eight arms.

13. Reach up high when traveling upstage and reach or scoop down when traveling downstage.

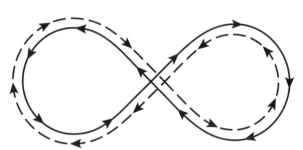

Figure 2.6   Two movers traveling.

14. When movers overlap at center stage, crossover arms can reach forward at shoulder height. The rising and lowering of the arms should be continuous.

Grades 4 Through 6 Variation 2: Vine-Inspired Movements While Traveling the Figure Eight

Now that students have successfully incorporated the simple arm pattern into their figure eights, it's time to add additional actions.

- Ask the duets to create figure eight movement phrases using the following elements:
  - Create actions that symbolize growth or change (moving slowly and quickly) or starting low and gaining height (roll and run, crouch and jump) and use both arms and torsos.
  - Use the traditional grapevine step or create original intertwining steps.
  - The pattern may have on-the-spot actions, but all traveling must follow the figure eight pathway.
  - The creations should be 24 or 32 beats long.
  - Finish with a twisted shape (create it together or apart).
- Allow duets approximately 15 minutes to create and practice.
- If time is an issue, invite two duets to present at the same time, with one duet on stage right and the other on stage left. If a group finishes before the other, ask that they stay frozen in the final shape until the music stops.

Discussion

- "Was everyone's choreography symmetrical (actions and spacing mirroring each other), or did some duets work differently?"

- "Were there some unique level and tempo changes? If yes, identify them."

- "Which shapes contained the most twists?"

Journal Entry for All Grades

"Draw a pattern inspired by intertwining vines and leaves." Show the class figure 2.7 for inspiration.

Figure 2.7 Vine patterns.

EXERCISE 2.4   TALL GRASSES

This exercise is inspired by tall stalks of bamboo, corn, and sugar cane and swaying fields of wheat, oats, and barley. Like exercise 2.1, this exercise helps students connect with their centers and balance, but instead of balancing on one foot, students will be tilting to create straight and curved lines while both feet remain on the floor.

Lesson Plan Suggestions

Kindergarten Through Grade 3

First lesson: Steps 1, 2, 3, 4, and 5 (follow the grade-appropriate variation)

Grades 4 Through 6

First lesson: Steps 1, 2, 3, 4, and 5 (follow the grade-appropriate variation)

Recommended Music: Track 16

Step 1: What We Know About Bamboo and Other Tall Grasses

Hundreds of species of bamboo grow in a wide range of sizes; panda bears eat the shoots and leaves of smaller species, while large species of bamboo can grow as wide as trees and over 90 feet (30 m) high. Those types of bamboo are used to build boats, bridges, and houses. Even though bamboo can grow as tall as trees, it's still classified as a grass. Tall grasses grow on every continent except for Antarctica. People domesticated tall grasses millennia ago; the grains and stalks continue to be an important food source for people and livestock.

Compile a list of other tall grasses your students are familiar with, including bulrushes (also called cattails), sugar cane, corn, oat, wheat, and barley.

Step 2: Stalks of Corn, Bamboo, or Cane

Instructions

1. Ask your class to find a spot in the room with everyone facing front, arm's-length apart.
2. Instead of standing in parallel position, ask everyone to move their feet so their heels come together and their feet form a V. This V shape is similar to first position in ballet, but the V shape is not as wide.
3. Invite your students to imagine that they are stalks of corn or bamboo; their feet are planted in the earth. Their legs are together and represent the lower stalk of the plant. The spine extends up from the legs, and the top of the head extends up to the sky.
4. Just like a stalk of corn or bamboo, your students are standing straight and tall without bending their knees or twisting their torsos.
5. Invite them to imagine a gentle breeze is blowing against their right side.

6. Corn and bamboo have strong stalks that don't bend. When the wind blows against the students' right side, they'll tilt to the left.

7. In order to tilt without bending, your students should keep their arms at their sides and their spines straight and tall (see the Tilting photograph).

8. The breeze has stopped, so everyone can return to center position.

9. Now there's a gentle breeze blowing against their left sides.

10. Tilt to the right without bending and keep the arms straight against the torso.

11. The breeze has stopped, so return to center.

12. Lead your class through two more tilts and have them return to center.

Tilting.

© Barry Prophet

Discussion

- "Were you comfortable tilting from side to side? If not, why not?"
- "Were you able to tilt from side to side without bending or falling over? If yes, what were your strategies?"
- If a number of students are having difficulty maintaining their balance, suggest that they try standing with their heels 1 or 2 inches apart.

Step 3: Conducting

Instructions

- Ask your students to return to standing with their feet in a V shape.
- Instead of using your voice to direct the tilts, you (and later volunteers) will conduct the class.
- Play music track 16.
- The music has a gentle pulse but also has a gentle, breeze-like quality.

  1. Stand in the front of the room.
  2. Let your class know that you'll be leading the direction, speed, and degree of their tilts, not with your voice but with your hands, like a conductor leading a choir or orchestra.
  3. As the conductor, feel free to follow the gentle pulse of the music or conduct the tilts independently of the score.

4. Start simply to make sure everyone is able to tilt from side to side without losing their balance or bending at the torso or knees.

5. Play with the rhythms and timing; keep students suspended in a tilt for 4 beats, then tilt them to the other side for 2 beats, and then tilt them back for 1 beat.

6. The more beats allowed for each tilt, the more time there is to increase the degree of the tilt.

7. Short and long tilts require strength and concentration.

8. If your class is having difficulty focusing, you can call out prompts while you conduct.

9. After a minute or so, stop and ask for two volunteer conductors.

10. Invite one volunteer to stand to the right side of the class and the other volunteer to the left side.

11. Ask students in the center of the room to create a space to delineate the right and left sides of the room and to make sure that there's no danger of students on either side bumping into each other.

12. Start the music and invite the volunteers to conduct their sides of the room.

13. The conductors will be working independently of each other. Students must stay focused on their conductor, not the other side's conductor.

14. After 20 to 30 seconds, repeat the process with two new volunteers.

15. After the second set of volunteers, suggest your class try tilting forward and backward.

16. Invite everyone to take a moment to try tilting in these new directions.

17. Going backward is very difficult. Try not to make those tilts too extreme.

18. Invite two new conductors to use all four directions to conduct the class.

19. After 20 to 30 seconds, have the class sit down and ask for feedback.

Discussion

- "Were you always able to follow the conductors? Identify when it was easy and when it was challenging."
- "Why is tilting backward so difficult?" (Hint: If our ankles were in the middle of our feet, it would be easier.)

Step 4: Waves of Wheat

Wheat, oats, and barley are much more flexible than bamboo, cane, or corn stalks, and they bend and sway with the wind.

1. To contrast the rigid bamboo and corn tilts, lead your class in a short swaying exploration.

2. Ask your students to bend and sway their torsos, heads, and arms while their feet are in the same position they used for their tilts.

3. To increase the range of the sways, try lunging to the right while swaying from the torso and reaching the arms to the right. Then bring the heels together to return to the V standing position as the arms and torso return to an upright position.

4. Lunging and straightening offer a greater range of movement for your students to play with.

5. Let your class practice swaying into a deep lunge to the right, rising up and returning with the feet in a V position, and then swaying to the left in a deep lunge.

Step 5: Creating Tall Grass Dances

Combine tilts and sways to create a dance phrase inspired by tall grasses.

Kindergarten Through Grade 3 Variation

- Make sure your students are standing arm's-length apart and are facing front. The structure for this dance is similar to the Maple Key dance. Let your class know that in this dance they will be:
  - Tilting—with a straight spine and legs and heels together to form a V with their feet
  - Swaying and bending with a curved spine and lunging from side to side
  - Moving throughout the room like the wind
- You will be the conductor of the tilts and calling out when to move like the wind.
- Each time your students finish dancing like the wind, they will be in a new position, but they should all face front so they can see you.
- Lead them for 2 to 3 minutes and play with different speeds and dynamics. Have one final strong wind section, then ask for gentle tilts. Finish the dance in stillness.

Grades 4 Through 6 Variation

Instructions

- Working in groups of five or six, ask your students to create a dance containing three phrases:
  - They need two different tilt and sway phrases; both phrases contain only on-the-spot actions that have the feet in V position and lunges (movers can tilt and sway at different times and move in different directions).
  - They need a traveling phrase inspired by the wind to be performed between the two tilt and sway phrases.
  - In the Tree exercise, each student improvised their own wind patterns, and now the wind will be choreographed and performed by the group.
- Allow 10 to 15 minutes for students to create and practice. Present two groups at a time and freeze them in their final positions until you stop the music.

Discussion

- "Did all the tilt and sway phrases use tempo changes or different rhythmic patterns? Identify some of the most eye-catching ones."
- "How did the groups deal with the wind section? Identify unique movements that were used to create wind."

Journal Entry for All Grades

"When the wind blows through a field of tall grass, the air is filled with the soft sound of the leaves and stalks rustling. If the grass was whispering to the wind, what would the grass be saying? Draw or write a poem or descriptive paragraph inspired by the grasses and the wind."

EXERCISE 2.5   THE THREE SISTERS

In the culminating exercise for plants, your class will combine many of the skills and choreographic ideas they explored and developed in this chapter to create dances inspired by the Three Sisters: corn, beans, and squash. American Indigenous People's Three Sisters agricultural tradition is a unique biodynamic system: Each plant protects and supports the others as they grow and enriches the earth with important nutrients so the soil remains fertile even after years of use.

The garden is planted in numerous mounds. Corn is planted in the center of each mound; the stalks support the bean vines as they climb and grow. Squash is planted on the perimeter of each mound; its broad leaves shade the soil and act like a living mulch to keep weeds out and prevent the soil from drying out in the sun. In addition, the prickly hairs on the squash vines discourage foraging insects and animals. The roots of the beans deposit nitrogen into the soil. Corn requires an abundance of nitrogen, so when partnered with beans, the earth is never depleted of that essential nutrient.

Lesson Plan Suggestions

Kindergarten Through Grade 3

First lesson: Step 1 (video: Three Sisters Garden, 2:00), 2, and 3 (follow the grade-appropriate variation)

Second lesson: Review the ideas from steps 3, 4, and 5, follow the grade-appropriate variation; journal

Grades 3 through 6

First lesson: Step 1 (video: Planting the Three Sisters Garden, 2:00), 2, and 3; follow grade-appropriate variation

Second lesson: Review the ideas from steps 3, 4, and 5 (follow the grade-appropriate variation); journal entry

Third lesson: A third lesson may be required if students need more time to create their culminating dance

Recommended Music: Select from compositions your students have worked with

Step 1: The Three Sisters

The Three Sisters is an agricultural tradition of American Indigenous People. From Nation to Nation, there are differing stories of how the Three Sisters came to be, but the planting practice is similar across the continent.

Watch the Planting the Three Sisters Garden video (2:00) from the list of video links in HK*Propel*. This instructive video is available to the public on the Chickasaw TV Video Network. The website contains a number of links for you and your class to learn about Chickasaw culture, history, language, and stories.

Step 2: Compile Ideas for Structuring a Dance to Honor the Three Sisters

After watching the video, create four columns on a flip chart. One column is for corn; one is for beans; one is for squash; and the fourth column is for additional ideas and information, including timing (the seeds are planted at different times) and spatial relationships (the seeds are planted in a specific spatial relationship; how can this be communicated in the dance?).

1. In exercise 2.4, your class explored a number of choreographic strategies for corn and tall grasses that you can put in the Corn column. Ask your class which of the movement ideas from exercise 2.4 they might use in this new dance. What about the edible part of corn? Can the tightly wrapped outer leaves, the silk, sweet corn, and husk inspire new ways of moving?

2. In exercise 2.3, your class created dances inspired by vines. The beans grown in a Three Sisters Garden are pole beans, and they grow vertically up the corn stalks. Ask your class which of the movement ideas from exercise 2.3 could be used to convey beans growing vertically or if they have new ideas to suggest.

3. Summer squash grows in low-lying bushes; their stems extend several feet outward in all directions. The stems are thick; the leaves are broad and semi-triangular and have jagged, somewhat prickly edges. Can the movement exploration inspired by thorns from exercise 2.2 be adapted?

4. Use the column headed Other to put additional ideas and insights—for example, beans and squash have flowers. The flowers on bean vines are small, but squash flowers are large. Ask students these questions: Could any of the flower ideas from exercise 2.2 be incorporated into the dance? And what about preparing the earth and planting the seeds? Should that be explored as well?

5. Make sure students have included ideas for level, tempo, shape, direction, and pathways that would help depict the unique character of each plant. Corn is tall, straight, and stately; beans are quick and intertwining; and squash is low, weighted, and wide.

Step 3: Explore All the Ideas in Each Column

Recommended Music

Use tracks your students have worked with and enjoyed from chapters 1 and 2. Invite them to suggest which composition should be used for corn, beans, and squash. Some classes will want different tracks for each of the sisters, while others prefer using one track throughout the dance. After compiling ideas, invite your class to explore movement ideas on their own and then share their discoveries.

Instructions

1. Ask your students to find a spot in the room that's arm's-length apart.
2. Remind everyone that when they are exploring movement ideas, they should stay in their own personal spaces.
3. If they are exploring traveling actions, your students should take small steps or work on-the-spot knowing that later on there will be opportunities for them to travel around the room.
4. Select a column—Corn, Beans, Squash, or Other—and call out all the ideas that are listed in that column.

5. Explore each column for 2 to 3 minutes.

6. Play the music. Call out prompts while your students are working.

7. After all the ideas from the first column have been explored, invite your class to share any new movement possibilities they discovered.

8. Continue the process by exploring all the columns and ideas listed.

9. Bring the exploration to a close.

Kindergarten Through Grade 3 Variation for Sharing and Discussion

Invite your students to come together after each exploration and share their ideas. Create new columns with the same headings to record your students' movement discoveries. (You'll need them for lesson 2.)

Grades 4 Through 6 Variation for Sharing and Discussion

1. Ask your students to work in their journals and record (write or notate) two to four movement ideas they discovered in the exploration.

2. After journaling, bring the class together to share and discuss.

3. Invite your students to contribute their movement ideas for the first item you called out. Listen to the first idea and write it down. Ask if anyone discovered a different way of moving for the same item. Write down any additional ideas, then move on to the next item. Continue sharing ideas item by item.

Continue Exploring For All Grades

1. Continue the process of exploring movement ideas for each column and sharing what they have discovered.

2. Let your class know that their next lesson will be dedicated to creating a Three Sisters dance using the movement ideas they've shared.

3. You'll need all the charts and journal notes for lesson 2.

Grades 4 Through 6 Variation

At the end of class, ask your students to think about possible structures for creating the Three Sisters dance by having them consider the following:

- Should the class work collaboratively and create the dance together?

- Should the class be divided into three groups, with each group creating a different movement section (one for corn, one for beans, one for squash)? Then afterward, the class can work together and find a way to connect them all.

- Should the class be divided into five or six groups, with each group creating their own Three Sisters dance?

Let your class know that at their next lesson, they'll review the options and decide how to proceed.

Step 5: Creating the Three Sisters Dance

Kindergarten Through Grade 3 Variation

Instructions

1. Bring out the flip charts compiled in the previous lesson.

2. Highlight three or four ideas from each of the columns that your class feels will best represent the individual plants and be what they feel confident performing.

3. Review those movements with your class as a warm-up.

4. Get ready to lead the dance.

As shown in the instructional video, corn is the first seed planted when creating a Three Sisters Garden. The corn stalk has to be mature enough for the bean vine to latch on to. Ask your class to consider the following items:

1. How should the Corn dance start (should students be spread out or close together, should they start as seeds in the ground, or should they create a phrase showing the seeds being planted)?

2. How should the corn grow (fast or slow, straight, swaying, or bending)?

3. Do they have ideas inspired by the shape of the corncob?

4. Write their ideas on the flip chart.

5. Choose how and where to start.

6. Ask your class to find their places.

7. Put the music on at a low level so your voice can be easily heard.

8. Using your students' ideas, talk your class through a Corn dance. Your students will interpret your directions in their own way, individually embodying the essence of corn and the important role corn has in the Three Sisters Garden.

9. When you feel the dance has reached its conclusion, ask your class the find a finishing position for their Corn dance.

Repeat the process with beans and squash. After all three sections have been danced, have your class consider the following:

- Would they like to try performing it again without stopping between each section?

- How can students move into their Bean dance after their Corn dance?

- What are some ideas for transiting between the sections? Try them out.

- Do they want to add additional sections to the front or end of the dance, such as preparing the earth before planting or preparing the vegetables for a stew?

Collaborative dance creations have a life of their own; a student can make a suggestion no one else has thought of, and it can open up a new area to explore. Whenever your class has collaborated on a multisectional dance, remind them that each one of them contributed to its creation by sharing ideas and supporting the ideas of others. Use the discussion to reflect on the choreography.

Discussion

- "What was your favorite part of the dance? Explain why."

- "Has the dance made you think about how food is grown?"

- "Have you ever thought about how plants feel when they're growing and how plants can help each other grow?"

Journal Entry

"How do you imagine the Three Sisters? Draw a picture of the Three Sisters helping each other grow."

Grades 4 Through 6 Variation

Instructions

Select the structure.

1. Bring out the charts compiled in the previous lesson.

2. Review students' ideas from the charts and their journals.

3. Ask your class which of the following structures they think is the best to create their Three Sisters–inspired dance.

   • Divide them into three groups and assign one of the Three Sisters to each group.

   • Work in smaller groups and have each group create their own Three Sisters dance.

Three Sisters.

   • Have the class work collaboratively to create the dance.

4. If the class has chosen to go into three groups, divide the class into groups then write "Corn," "Beans," and "Squash" on separate pieces of paper. Fold the paper, mix them up, and invite a representative from each group to select one. Follow the instructions for structure 1 below.

5. If your class has decided to work in small groups and create their own Three Sisters Dance, divide the class into smaller groups of six or seven students. Follow the instructions for structure 2 below.

6. If the majority of students want to work together and create the dance collaboratively, follow the structure laid out in the Kindergarten Through Grade 3 variation outlined previously and reviewed below as structure 3.

Structure 1   Divide the class into three groups. Each group creates a dance inspired by one of the Three Sisters. Depending on class size, there may be 9, 10, or 12 students in each group. If the group has 10 or more students, you may suggest that the groups subdivide so smaller numbers of students create specific sections and teach them to the others in the group. For example, if half the students doing Squash create the choreography for the shape and textures of the flowers and squash, the other half can create choreography inspired by the protective aspect: broad leaves, strong stems, and shade. After teaching what they've created to each other, they can decide on the best spatial relationship to use and develop additional details.

Structure 2   Students working in small groups will need to discuss ideas for creating their choreography, but don't let them take too much time talking. After five

© Barry Prophet

minutes, encourage everyone to get up and start moving. Let them know they can start anywhere in the dance and that ideas will evolve once they get moving. For example, someone may have a great idea for bean vines traveling upward—the group can start there, and perhaps while creating and practicing that choreography, a student gets an idea for the squash section. One important thing to mention when using structure 2 is that your students should explore ways to make the section for corn as rich and varied as the sections for beans and squash.

Structure 3   The structure outlined in the Kindergarten Through Grade 3 variation can produce dances of depth and complexity. As the facilitator, your job isn't to teach; it's to ask questions, listen to students' answers, observe and record the choreography, and offer prompts and possible solutions when students are at an impasse. Let your students know that they are responsible for the choreography. Start by collaborating on the Corn dance and proceed from there.

Monitor the Process

1. If your class is using structures 1 or 2, check in on them regularly throughout the process.
2. Remind them that if there is a disagreement, they should not let it escalate. They should come to you for help.
3. After 15 or 20 minutes, stop the class and ask how things are going.
4. There was no beat limit to the choreography, but remind students not to make their dances so long that they have difficulty remembering them.
5. If there is only a short amount of time left and the dances aren't finished, ask everyone to go to their journals and write or notate the dance as they remember it. They'll refer to those notes in their next lesson.
6. Finish, rehearse, and share the dances on the third lesson.
7. If your class used structure 3 and created their dance in their second class, make a video of it so they can watch and reflect on the process and the product.

Discussion

- "What was your favorite part of your dance? Explain why."
- "What was your favorite part of one of the dances you watched? Explain why."
- "Have you ever spent this much time thinking about how plants grow?"
- "Have you ever thought about how plants support each other?"

Journal Entry for Grades 4 Through 6

"There are hundreds of thousands of plants in the world, and today we only explored a few of them. Select a plant and give three reasons you think it would make an interesting subject for a dance."

SUMMARY

The Three Sisters provided your students with a choreographic vehicle to demonstrate some of their new movement skills and aesthetic sensibilities. Each chapter builds on the knowledge introduced in the previous chapters.

The skills students have acquired in the first and second chapters will strengthen and grow in chapter 3 as they interpret the movement patterns of animals through dance.

Go to HK _Propel_ to find audio files, reproducible forms, and a list of video links corresponding to chapter exercises.

© Janice Pomer

CHAPTER 3

Animals

Has there ever been a time when people were not studying animals? Animals have always been a source of food, clothing, transportation, and wealth. We love, fear, and admire animals; their extraordinary abilities to leap, fly, run, transform, navigate, build, adapt, and survive have inspired fighting styles, health practices, dances, architecture, and technologies. In the 21st century, animals continue to have much to teach us about our bodies and the world we live in.

This chapter is unique in its structure; the first six exercises follow the same template:

1. Introduce the animal group to be explored.
2. Compile a list of actions that are unique to those animals.
3. Compile a list of qualities attributed to the animals using multiple sources (contemporary, historical, cultural).
4. Teach the 16-beat dance inspired by the animal group.
5. Learn and perform the original 16-beat dance.
6. Apply the appropriate variation to the dance.
7. Use the variations as inspiration and create new dances.

8. Kindergarten through grade 3 will work collectively to create a new dance with their teacher (some grade 3 teachers may wish to follow grades 4 through 6 lesson plans).

9. Grades 4 through 6 will work in small groups creating and presenting original dances that communicate what they know about the animal.

10. Kindergarten through grade 3 and grades 4 through 6 have different culminating exercises.

There are so many amazing animals to explore that the subject could fill an entire book. The process of exploration and creation in these exercises can easily be repeated with other animals. If your class is studying an animal or if a student has a particular interest in an animal that is not included in these exercises, simply use the template introduced in this chapter and create a dance for it.

Inspire Versus Imitate

When your class begins exploring animal movements, the word *inspired* should be emphasized, especially with younger students. For example, while exploring exercise 3.2, which focuses on lions, tigers, and other wildcats, young students may want to imitate a lion by moving on all fours. Moving with both hands and feet on the ground can be a beneficial stretch, but it limits movement possibilities and makes it difficult for the human body to emulate the strength, agility, and majesty of lions and tigers.

In this chapter, your class will be asked to identify specific animal movement qualities and translate them for the human body. This approach to movement exploration and creation has been used for thousands of years. One example of how animal actions have been translated into movement for the human form is kung fu, an ancient Chinese martial arts form.

The five main kung fu styles were inspired by these animals:

- Tiger: Focuses on frontal assault, aggression, and power, so movements are short and follow ripping or tearing motions (like a tiger's powerful paws and claws).
- Leopard: More precise than the tiger; the arm and hand work is faster and tighter (speed is key to the leopard's strength).
- Crane: Balance and flexibility can be used to disturb the opponents' balance. The arms (like the crane's wings) are used as counterbalance and for attack.
- Dragon: This uses zigzag, swinging (like the dragon's tail), and floating movements.
- Snake: Movements emphasize flowing and rippling arms, hands, and fingers (like the snake's mobile spine). The snake style of kung fu doesn't require practitioners to slither on the ground; instead, the snake's fluid, rippling actions are applied to the hands and fingers.

There are other animal-based kung fu forms, including styles inspired by the praying mantis, monkey, and eagle. Kung fu isn't the only ancient movement form that's been inspired by animals. Yoga poses are inspired by nature, and many of the poses are based on animals, including:

- The pigeon (eka pada rajakapotasana)
- The cobra (bhujangasana)

- The butterfly (bhadrasana)
- The camel (ustrsana)

Ballet steps inspired by animals include these:

- Pas de chat (cat's step) and saut de chat (cat leap)
- Pas de cheval (horse step, resembles pawing the ground)
- Poisson (a stylized fish performed while standing tall with the legs together and back arched)

Popular mid-20th-century dances inspired by animals include these:

- The Bunny Hop (a variation of the conga line popular in the 1950s and 1960s)
- The Pony (Chubby Checker sang the song "Pony Time" in the 1960s)
- The Chicken (originally from the 1950s and re-emerged in the 1970s)

Animal Symbolism

Besides looking at the kinetic actions of animals, students may also want to consider the attributes humans associate with animals. It's important to look at many cultures to provide a diverse perspective of how specific animals are viewed. For example, in Greek mythology, Athena, the goddess of wisdom, is often depicted with a small owl, and both the owl and Athena are associated with truth and wisdom. In the Celtic tradition, owls are considered warriors and defenders of truth and honor. In many African traditions, owls were considered bad luck; in early Christianity, owls were thought to be evil. In Afghani mythology, the owl helped humanity by giving man flint to make fire.

Owl eyes.

Ancient owl symbols are still strong in the 21st century. Rapper Drake features an owl in his OVO brand label. The letters *OVO* could be seen as two large owl eyes and a beak. (OVO stands for October's Very Own—October being Drake's birth month.) The owl image he uses is styled after an ancient Egyptian hieroglyph, an image that's more than 5,000 years old.

Before you introduce exercise 3.1, share the inspiring video How to Dance Like Animals (1:53) from the list of video links in HK*Propel*. Critically acclaimed dance artists Jared Grimes and Lil Buck are featured in this short clip excerpted from their work with award-winning jazz artist Wynton Marsalis' jazz composition, *Spaces*. In less than two minutes, your students will see dancing inspired by a chicken, tree frog, and lion (and at the top of the video, there's a moment from the elephant dance).

EXERCISE 3.1   BIRDS OF A FEATHER

Lesson Plan Suggestions

Kindergarten Through Grade 3

First lesson: Steps 1, 2, 3, 4, and 5

Second lesson: Warm up by reviewing step 3, review the notes from step 5, and perform step 6 (follow grade-appropriate variations)

Grades 4 Through 6

First lesson: Steps 1, 2, 3, 4, and 5. (At the end of the first lesson you may wish to divide your class into groups and assign each group their animal. Students may wish to work on their own or in their groups to research their animal before their next dance class.)

Second lesson: Warm up by reviewing step 3, introduce the new dance requirements at the top of step 6 (follow grade-appropriate variations), and work in groups to create and present original dances; journal

Recommended Music: Track 4 (fast) or track 16 (moderate)

Step 1: What We Know About Birds

Instructions

Make a list of birds your class is familiar with, including songbirds (robins, cardinals, finches, jays, orioles), birds of prey (hawks, owls, eagles, falcons), and carrion (scavenger) birds (vultures, crows, condor). There are flightless birds such as emus and ostriches (see Other Wonders, chapter 8), but this exercise focuses on birds that fly.

Compile a list of movement characteristics that all flying birds share, such as the ones that follow and invite your class into the performance area to explore the movements together.

- Smooth gliding movements
- Flapping wings
- Perching or balancing on one foot
- Scratching and pecking the earth
- Grabbing prey with claws and beaks
- Nest building
- Turning and tilting the head
- Shaking or fluffing the tail and wings

Step 2: What Can Birds Symbolize?

Instructions

As mentioned at the beginning of the chapter, depending on the cultural tradition, the owl can represent or symbolize a wide range of attributes. Compile a list of qualities that are attributed to other birds, such as love, beauty, peace, freedom, grace, and longevity.

Step 3: Foundation Bird Dance

This Bird dance is designed to provide your class with inspiration for the original dances they'll be creating later in the exercise. You're welcome to create your own foundation Bird dance, and you may change parts of the dance or use it in its original form. What's most important is that all your students learn a foundation Bird dance so they are able to explore the choreographic variation in step 4 and that some of the movement characteristics of birds your class identified in step 1 are translated into dance.

Recommended Music

Track 4. This 16-beat dance phrase uses the following movement characteristics of birds:

- Quick, staccato head turns
- Balancing on one leg to create a sense of being suspended in the air
- Playful hops and shaking to represent ruffling feathers

Instructions

Start in parallel position (flex the wrists so the hands extend outward at the hips to create a tail)

1. Turn the head to the right on beat 1, return it to center on beat 2, turn the head to the left on beat 3, and return it to center on beat 4.

2. Step to the right, lift and stretch the left leg to the back as the arms reach out to either side on beat 5, and hold the position (gliding through the air) for beats 6, 7, and 8 (as shown in the Birds photograph).

3. Step to the left, lift and stretch the right leg to the back as the arms reach out to either side on beat 1, and hold the position for beats 2, 3, and 4.

4. Hop onto the right foot on beat 5, and hop onto the left foot on beat 6.

Birds.

© Janice Pomer

5. Return to parallel position and shake the wings and tail while moving quickly up and down on beats 7 and 8.

Repeat entire sequence starting to the left and practice two or three times on each side.

Step 4: Flying in Flocks

All Grades (kindergarten through grade 3 teachers may wish to divide their class into two groups instead of four)

Recommended Music

Track 16

Instructions

1. Divide your class into four groups.
2. Ask each group to stand in a different corner of the performance area.
3. The group upstage right is group 1, downstage left is group 2, upstage left is group 3, and downstage right is group 4 (refer to the stage map in chapter 1).
4. Group 1 will enter the performance area together as a flock and have 16 beats to travel through the open space to reach the center area.
   - Kindergarten through grade 3 students can improvise how they travel.
   - Teachers working with students in grades 4 through 6 may give their class time to explore traveling ideas and practice in their groups or ask your students to improvise their 16-beat flying phrase. The traveling movement phrase should be 16 beats long and communicate flight.
5. In the center, they will perform the 16-beat foundation Bird dance once.
6. After they have finished performing the foundation dance, they have 16 beats to repeat their original traveling phrase and return to their corner before the next flock enters.
7. Continue the process until each flock has presented.

Discussion

- "Did some groups decide to create a unison traveling pattern? If yes, explain why you chose to work in unison and how you selected your traveling pattern."
- "Did it seem as if different types of birds were flying together when individuals performed the traveling section differently?"

Many birds migrate in flocks and separate once they reach their summer or winter locations, some birds stay in flocks all year, and other birds are solitary.

Step 5: Solitary Birds

Make a list of solitary birds, including owls, eagles, herons, hummingbirds, and woodpeckers. Each of these birds has unique characteristics. Create separate lists for each of these birds. Here are some interesting facts to include:

- Owls are nocturnal, can rotate their heads as much as 270 degrees in either direction, and are the only birds that can fly soundlessly.
- Eagles have large and strong wings, enabling them to fly in a straight line against prevailing air currents (something most birds cannot do).
- Herons are the only wading bird on the list; wading birds have very long legs and necks, and their movements and resting positions are distinct.

- Hummingbirds are the only birds that can fly forward, backward, side to side, and upside down and hover in the same spot while in the air.
- Woodpeckers don't just peck at the earth; their heads and beaks are so strong that they hammer holes into trees.

Grades 4 through 6 teachers may wish to divide their classes into groups and assign each group an animal so that students may work on their own or in their groups to research their animal before the next dance class.

Step 6: Creating Original Bird Dances

Kindergarten Through Grade 3 Variation

Instructions

Work together to create a new dance that communicates some of the unique characteristics of solitary birds. To generate ideas, put both music suggestions on and ask students to improvise the actions compiled in your list from steps 1 and 2 as well as the following:

- Owl head turns and swoops
- Heron walks
- Soaring like an eagle
- Woodpecker head isolations
- Fast hummingbird wings

After improvising, ask your students which movement ideas they would like to include in their new Bird dance. Compile the list and establish an order (make sure there are some full-body actions between isolations). Practice and memorize the dance.

Discussion

"What movements felt most birdlike? Explain why."

Journal Entry for Kindergarten Through Grade 3

- Have the class create a poem inspired by birds. Older students should work independently; for younger students, create the poem (or poems) collaboratively. Use words from the lists compiled in steps 1 and 2.
- Save the poems. They'll be used in the culminating exercise for this chapter.

Grades 4 Through 6 Variation

Instructions

Create dances to communicate the unique qualities of the five solitary birds: owl, eagle, heron, woodpecker, and hummingbird.

- If you haven't already, divide your class into five groups and assign a different solitary bird to each group.
- In their groups, students will explore ways to communicate their bird's unique characteristics through movement in a 20- to 32-beat movement piece.
- Each group's choreography should combine full-body traveling actions with on-the-spot isolations that are unique to their birds.
- They may use either the fast or slow composition for their presentation.

After each group has presented, discuss the process and dances.

Discussion

Ask each group to describe the following:

- What they learned about their bird
- The unique features and abilities they wanted to highlight
- How they communicated their bird's actions and attributes through movement

Journal Entry for Grades 4 Through 6

"If you were a bird, what bird would you be? Remember to let the reader know why you'd like to be that bird."

EXERCISE 3.2   WILDCATS

Lesson Plan Suggestions

Kindergarten Through Grade 3

First Lesson: Steps 1, 2, 3, and 4, and if time allows, introduce step 5 (follow grade-appropriate variations)

Second Lesson: Warm up by reviewing step 3, do step 5 (exploring new actions and creating an original dance), and complete the journal entry

Grades 4 Through 6

First Lesson: Steps 1, 2, 3, and 4, and introduce step 5 (follow the grade-appropriate variation).

Second Lesson: Warm up by reviewing step 3, review the dance requirements in step 5, and work in groups to create and present original dances; complete the journal entry

Recommended Music: Track 8

Step 1: What We Know About Wildcats

- Make a list of the wildcats your students know. The list will include lions, cheetahs, tigers, panthers, jaguars, cougars, snow leopards, and lynx.
- Compile a list of movement characteristics these animals share, such as the following, then invite your class into the performance area to explore the movements together:
  - Sneaking and creeping quietly
  - Stalking and running after prey
  - Pouncing suddenly
  - Bounding leaps
  - Opening and closing large powerful jaws
  - Reaching and swiping with front paws

Step 2: Compile a List of Qualities Attributed to Wildcats

In exercise 3.1, we learned that different cultures view owls in different ways. Interestingly, the lion has symbolized strength and nobility for thousands of years in many parts of the world. Lions can be found on African and European coats of arms, the Sri Lankan flag, the Cambodian royal arms, Israel's coat of arms, and India's national emblem.

Instructions

Create a list of qualities wildcats are known to represent, such as strong, fierce, courageous, noble, and proud.

Step 3: Foundation Lion Dance

This Lion dance is designed to provide your class with inspiration for the original dances they'll be creating later in the exercise. You're welcome to create your own foundation Lion dance, and you may change parts of the dance or use it in its original form. What's most important is that all your students learn a foundation Lion dance so they are able to explore the choreographic variation in step 4 and that some of the movement characteristics of wildcats your class identified in step 1 are translated into dance.

Recommended Music

Track 8

Instructions

Teach the following Wildcat dance to your class:

1. Start by standing in parallel position with knees slightly bent.
2. Reach your right hand forward and swipe the air diagonally from head height to hip height, from right to left, on beat 1 (big paw with claws).
3. Swipe your left hand (big paw with claws) diagonally from head height to hip height, from left to right, on beat 2.
4. Repeat the big-claw swipes on each side for beats 3 and 4.
5. Turn the head and torso, straighten the knees, raise the paws overhead, and show a fierce face to the right for beats 5 and 6. Then repeat this movement to the left on beats 7 and 8.
6. Creep (with knees bent) with the left foot and move the right arm or claw forward on beat 1.
7. Move the right foot and left arm or claw forward on beat 2.
8. Repeat creeping two more times for beats 3 and 4.

Lions.

© Janice Pomer

9. Deeply bend both knees and bring the arms and claws close to the torso on beats 5 and 6.

10. Big jump forward with claws reaching up on beat 7.

11. Land, bring what your big claws have caught up toward your face, open the jaws, and bite on beat 8.

If you're tight for space, the 4 beats of creeping can be performed on-the-spot instead of traveling forward. Repeat the sequence 4 times so everyone is performing the dance with confidence and lion energy.

For an additional challenge ask students to perform the sequence the first time facing front. The second time, use the claw swipes to quarter turn to face the right side of the room. The third time they repeat the phrase, they use the claw swipes to turn them so they face the back of the room, and the final time they repeat the phrase, they'll face the left side.

Step 4: Hunting Habits

Kindergarten Through Grade 3 Variation

Teachers working with kindergarten through grade 3 students should divide their class into two prides of lions and let each group perform their Wildcat dance for each other. After presenting the dance to each other, your students may have additional ideas to add to the dance or they may wish to improvise their own Lion dances.

Grades 4 Through 6 Variation

Wild and domestic cats are solitary hunters. Only lions hunt in groups, and female lions are the dominant hunters. Instead of having everyone perform the Wildcat dance in unison, try doing it in a round.

Instructions

1. Invite half the class to watch while the other half presents.

2. Ask those in the performance area to go into small groups of three or four. Each group will represent a small pride of lions.

3. Make sure the prides are placed throughout the performance area.

4. Assign each pride a number. If pride 1 is upstage right, pride 2 should be downstage left, pride 3 can be upstage left, and pride 4 can be downstage right so the action is scattered across the savannah.

5. Each pride will begin every 4 beats, and when they have finished the 16-beat phrase, they should freeze until the music ends.

6. After the four prides have finished, ask students in the viewing area to change places with those who just presented.

7. After the second group of students have presented, sit together and discuss.

Discussion

- "What was the most eye-catching moment in the Lion dance—the big pounce, the slow creeping, or the side-to-side snarls? Explain why you felt one was more powerful than the others."

- "Review the list of wildcat actions. Are there some actions on the list that weren't used in the dance?"

Step 5: Creating Original Wildcat Dances

Kindergarten Through Grade 3 Variation

Instructions

- Review your list of wildcats. Ask students, "Do many of them live in the same habitat as lions? Are there any wildcats on your list that live in a cold, mountainous habitat?"
- Work collaboratively to create new a dance that communicates the unique characteristics of the snow leopard. To generate ideas, put the music on and ask students to improvise movement ideas based on the following and other snow leopard actions:
  - Snow leopards are powerful leapers.
  - They live in the mountains and are good rock climbers.
  - Their paws are like snowshoes—they can walk on snow without sinking down.
  - Their tails are longer than the tails of other wildcats; they wrap their tails across their noses to stay warm when sleeping or resting.
  - They can't roar.
  - They can travel more than 25 miles in a single night.
- After improvising, ask your students to share and possibly teach some of their movement discoveries to the class. Afterward, discuss which movements should be used in their new Snow Leopard dance. Compile the list, establish an order (make sure there are some calm actions between leaps and runs), learn the combination, and perform it for each other.

Discussion

- "What was your favorite wild cat action to perform?"
- "What was the most exciting part of the dance to watch?"

Journal Entry for Kindergarten Through Grade 3

- Have the class create a poem inspired by wildcats. Older students should work independently; for younger students, create the poem (or poems) collaboratively. Use words from the lists compiled in steps 1 and 2.
- Save the poems. They'll be used in the culminating exercise for chapter 3.

Grades 4 Through 6 Variation

In the Wildcat foundation dance, students focused on being lions and hunting together. Now your students will research and create dances inspired by solitary hunters.

Instructions

- Divide your class into five groups. Assign each group one of the following wildcats for their dance: jaguars, lynx, cheetahs, ocelots, or snow leopards. (The kindergarten through grade 3 variation focuses on snow leopards; see accompanying list of their unique traits).
  1. Invite the groups to start brainstorming ideas for their dances and to record the ideas in their journals.
  2. In their next lesson, students will create, rehearse, present, and discuss their original Wildcat dances.

3. Groups may need to research their wildcat outside of dance class so they might have new movement ideas to explore at their next dance lesson (provide class time or make it a homework assignment).

4. Focus your students' research by assigning these questions:
   - Does your wildcat have unusual habits or skills? For example, does it swim, climb trees, or enjoy the cold?
   - What is their habitat like?
   - What do they hunt or eat?
   - What time of the day or night do they hunt?

- When your students begin working on their dances, ask them to create a 28- or 32-beat dance that highlights some of the unique abilities of their wildcat.

- After each group has presented, discuss the process and the dances.

Discussion

Ask each group to describe the following:

- What they learned about their animal

- The unique features and abilities they wanted to highlight and how they communicated them through movement

Journal Entry Grades 4 Through 6

"Do you have any wildcat character traits? Are you strong and fierce? What makes you feel proud? What makes you want to roar? When do you purr? Write a short paragraph about the wildcat within you."

EXERCISE 3.3   HORNS, ANTLERS, HOOVES, AND HERDS

Lesson Plan Suggestions

Kindergarten Through Grade 3

First Lesson: Steps 1, 2, 3, 4, and 5 (videos: Springbok Pronking, 2:57, and Wolves Versus Herd of Muskox | Snow Wolf Family and Me, 4:15; follow the grade-appropriate variation)

Second Lesson: Warm up by reviewing step 3, review the notes from step 5 (show the video if there wasn't time in the previous lesson), do step 6, and make a journal entry

Grades 4 Through 6

First Lesson: Steps 1, 2, 3, and 4, and introduce step 5 (videos: Springbok Pronking, 2:57, and Wolves Versus Herd of Muskox | Snow Wolf Family and Me, 4:15; follow the grade-appropriate variation); divide the class into working groups, assign each group their animal, and ask students to research their animal before the next class

Second Lesson: Warm up by reviewing step 3, review the dance requirements in step 5, have students work in their groups for step 6 to create and present original dances, and make a journal entry

Recommended Music: Tracks 3 (for step 2 and antelope, gazelle, and impala) and 20 (for musk ox and buffalo)

Step 1: What We Know About Migrating Herds With Horns and Hooves

- Make a list of the wild animals with hooves, horns, or antlers that live in herds. The list should include buffalo, deer, caribou, gazelle, antelope, impala, yak, and musk ox. Other animals live in herds, but for this exercise we're focusing on migrating animals that have horns (or antlers) and hooves.

- Compile a list of movement characteristics these animals share, including the following, then invite your class into the performance area to explore the movements together.

  · Stomp and paw the earth

  · Feed on ground vegetation

  · Chew cud

  · Run and gallop

  · Kick with back legs

  · Powerful necks

  · Antlers and horns (ask students what the animals use them for)

Step 2: Qualities

Create a list of qualities attributed to these animals, including majestic, powerful, prosperity, elegance, and grace.

Step 3: Foundation Caribou Dance

This Caribou dance is designed to provide your class with inspiration for the original dances they'll be creating later in the exercise. You're welcome to create your own foundation Caribou dance. You may change parts of the dance or use it in its original form. What's most important is that all of your students learn a foundation dance so they are able to explore the choreographic variation in step 4 and that some of the movement characteristics of herd animals with horns and hooves your class identified in step 1 are translated into dance.

Recommended Music

Track 2

Instructions

- Teach the following dance to your class:
    1. Starting position: Stand with feet in parallel position with both hands in fists (to represent hooves) and arms straight, extending in front of the torso at a 45-degree angle.
    2. Stand on the right foot and paw the earth with the left (as shown in the Hooves photograph) two times on beats 1 and 2.
    3. Bend the left knee to hip height and bend the elbows on beat 3.
    4. Straighten the left leg and elbows as the foot stomps down slightly forward of parallel on beat 4.
    5. Stand on the left foot and paw the earth with the right two times on beats 5 and 6.
    6. Bend the right knee to hip height and bend the elbows on beat 7.
    7. Straighten the right leg and elbows as the foot stomps down into parallel on beat 8.
    8. Leading with the right foot, take two gallop steps to the right (DSR) on beats 1 and 2.
    9. Kick back the left leg and toss the head on beats 3 and 4.

Hooves.

© Janice Pomer

10. Turn to face the left corner (DSL) and take two gallop steps diagonally left on beats 5 and 6.

11. Kick back the right leg and toss the head on beats 7 and 8.

12. Bring the feet to parallel position and face the front to repeat to the second side.

- Repeat the sequence starting on the second side (standing on the left foot), then repeat the sequence again on both sides until everyone is confident before adding the variation.

Step 4: Migration

All Grades

Instructions

Migrating animals travel long distances from one feeding area to another. Caribou travel as far as 3,000 miles (5,000 km) from northern forests to their summer feeding grounds on the tundra. Try adding a traveling pattern between the first and second sides of the dance to represent a migration. After tossing the head and kicking the right leg (beats 15 and 16), gallop in a circle to the right with the right leg leading for 8 beats. On the beat 8, students should be facing front, ready to repeat the dance on the second side. If you're working outside or in the gymnasium, the circle can be larger and take 16 beats. After the first circle, perform the dance on the second side. Finish by galloping for 8 (or 16) beats, circling to the left to finish facing front. Divide your class into two or three groups so there's enough room in the circular gallop pattern for everyone to work safely.

Discussion

- "Did galloping together in large circles help communicate the life of a migrating herd? If yes, how? If no, why not?"
- "What else could you add to the dance to communicate the lives of migrating herds?" Write down the suggestions to explore later.
- "While dancing, did you imagine having antlers on your head?"
- "What would antlers feel like? Are they heavy or cumbersome? Are antlers like crowns? Would they make you feel proud?"
- "Take a moment to explore antler shapes with your arms. Caribou antlers can grow to more than 40 inches (over a meter) in length! Stretch your arms wide and hold the position for 10 to 15 seconds."
- Caribou or reindeer (they are the same species but are called reindeer when domesticated) grow new antlers every year. An adult male's antlers can weigh up to 20 pounds (9 kg). The males shed their antlers in late November, but females keep their antlers all winter. ("What does that tell us about Santa's reindeer?")

Step 5: Create Original Herd Dances

Before creating original dances, share these two videos with your class.

- Watch the video Springbok Pronking (2:57) from the list of video links in HK*Propel* to see the amazing leaping powers of the springbok antelope. The springbok has a unique leap called pronking.

- Watch the video Wolves vs Herd of Muskox | Snow Wolf Family and Me (4:15) from the list of video links in HK*Propel*. In this fascinating video, a herd of musk ox face a pack of hungry Arctic wolves. The herd works as a team, with incredible defensive moves and strategic positioning to protect their young.

Kindergarten Through Grade 3 Variation

Instructions

- Work together collaboratively to create a new dance inspired by some of the unique characteristics of the springbok antelope.
- Ask your students for movement suggestions. These suggestions could include the following:
  - Arms raised as long horns and lift the head up and down and side to side
  - Gallops with arms lifted in horn positions
  - Traveling across the floor using a leap, run, leap combination
  - Lower heads to show grazing
  - Lifting heads up and looking from side to side in case of danger
- After several minutes of exploring these movement ideas collectively, ask your students which ideas they would like to include in their new Herd dance. You can use sections of the foundation dance or create an entirely new dance.
- Establish an order to perform the selected movements (make sure there are some full-body actions between head isolations) and practice the dance until everyone is confident performing it.
- Divide into two groups and perform it to each other.

Journal Entry Kindergarten Through Grade 3

- Create a poem inspired by antelope.
- Work independently or, for younger students, create the poem (or poems) collaboratively. Use words from the lists compiled in steps 1 and 2.
- Save the poems. They'll be used in the culminating exercise for this chapter.

Grades 4 Through 6 Variation

Instructions

- After watching the two videos, lead a class discussion about gazelles, antelope, impalas, buffalo, yak, and musk ox. Compile two lists: a list of the qualities they share and a list of characteristics and abilities that are unique (for example, pronking is unique to the springbok antelope). Brainstorm ways to highlight their differences in movement, such as the following examples:
  - Gazelles, antelope, and impalas are swift, agile leapers, while musk ox, buffalo, and yaks are strong and sturdily built.
  - Students can use changes in timing and energy to highlight the differences: slower, heavier steps for buffalo, yak, and musk ox; faster, lighter steps for gazelle, antelope, and impala.
  - Gazelle, antelope, and impalas have long vertical horns while buffalo, yak, and musk ox horns are thicker and stay close to their heads.
  - Students creating dances inspired by gazelles and impalas may wish to use their arms in stylized positions for gazelles, antelope, and impala while they leap.

Herds.

- · Students doing buffalo, yak, and musk ox could consider ways to make their shoulders appear broader.
- Divide the class into groups of five or six. Ask half of the groups to create dances inspired by gazelles, antelope, or impalas while the other groups create dances based on musk ox, yak, and buffalo.
- If needed, provide the students with some class time or ask them to research on their own before their next dance lesson.
  1. If there is time, invite groups to start brainstorming and record ideas in their journals.
  2. At the next dance lesson, your students should be ready to work in their groups to identify movement qualities, explore ideas, and create their dance.
  3. The dances can be 28 or 32 beats long and should highlight three of the animal's unique characteristics and movement abilities.
  4. Those creating dances for musk ox or buffalo should choreograph to track 20; those creating dances for antelope, impala, and gazelles should use track 3.

Discussion

After all groups have presented their choreography, discuss the process and dances. Ask each group to describe the following:

- What they learned about their animal
- Which unique features and abilities they felt were important to highlight
- How they communicated those features and abilities through movement

Journal Entry for Grades 4 Through 6

"Is teamwork important when you're part of a herd? Could these animals survive without living with each other? When is teamwork important for you, your family, and your community? Write a descriptive poem or paragraph about teamwork."

EXERCISE 3.4   REPTILES WITH SCALES AND SHELLS

Lesson Plan Suggestions

Kindergarten Through Grade 3

First Lesson: Steps 1, 2, 3, 4, 5 (follow the grade-appropriate variation), and 6 (videos: Frill-Necked Lizard Escapes Python | Wild Monsoon, 2:16, and Fast Tongues | Chameleons in Slow Motion, 2:19)

Second Lesson: Warm up by reviewing step 3, review the notes from step 5, do step 6 (exploring new actions and creating an original dance), and make a journal entry

Grades 4 Through 6

First Lesson: Steps 1, 2, 3, 4, 5 (follow the grade-appropriate variation), and introduce step 6.

Second Lesson: Do the spine warm-up and review the Rattlesnake dance in step 3, review the grade-appropriate dance requirements in step 6, work in groups to create and present original dances, and make a journal entry

Recommended Music: Tracks 9 (for snake), 14 (fast lizards), and 8 (slow tortoises)

Step 1: What We Know About Reptiles With Scales or Shells (birds can be classified as reptiles but are not the focus of this exercise)

- Make a list of all the reptiles with scales and shells your students know. The list will include snakes, iguanas, chameleons, crocodiles, turtles, and tortoises.
- Compile a list of movement characteristics they share, including the following, then invite your class into the performance area to explore the movements together:
  - Snakes and crocodiles have mobile spines that can ripple and curve.
  - Snakes and some lizards have darting tongues.
  - Twisting necks and torsos are common.
  - Some lizards have incredibly long and powerful tongues.
  - Flicking and swinging tails are found on these reptiles.
  - Lizards' front legs are short, and their back legs are powerful.
  - Turtles and tortoises have hard armored shells for protection.

Step 2: Create a List of Qualities Attributed to These Reptiles

The qualities include wise, rebirth, dangerous, patient, and tempting.

Step 3: Special Warm-Up Before the Rattlesnake-Inspired Dance

During their Reptile dances, your students may want to use curving and rippling moves with their torso. Use this warm-up to stretch and loosen the spine.

1. In parallel position, reach up and stretch your fingers toward the ceiling. Lengthen the spine, look straight ahead, and keep the back of the neck long. Hold for 8 beats.

2. Take 4 beats to lower the head and arms as you roll down through the torso (bend your knees slightly) on beats 1, 2, 3, and 4.

3. Keep rolling down and touch the floor, keeping the head down and the back of the neck long on beats 5, 6, 7, and 8.

4. Roll up through the spine as you slowly straighten the knees on beats 1, 2, 3, and 4.

5. Reach the arms overhead, stretch the fingers, and lengthen the spine for 5, 6, 7, and 8.

6. Repeat the reach, roll down, release the spine, and roll up again.

7. Bring the left arm up overhead for beats 1 and 2.

8. Reach the left arm overhead to the right, let the upper torso curve to the right, and stretch away from the left hip on beats 3, 4, 5, and 6.

9. Bring the torso back to center and bring the left arm down on beats 7 and 8.

10. Bring the right arm up overhead on beats 1 and 2.

11. Reach the right arm overhead to the left, let the upper torso curve to the left, and stretch away from the right hip on beats 3, 4, 5, and 6.

12. Bring the torso back to center and bring the right arm down on beats 7 and 8.

13. Repeat reaching and stretching on the second side.

14. Repeat the entire sequence on both sides.

Step 4: Snake-Inspired Dance

Recommended Music

Track 9

Instructions

- For this movement, the sequence of the hand movements are inspired by the actions of the head, tongue, and tail of the snake.

- Start facing front with the knees bent (students will be standing at level 6 or 7) and reach the hands forward and bring the palms together.

    1. Step right and ripple the arms downstage right, (hands leading like the head of the snake) on beat 1.

    2. Step left and ripple the arms downstage left (hands leading like the head of the snake) on beat 2.

    3. Repeat the step downstage right and ripple the arms (keep the knees bent) on beat 3.

    4. Repeat the step downstage left and ripple the arms (keep the knees bent), on beat 4.

5. Step to the right and keep rippling the arms as you take 3 steps with bent knees in a small circle (imagine a snake coiling up) on beats 5, 6, and 7.

6. Take one more step to complete the circle and face front on beat 8.

7. Do a deep lunge diagonally right (if you wish, the back knee may touch the ground; see the Snake photograph) and dart the right hand on beat 1. Then do the left hand on beat 2 (imagine the snake's tongue flicking).

8. Do a deep lunge diagonally left and quickly dart the left hand on beat 3, then do the right hand on beat 4 (imagine the snake's tongue flicking).

9. Step into a slightly higher lunge with the right leg forward, the back leg straight, and the knee off the ground. Reach the right arm front, stretch the left arm behind, and shake both hands on beats 5 and 6 (the snake shaking its tail).

10. Lunge the left leg forward, reach the left arm to the front, stretch the right arm behind, and shake both hands on beats 7 and 8 (the snake shaking its tail).

• Repeat the combination to the second side and practice until everyone is confident performing the combination.

Snake.

Step 5: Snake Nest

Birds and snakes have nests and lay eggs. Rattlesnakes can lay up to 25 eggs at a time, and some snakes lay up to 100 eggs in a single clutch!

Kindergarten Through Grade 3 Variation

Instructions

• Invite your class to work in two groups.

• Ask the presenting group to start close together and move away from each other as they perform the dance.

Discussion

• "Did the opening section of the dance look like a nest of snakes leaving their nest?"

• "Which movement looked the snakiest: the rippling arms, darting hands, or rattling hands?"

Grades 4 Through 6 Variation

Instructions

Classes should divide into two groups.

1. Ask the performing group to start in a tight, outward facing circle in the center of the performance area.

2. Ask the viewing group to sit in a large circle around the outside of the performance area.

3. As the dance begins, the dancers will appear to be rippling in their nests and slowly begin to travel outward.

4. When they circle on-the-spot, it will appear that they're returning to their nests, but suddenly their arms dart (tongues), and they begin to travel outward again.

5. The two big lunge steps with rattling arms should take the dancers even farther away from their nests, spreading throughout the performance area in all directions.

6. Ask the dancers to repeat the phrase 4 times (if there's enough room).

7. Each time the dancers perform the forward lunges, they move closer to the viewers.

8. Change groups so everyone performs and views.

Discussion

- "As a dancer, did it feel like you were in the snake's nest at the start of the dance?"

- "While you were watching, how did you feel as the snakes moved closer and closer toward you?"

Step 6: Create Your Own Reptile Dance

Kindergarten Through Grade 3 Variation

Recommended Music

Track 14 for fast lizards and track 8 for slow tortoises

Instructions

- Collaboratively create a new dance that communicates some of the unique characteristics of reptiles other than snakes. To generate movement ideas, ask students to improvise the following actions and other actions compiled in your list:

- Turtles and tortoises

  · Reach the head up and pull the head in

  · Slow, plodding walks

- Crocodiles and alligators

  · Huge jaws open and slam shut (use arms)

  · Waits in stillness, attacks quickly

- Lizards

  · Long, fast tongues

  · Side-to-side locomotion

- Watch the video Frill-Necked Lizard Escapes Python | Wild Monsoon (2:16) and Fast Tongues | Chameleons in Slow Motion (2:19) from the list of video links in HK*Propel* to get a sense of the speed and strength of lizards' tongues and legs and the colors and eye movements of chameleons.

- After exploring, invite your students to share their favorite movement ideas and then decide which to use in the dance using the following template:

  1. Compile the list of actions.

© Janice Pomer

Alligators.

2. Establish an order.
3. Explore ideas for spacing.
4. Practice the dance together.
5. Divide into two groups.
6. Perform it for each other.

Journal Entry for Kindergarten Through Grade 3

- After dancing, create a poem.
- Ask students: "Can you create a poem inspired by reptiles with scales and shells?"
- Work independently or, for younger students, create the poem (or poems) collaboratively. Use words from the lists compiled in steps 1 and 2.
- Save the poems. They'll be used in the culminating exercise for this chapter.

Grades 4 Through 6 Variation

Now that students have performed the Snake dance, it's time to explore other reptiles. Students will work in small groups and select their own reptile.

Instructions

- Review the list of reptiles your class compiled at the beginning of the exercise. Work collectively to identify some of the characteristics unique to iguanas, chameleons, crocodiles, turtles, tortoises, and other reptiles with scales or shells.
- Ask your class to work in groups of four or five students.
- This will be the first time your students are choosing their own animals.
- Allow groups 2 to 3 minutes to decide on their reptiles. Remind them they're part of a team, and even if the reptile the group picks isn't their favorite, every member of the group must contribute and work to their optimum.
- It's all right if more than one group selects the same animal because it's interesting to see how two groups approach the same reptile and see which qualities they focus on and how they translate the animals' movements into dance.

- Remind students that even though reptiles stay low to the ground, they needn't be moving on the floor. The challenge is to translate and modify reptiles' movements for the human body. The following list has examples:
  - Outstretched arms can become an alligator's long mouth and snout.
  - Work with wide legs, bent knees, and a rounded spine to create a turtle shell.
  - Lizards that run upright have a unique gait (go the Frill-Necked Lizard Escapes Python link from the list of video links in HK*Propel*).
- By now, your class should be comfortable with the process of researching, exploring, and creating their animal-inspired dances, but it's still important to check in with each group to make sure they're staying on track.
- The dances should be 28 or 32 beats in length.
- Invite the students to use track 14 if they're creating a fast Lizard dance or track 8 for a slow Reptile dance.
- After each group has presented, sit together and discuss the creation process.

Discussion

- As creators, ask each group to explain the reasons they selected their reptile, what characteristics they decided to highlight, and why.
- Ask viewers to identify any movements they thought were eye-catching and unique in others' presentations.
- Did some groups select the same reptile? If yes, identify the similarities and differences between their dances.
- "Was creating a dance phrase for reptiles more challenging that the previous animal dances? If yes, explain why." (*It was hard to translate low-level movement to higher levels, it was hard to show chameleons changing color.*)

Journal Entry for Grades 4 Through 6

"Did this exercise introduce you to new reptiles or new reptile facts? If yes, what did you learn? If you already knew all about reptiles, can you share two of your favorite reptile facts or dispel any reptile myths?"

EXERCISE 3.5   SPIDERS AND INSECTS

Lesson Plan Suggestions

Kindergarten Through Grade 3

First Lesson: Steps 1, 2, 3, and 4, and compile ideas in step 5 (video: Crystal Pite's Emergence, Pacific Northwest Ballet, 3:01; follow the grade-appropriate variation)

Second Lesson: Warm up by reviewing step 3, review the notes from step 5 (exploring actions, create an original dance, write poems); step 6 is optional (video: Anansi the Spider and His Six Sons, 6:45); journal

Grades 4 Through 6

First Lesson: Steps 1, 2, 3, and 4 and introduce step 5 (video: Crystal Pite's Emergence, Pacific Northwest Ballet, 3:01; follow the grade-appropriate variation); divide the class into working groups where they will select their own insects and compile their own list of movement characteristics

Make sure students have time to work on their own or in their groups during class time to research their animal before the next class.

Second Lesson: Warm up by reviewing step 3, review the dance requirements in step 5 (follow the grade-appropriate variation), and work in groups to create and present original dances; step 6 is optional; journal

Recommended Music: Tracks 17, 18, and 19

Step 1: What We Know About Spiders

The first half of the exercise focuses on spiders (arachnids) and the latter half on insects. Anatomically, insects and spiders are different; spiders have eight legs and two main body sections. Insects have six legs and two antennae, and their bodies have three main sections.

Instructions

There are many different types of spiders, but most people tend to put spiders into two categories: poisonous and nonpoisonous. You can ask your class if they know the names of specific spiders or go immediately into creating the list of the movement characteristics all spiders share. Then invite your class into the performance area to explore the movements together.

- Articulate legs
- Wonderful balance
- Can climb up smooth vertical surfaces
- Ability to jump forward, backward, and side to side
- Swing on invisible web strands
- Build webs out of silk threads they produce in their body

Step 2: Qualities

Spiders play a significant role in human folklore. Tales and legends from diverse traditions associate spiders with artistry (Ancient Greece), stories and wisdom (Ashanti and other African cultures), bringers of light (Cherokee), weavers of fate (Celtic), and creators of the world (the Hopi of North America and the Kiribati Islanders in the South Pacific). No list about spider tales is complete without mentioning E. B. White's mid-20th-century classic novel *Charlotte's Web*.

Create a list of the qualities attributed to these animals, including planning, patience, curiosity, storytellers, creativity, and intelligence.

Step 3: Spider Dance

This Spider dance is designed to provide your class with inspiration for the original dances they'll be creating later in the exercise. You're welcome to create your own foundation Spider dance, change parts of the dance, or use it in its original form. What's most important is that all your students learn a foundation Spider dance so they are able to explore the choreographic variation in step 4 and that some of the movement characteristics of spiders your class identified in step 1 are translated into dance.

Recommended Music

Track 18

Dance Inspired by Common Spiders

1. Start with the legs wide apart and the feet turned out slightly.
2. Bend the knees and place the hands on the knees with the elbows bent. Lean slightly forward. The position is at level 4 to 6, depending on flexibility. See the Spider photograph.
3. Keeping the knees and elbows bent, lift both heels off the floor and reach the hands in the air on beat 1.
4. Lower the heels to floor and return the hands to the knees on beat 2.
5. Repeat the heel and hand lift and lower back down on beats 3 and 4.
6. Keep the legs wide and the knees and elbows bent. Jump up and bring forearms and hands up on beat 5 and land on beat 6.
7. Jump again, maintaining the same shape, on beat 7. Land and put the hands back on the knees on beat 8.
8. Lift the right hand, keeping the elbow bent and the arms wide. Look up at the hand (begin to climb the web) on beat 1.
9. Lift the left hand a little higher than the right, still keeping the elbow bent and the arms wide. Look up as you climb a little higher on beat 2.
10. Lift the right hand higher than the left and straighten the right arm and leg on beat 3.

Spider.

© Barry Prophet

11. Lift the left hand higher than the right and straighten the left arm and leg on beat 4.

12. Take a big side leap to the right on beat 5 and land in an original spider shape on beat 6.

13. Jump or side leap to the left on beat 7 and land in an original spider shape on beat 8.

Repeat the dance phrase 2 or 3 times. Encourage students to create original spider shapes for the landing positions of the last two side leaps.

Step 4: For All Grades

Recommended Music

Track 19 for poisonous spiders

Instructions

Most spiders are nonthreatening to humans, but some, like the Texas recluse and black widow spiders, are poisonous. Imagine being a hungry, poisonous spider when you repeat the dance sequence from step 3 using track 19. Perform it 2 or 3 times with the new music, then discuss the differences.

Discussion

"Did the idea that you were dangerous and poisonous alter the way you performed the dance? Did the music help? If yes, give examples."

Step 5: Insects

The foundation dance in this exercise was unique to spiders. Now it's time to explore insects.

- Watch Crystal Pite's Emergence (Pacific Northwest Ballet) (3:01) from the list of video links in HK*Propel* to see the Pacific Northwest Ballet Company rehearse and perform *Emergence*, Crystal Pite's acclaimed contemporary ballet inspired by bees. If time is available, watch Crystal Pite's Emergence—Excerpt (1:29) from the list of video links in HK*Propel* to see the final moments of the ballet with the entire company is on stage. You can feel (and hear) the entire hive buzzing.

- Compile a list of insects. The list should include ants, mosquitoes, flies, cockroaches, praying mantis, ladybugs, bees, wasps, and grasshoppers. Your class will probably include butterflies, but since there is a special exercise on butterflies and dragonflies in chapter 8, encourage your class to focus on other insects at this time.

Kindergarten to Grade 3 Variation

Recommended Music

Tracks 17 or 18

Instructions

- Work with your class to create a new dance that communicates some of the unique characteristics of insects.

- Take a moment to generate a list of insect movements. The list will probably include the following:
  - Jumping like a grasshopper
  - Flying like a bee (from flower to flower)
  - Opening wings like a ladybug (shell opens to reveal wings)
  - Eating (plants, other insects, blood, garbage, fabric)
  - Carrying food (individually and through teamwork)
  - Benefiting other living things (bees pollinate, insects are food for larger animals)
- Invite your class to explore the movements on their list.
- Call out prompts to support their work: "Are you jumping through tall grass or onto a rock?" "Do you enjoy flying from flower to flower?" "What happens to your wings when you're not flying?" "How do you carry the food back to the colony?"
- After exploring, invite your students to share their favorite movement ideas and then decide which ones to use in the Insect dance. Use the following template:
  - Compile the list of actions.
  - Establish an order.
  - Explore ideas for spacing.
  - Practice the dance.
  - Divide into two groups.
  - Present the dance to each other.

Journal Entry for Kindergarten Through Grade 3

- After dancing, create a poem.
- "Can you create a poem inspired by spiders or insects?"
- Work independently or, for younger students, create the poem (or poems) collaboratively. Use words from the lists compiled in the earlier steps.
- Save the poems. They'll be used in the culminating exercise for this chapter.

© Barry Prophet

Mosquito.

Grades 4 Through 6 Variation

Recommended Music

Track 17 (moderate tempo) or 18 (fast)

Instructions

- Ask your class to work in groups of four or five. Make sure students are working with different classmates from the previous exercise.
- Each group will select their insects and create their own list of movement characteristics they'll use to inspire their dance.

- Depending on their insect choice, the list they compile may contain some of these movement characteristics:
  - Antennae on head is used to detect surroundings, food, and enemies.
  - They have articulated legs.
  - Most insects have wings; some wings are concealed, but others are not.
  - Insects can fly, jump, walk, and swim.
  - How many eyes do insects have? Can the way they see be translated into movement?
  - Some insects eat vegetables, some eat other insects, and some suck blood.
  - Some insects are solitary, and others live in large colonies.
  - Some hibernate during the winter.
  - Some are uniquely camouflaged.
- This is the second time students are choosing their own animal and compiling their movement lists on their own.
- Allow time for students to compile their lists; explore movements; create their dances; and rehearse, present, and discuss their process.
- After every group has presented their dances, ask them to describe the following:
  - What they learned about their insect
  - The unique features and abilities they wanted to highlight
  - How they communicated their insect's actions and attributes through movement

Step 6: Folktale for All Grades—Optional

Watch the video Anansi the Spider and His Six Sons (6:45) from the list of video links in HK*Propel*. This video adaptation of the Ashanti story was created and performed by grade 4 students from Penn Beach, in the United States. It may inspire your class to do their own multiarts presentation.

Journal Entry for Grades 4 Through 6

- "Insects are the largest and most varied animal group in the world. Some have wings, some live underground, some are beautifully decorated or camouflaged, and some are deadly. Did you know that there are about 900,000 different kinds of insects in the world?"
- "Imagine you've discovered a new insect. Is it a friend or foe? What does it look like? What does it eat? Describe its habits and habitat in words or an illustration."

EXERCISE 3.6   RODENTS

Lesson Plan Suggestions

Kindergarten Through Grade 3

First Lesson: Steps 1, 2, 3, 4, and (follow the grade-appropriate variation)

Second Lesson: Warm up by reviewing step 3, review the notes from step 5 (exploring new actions and creating an original dance), and create a journal entry

Grades 4 Through 6

First Lesson: Steps 1, 2, 3, and 4; introduce step 5.

Second Lesson: Warm up by reviewing step 3, review the dance requirements in step 5 (follow the age-appropriate variation), and have students work in their groups to create and present original dances; make a journal entry

Recommended Music: Tracks 4 and 17

Step 1: What We Know About Rodents

- Make a list of rodents, including squirrels, field mice, beavers, chipmunks, and lemmings. Because we're focusing on wild animals, the list will not include pets such as hamsters, though many characteristics are the same.

- Compile a list of movements associated with these animals, including the following. Then invite your class into the performance area to explore the movements together:
  - Scurrying and skittering
  - Sudden freezes
  - Small jumps
  - Digging (borrowing holes for shelter or to bury food)
  - Using their sharp, tiny claws
  - Gnawing with their strong front teeth, which can gnaw through trees
  - Cleaning and eating with their forepaws
  - Carrying food in their cheeks

Step 2: Qualities

Create a list of qualities attributed to rodents, such as gatherers, industrious, family-based, persistence, and clever.

Step 3: Field Mouse Dance

This Field Mouse dance is designed to provide your class with inspiration for the original dances they'll be creating later in the exercise. You're welcome to create your own foundation Field Mouse dance. You may change parts of the dance I've written or use it in its original form. What's most important is that all your students learn a foundation Field Mouse dance so they are able to explore the choreographic variation in step 4 and that some of the movement characteristics of rodents that your class identified in step 1 are translated into dance.

Recommended Music

Track 4

Instructions

1. Start at mid-level (level 5), keeping the knees bent and close together. Let the torso come slightly forward, bring the elbows close to the torso, and lift the hands in tiny claw position.
2. Quickly rub the hands together and look right on beats 1 and 2.
3. Keep rubbing the hands together and look left on beats 3 and 4.
4. Scurry forward (tiny runs on the balls of the feet) on beats 5 and 6.
5. Make a tiny jump on-the-spot (stay in mouse position) on beat 7.
6. Land (in the mouse starting position) on beat 8.
7. Crouch forward and reach down on beats 1 and 2.
8. Dig (just above the floor) on beats 3 and 4.
9. Come up to mid-level, bring the hands toward the mouth, and chew on beats 5 and 6.
10. Make a tiny jump on-the-spot (stay in mouse position) on beat 7.
11. Land (in the mouse starting position) on beat 8.

Repeat the combination 4 times to make sure everyone is confident performing it.

Step 4: Gathering and Storing

Instructions

Mice and other rodents live in family units, gathering and storing food to eat through the winter. Ask your students to repeat the foundation dance starting in clusters of four to six, facing different directions. When it's time to scurry forward, they will move away from each other and dig for food (possibly buried nuts and seeds). When they repeat the dance a second time, they should travel back to where they started to return to their family with food.

© Janice Pomer

Tiny mice.

Discussion

Compile a list of what students already know about the food chain and what they would like to study further. Lead a grade-appropriate discussion with your class about ecosystems and food chains.

- Some people have only negative thoughts about rodents, but in the wild, rodents are responsible for seed dispersal, pollination, and controlling the growth of fast-growing plants. In addition, rodents are a vital food source for larger animals.

- Rodents are at the low end of the food chain. Just like with buildings, if the bottom is weak, the top will collapse. Without rodents, other animals will perish.

Step 5: The Food Chain

Kindergarten Through Grade 3 Variation

Recommended Music

Track 3 or 17

Instructions

- Collectively create a dance to illustrate two different animal groups: one for rodents and another dance of an animal that relies on rodents for food.

- Gather suggestions for which two animal groups to select. Lizards and snakes eat rodents, and so do owls and eagles. If you decide to work with rodents and snakes, follow this procedure:
  - Brainstorm ideas with the class. Ask them if you should start with rodents dancing, then do the Snake or Lizard dance and then create a dance to show the reptile hunting a rodent.
  - Improvise those ideas together. Ask them if the reptile catches the rodent.
  - Select the most successful ideas.
  - Practice the dance together.
  - Divide into two groups and perform for each other.

- Create a poem about rodents collectively or individually. Save them for exercise 3.7.

Grades 4 Through 6 Variation

Instructions

- Divide your class into four or five groups and ask them to create a dance inspired by the food chain featuring two animals: one that relies on another for food. Try owls and rodents, lizards and insects, lions and antelope, or other animals.

- The dance should include these elements:
  - Use distinct animal movement phrases for each animal group (phrases can be newly created for this dance or excerpted from past exercises).
  - Use timing, levels, and actions to highlight differences between animals.
  - Incorporate a movement phrase to represent the habitat (the phrase may be original or inspired by the trees and plants explored in chapter 2).

- · Have movement phrase(s) showing the relationship between two different animals, for example, hunting and hiding.
- · There's no beat limit to the dance, but it shouldn't be so long that learning and memorizing becomes too time consuming.
- Use what time remains from lesson 1 for students to brainstorm ideas and record them in their journals. In lesson 2, they can create and present their dances.
- After everyone has presented, learn the details behind each group's process.

Discussion

This was the first dance your class has created featuring two or more animals. Ask each group which animals they selected and why. How did they use levels, timings, and qualities to differentiate between the animals?

Journal Entry for All Grades

"Write a descriptive paragraph or create a drawing highlighting the animals' relationship in your food chain–inspired dance."

EXERCISE 3.7 ANIMAL ANTHOLOGY (KINDERGARTEN THROUGH GRADE 3)

Lesson Plan Suggestions

Kindergarten Through Grade 3 Only

First Lesson: Steps 1, 2, and 3 (there will be additional work to collate the material)

Step 1: Select the poems

Use the poems your class has created at the end of each exercise to create a book (hard copy or digital) or video as their culminating exercise for chapter 3. Kindergarten and some grade 1 classes will have created their poems together. If you only created one to three poems for each animal, you may wish to use them all. Grades 2 and 3 students created their own poems. Ask your students to select their three favorite poems. Use five to seven poems for each animal so each student will have two of their poems in the book or video.

Step 2: Video or Book?

Once the poems have been selected, the next step is to decide the format for your animal anthology. For the video, you and your class will want to review the foundation dances or their original choreography created as a class and perform them. (The poems can be recited and recorded separately by individual students and played before or during the dances). For a book format (digital or hard copy), do a photo shoot using poses from their dances to illustrate the poems. In either case, you don't want the entire class dancing or posing at the same time.

To create the video or book, do the following:

1. Invite students to independently select their two or three favorite animal dances.
2. Review your students' choices.
3. Create the groups.
4. Video or photograph the students in small groups.
5. Edit the video or photographs.

Step 3: Add Text and Finalize Format

- For videos, record students reciting their poems.
- For books, lay out the poems (typed on the computer or handwritten and scanned).
- For both videos and books, combine the images and text.
- Share the videos and books with your class and their families.

Journal Entry

This entry is an opportunity for your class to reflect on their animal anthology and all they accomplished in chapter 3. Invite them to write or draw one of their favorite memories from the animal-inspired dances they created.

EXERCISE 3.8   ENDANGERED SPECIES (GRADES 4 THROUGH 6)

Lesson Plan Suggestions

Grades 4 Through 6 Only

First Lesson: Steps 1, 2, 3, and 4

Second Lesson: Steps 5 and 6

Recommended Music: Students' choice

Step 1: Animals on the Endangered Species List

Review the list of animals your class has explored and highlight those that are on the endangered species list. Add other endangered animals to your list. If you don't have a list of endangered species, visit the World Wildlife Fund at worldwildlife.org for a current list.

Step 2: Some of the Reasons Animals Are Endangered

Ask your class to compile a list of factors that have attributed to animals' decline. The list will include the following causes:

- Loss of habitat caused by deforestation, urban sprawl, polar regions warming
- Overhunting or fishing
- Pollution such as pesticides, oil, and chemical spills
- Interferences during migrations, such as brightly lit office towers in North America killing millions of migrating songbirds every year

Step 3: Communicating Loss of Territory Through Movement

Recommended Music

Track 8

Instructions

Use this movement structure to provide your students with an example of how dance can communicate factors that are endangering animals:

1. To communicate loss of habitat, ask 10 to 12 volunteers to perform the foundation Caribou dance from exercise 3.3 with the migrating variation.
2. Give the dancers several minutes to review and practice the dance.
3. Ask six students to stand in parallel position at the sides of the performance area (three are on stage right and three on stage left).
4. Ask the 10 to 12 students who will be dancing to spread throughout the performance area—they should have room to move and travel freely.

5. After they have performed the Caribou dance once, ask the students standing at stage right and stage left to take two large steps into the performance area and spread their arms wide to create a barrier.

6. The dancers, especially those working near the sides, will have to move in toward the center.

7. Ask the dancers to perform the Caribou dance again. Ask viewers to watch for any changes in the way dancers are moving by asking them these questions: "Do they still have enough room to do the full migration circle? Are some dancers affected by the smaller space while others are not?"

8. Ask the students standing at the sides to take two more steps into the performance area, forcing the dancers to move even closer together. Dancers will have much less room.

9. Tell the dancers to modify their actions (don't travel as far or stretch out as wide) and work safely. Ask viewers to focus on the changes the dancers have to make by asking them these questions: "Can they extend their legs fully or move as easily? Do the dancers look like they are in danger of bumping into each other?"

10. Once again, ask the students at the sides to come even farther into the performance area. Ask the viewers these questions: "Is it even possible for the dancers to perform? Are they getting frustrated? Are the dancers able to keep moving or are they ready to give up?"

11. If it's impossible to do the dance safely, ask some of the dancers to leave so a remaining few are safe.

12. How many dancers had to leave to create enough space for the dance to be performed properly?

Discussion

- "The dancers who left so that others could perform safely had somewhere safe to go when they left the performance area, but where do animals go when there's no room left for them in their natural habitat?"

- "The dancers were unable to gallop in large circles, and that means they couldn't complete their migration. What will migrating animals do when it's time to travel to their winter or summer location? If they can't get to the location where they normally mate and raise their offspring, what will happen to the species?"

- "Whether animals are migratory or live in localized habitats less space means less food. When their habitat decreases, less food becomes available. What will they eat?"

- "The dancers found it frustrating, so how do the animals in the wild feel? Are they fighting among themselves? Giving up? Changing their behaviors?"

Step 4: Explore Movement Ideas to Communicate Human Actions Responsible for Habitat Loss

Instructions

- Ask your class to brainstorm movement ideas to communicate urban sprawl, mining, and deforestation.

- In step 3, students stood with their arms outstretched, creating a barrier to prevent migration. It was effective but ask students if they can create more descriptive actions.
- Compile a list of movement ideas that students could perform, including the following:
  - Digging
  - Construction
  - Cutting down trees
- Ask everyone to work on their own to create an 8-beat repeatable movement phrase to communicate one of the activities identified in the list.
- Music: Track 8
  1. Allow 3 to 5 minutes for students to explore, create, and practice their movement phrases.
  2. Bring the class together and ask six to eight volunteers to go into the performance area and share their movement phrases.
  3. Ask performers to freeze in their first position to create tableaus and to freeze in their final position after they have repeated their phrase twice.
  4. Keep the music going until everyone has stopped moving.
  5. After the first group has shared their phrases, ask others to share theirs and continue sharing until everyone has presented.

Discussion

"Were some phrases especially effective?" If yes, discuss why. (*You could immediately tell what the person was doing because her actions were so clearly defined, he slowed his actions down to help us feel how big and heavy the equipment was.*)

Step 5: Toxic Air and Water's Impact on Animals

Brainstorm ways to show water and air pollution, what causes it, when it's visible, and when it's invisible. Create a list of ways the impact of air and water pollution could be communicated through movement.

Step 6: Creating Endangered Species Dance

Invite students to go into groups of six to nine dancers. In their groups, they will do the following:

1. Select an endangered animal the class has not explored.
2. Create a movement phrase inspired by the animal's natural movements.
3. Show changes to the animal's habitat (pollution or encroachment).
4. Show the impact those changes impose or inflict on the animal.
5. Be prepared to do a brief presentation after your dance that introduces the endangered animal, their habitat, and the factors that have caused their population to decline so severely.

- Your students will need time to research, create, practice, and present, so plan accordingly.

Journal Entry

Ask students to suggest ways humanity can reduce its impact on the environment and living things. Research the following stories:

- Flap Canada educates the public about the dangers brightly lit office towers at night have on migrating birds.

- Communities build frog and toad tunnels under highways to provide safe passage when reptiles are laying eggs.

- Go to the Cornell University website and type in "Hargila Stork" to read an inspiring article about a scientist who saved an endangered species by teaching a community about the benefits of local wildlife instead of seeing them as a threat.

SUMMARY

In this chapter, your students have pounced and leaped, flapped and glided, stomped and kicked, slithered, skittered, and scurried. Each animal exploration inspired new movement ideas and the acquisition of new movement skills. Primary and junior grades had their own culminating exercises, and all grades are ready to apply their new dance creation skills to the exercises in chapter 4.

If your school celebrates World Wildlife Day (March 3), your students can create posters and invite guest speakers to visit your school. Younger classes can perform their animal-inspired dances for each other. Junior grades can use their endangered wildlife dances to raise awareness about dwindling habitat and how it affects wildlife.

Go to **HK***Propel* to find audio files, reproducible forms, and a list of video links corresponding to chapter exercises.

© Janice Pomer

CHAPTER 4

Water

Water is essential to all living things. Without water, life as we know it would cease to exist.

When viewed from above, Earth is embraced by a breathtaking blue ocean covering over 70 percent of the planet. Images of Earth from outer space can mislead us into believing that water is a limitless resource, but more than 96 percent of Earth's water is undrinkable ocean water, and more than half of Earth's fresh water is deep underground or frozen in icebergs.

It's easy for people living with access to fresh water to take it for granted, but billions of people around the world live without a secure source of drinking water. The exercises in this chapter explore the beauty and power of water and invite students to consider the many ways they interact with it each day.

EXERCISE 4.1   WATER WORDS

Lesson Plan Suggestions

Kindergarten Through Grade 3

First lesson: Teach steps 1, 2, and 3 (follow the grade-appropriate variation)

Second lesson: Warm up with step 2; review the word and movement phrases created in step 3, and do step 4 to create additional text and movement choreography (follow the grade-appropriate variation); journal

Grades 4 Through 6

First lesson: Teach steps 1, 2, and 3 (follow grade-appropriate variations)

Second lesson: Warm up with step 2, go into groups and begin step 4 to explore variation 1; if time allows, begin variation 2

Third lesson: Warm up quickly with step 2 and work in groups to complete variation 2; present and discuss; journal

Recommended Music: Tracks 5 and 10

Step 1: How Water Moves

Instructions

Compile a list of words that describe the many ways water moves, including swirls, splashes, spreads, ripples, rolls, sways, drips, drops, falls, crashes, curls, bubbles, flows, freezes, melts, evaporates, puddles, and cascades. Grades 3 and up should have no trouble compiling more than 40 words in just a few minutes. Younger grades may need prompts: "What happens to water when it gets hot?" (bubble, boil, steam) "What about when it gets cold?" "How does water move in large rivers, small streams, and oceans?" "How does water move in swamps and ponds?"

Keep your chart of water words available to students while your class is working on this exercise and invite everyone to add new words to the list each day. It's not uncommon for water word lists to fill several flip chart pages over the course of the exercise.

Step 2: Warming Up with Water Words

Some actions on their water word list, such as roll, freeze, and spin, have been used in early choreography. Encourage students to approach known skills from the perspective of water and expand their movement vocabulary.

Recommended Music

Track 10

Instructions

Follow the exploration template established in previous chapters.

1. Ask your class to stand in parallel position throughout the room.

2. Remind everyone that during the movement exploration they're to stay in their personal bubbles and not interfere with other people while they work. That can be tricky when working with water actions. It's easy to get caught up with splashing, crashing, and swirling around the room.

3. Put the music on.

4. Call out one of the water words on the list.

5. Give your class time to explore the first word using full-bodied actions and smaller isolations (arms, torso) before the next word is called out.

6. Continue calling out words every 30 to 40 seconds (depending on how old students are).

7. Call out contrasting water words to help students identify the unique qualities of each action. Try *flows*, *drips*, *rushes*, *drifts*, *cascades*, *evaporates*, and *splashes*.

8. Use prompts such as the following: "Can you make the movement smaller?" "How can you make the action stronger?" "Should you stay low, high, or use multiple levels?" "Does water always flow in one direction?" "Can water squeeze into spaces?"

9. Remind students to use isolation as well as full-body movements: "Can your shoulders bubble?" "Can your spine ripple?" "Jump high into the air for the geyser." "Can foot taps sound like the pitter-patter of rain?"

10. After 6 to 8 minutes, bring the exploration to a close. Finish with a restful word, such as *settles* or *reflects*, then invite students to sit down.

Discussion

- "Did you have a favorite action? If yes, what was it? Explain why."

- "Were there any words that were hard to communicate through movement?" If there are a number of words your class had difficulty translating into movement, brainstorm ideas for using movement.

- Did anyone think of other water action words to add to the list while they were moving? If yes, add them to the list.

Step 3: Creating Water Word and Movement Phrases

Variation for Kindergarten Through Grade 3

Instructions

- Use the words your students compiled in step 1 to create waterword phrases that can be combined with movement.

- Introduce your class to two examples of word and movement phrases that were created by grade 1 students.

- Teach the first spoken word phrase:
  - "Bubble, bubble, bubble, bubble, bubble, bubble, bubble, bubble."
  - "SPLASH, CRASH, SPLASH, SWIRL!"
  - Practice the word phrase several times until your students are confident reciting it in unison.

- Then add the accompanying movement phrase as follows:
  - During the eight bubbles, students pulse their shoulders up and down.

- · SPLASH is a big jump with the arms reaching up.
  - · CRASH is when students land and push both arms downward.
  - · SPLASH is a big jump with the arms reaching up.
  - · Land and SWIRL on-the-spot.
  - · Practice the words and movement together 3 or 4 times until everyone is confident.

Splash.

© Janice Pomer

- Introduce the second phrase.
- Teach the second spoken word phrase:
  - · "FREEZE! Mmelltt. FREEZE! Mmelltt. FREEZE! Mmelltt. Pppppuuuuddddle." (Say the word *puddle* softly and slowly, stretching it out even longer than "Mmelltt.")
  - · Practice the word phrase several times until your students are confident reciting it in unison.
- Then add the accompanying movement phrase:
  - · Start in parallel position.
  - · "FREEZE!" Students should quickly freeze in a high angular shape for 4 beats.
  - · "Mmelltt." Students soften their angles and melt to mid-level for 4 beats.
  - · "FREEZE!" Students should quickly freeze in a mid-level angular shape for 4 beats.
  - · "Mmelltt." Students soften their angles and melt to a low level for 4 beats.
  - · "FREEZE!" Students should quickly freeze in a low-level, angular shape for 4 beats.
  - · "Mmelltt." Students soften their angles and melt almost to the floor for 4 beats.
  - · "Pppppuuuuddddle." Students lie on the floor and slowly extend their arms and legs outward for 8 beats.
  - · Practice the text and movement together 3 or 4 times until everyone is confident.
- Discuss the first and second word and movement phrases, highlighting the similarities and differences.
  - · The first phrase repeats the word *bubble* 8 times and uses shoulder isolations for 8 beats.

- The second phrase repeats *freeze* and *melt* 3 times. The actions are repeated, but the shapes and levels are different.
  - The first phrase has a very strong ending with jumps and swirls.
  - The second phrase has a very quiet ending with the puddle slowly spreading outward.
- Discuss what elements in nature could have inspired the phrases.
  - The first phrase could be a hot geyser bubbling and erupting.
  - The second phrase could be snow and ice slowly melting.
- Invite your class to create their own word and movement phrases. Kindergarten and grade 1 students can work collaboratively as a class, while grades 2 and 3 students can work in small groups. Use the following procedure:
  1. Review the words on your water word list.
  2. Work collaboratively or in small groups and select four words to use in your phrase and establish the word order.
  3. Play with the words and determine if any of the words should be repeated or emphasized in a particular way.
  4. You may need to try several variations before the words and rhythm come together.
  5. Once the word phrase has been set, create the movement phrase.
  6. Combine the actions with the words and practice until everyone is confident performing the phrase.
  7. Present to the others one by one for grades 2 and 3. For kindergarten and grade 1, divide the class into two groups and perform for each other.

Journal Entry Before Finishing Lesson 1 for Grades 2 and 3

Ask students to map out or draw the words and movement phrase they created.

Grades 4 Through 6 Variation 1

Instructions

- Introduce this short water word and movement phrase created by grade 4 students: "Rip-ple…rip-ple…rock, rock, ROCK, RR-OO-LL-LL, *rip-ple…rip-ple*…rock, rock, ROCK, RR-OO-LL-LL."
- Invite two student volunteers to demonstrate the movement phrase.
  1. Starting in a wide A stance, ripple: Arms and spine softly ripple, then pause in stillness/silence (invite students to bend and straighten their knees while their arms ripple to emphasize the undulating quality of water and keep legs still during the stillness/silence).
  2. Ripple: Arms and spine softly ripple, then pause in stillness/silence.
  3. Rock: With a gentle tilt to the right, the left foot lifts slightly and arms stay at the sides.
  4. Rock: With a stronger tilt to the left, the right leg lifts slightly and arms reach up diagonally to the left.
  5. ROCK: With a large tilt to the right, reach up diagonally to the right and the left leg lifts higher.
  6. RR-OO-LL-LL: One student performs 2 or more floor rolls to the left while the other student stays upright, performing two more traveling turns to the left.

The students who created this word and movement phrase integrated sounds and silences with stillness and action. Their use of layering a floor roll with a standing turn created the image of two strong waves rolling over each other.

- Invite your students to work in pairs for this exercise.
  - Create a water word phrase containing three to five words from the class list.
  - Create a movement phrase inspired by their word phrase.
  - Rehearse the spoken word and movement phrase together to combine the sonic and kinetic dynamics.

1. Give your students time to create and rehearse their word and movement phrases. By the end of the rehearsal period, the room should be filled with sound.
2. If your class is reluctant to vocalize while rehearsing, ask everyone to stop moving and to speak their phrases at the same time on the count of 3.
3. Repeat the group vocalization several times and encourage everyone to make the vocal component of the phrase as expressive as the movement.
4. Use the final few minutes of rehearsal time to practice the movement and text at full volume.
5. Ask each duet to present their phrases and briefly discuss the process.

Discussion

Ask each duet to identify which of the other duet phrases significantly contrast theirs and give an example of how they contrast.

Grades 4 Through 6 Variation 2: Combine Water Phrases

Instructions

1. Team up contrasting duets to create quartets.
2. If there is an uneven number, ask one of the strong duets to separate and team up with different duets to create two trios.
3. Ask the newly formed quartets (or trios) to learn each other's word and movement phrases.
4. After the quartets have learned each other's text and movement phrase, they can connect the phrases and practice performing them in unison, one phrase after another without a pause.
5. A step, roll, turn, or other simple action may be needed to connect the phrases, but the adjustment or linking action should be minimal.
6. After 5 minutes, check to see if everyone has finished.

Water journal example.

© Janice Pomer

7. Make sure your class is using full volume for the last minute of rehearsal.

8. Invite the groups to present their expanded phrases with the spoken word.

Discussion

Did the group face challenges when they combined the contrasting word and movement phrases? If yes, identify them, and if the problems still exist, brainstorm ways to solve them.

Journal Entry Before Finishing Lesson 1

Ask students to independently record their word and movement phrases they performed in their journals.

Step 4: Water Symphony

Use the journals and review the word and movement phrases created in step 3. Kindergarten and grade 1 students can work collectively, and older grades should work in their small groups.

Kindergarten Through Grade 1 Variation

Create additional phrases to communicate different aspects of water.

1. "Look at the water word list."

2. "Which words would best describe an ocean?" (Swell, currents, tides.)

3. "Which words would best describe a waterfall?" (Crash, fall, churn.)

4. Have students identify other water events (tsunami, hurricane, spring rainfall).

5. Have students identify water environments (everglades, pond, stream, tidal pool).

6. Look at your list of water events and environments. With your students, select three or four contrasting environments and create word and action phrases for each one using the process established in step 3.

7. Some words may belong in several groups. (Rivers and oceans have currents and rough water.) Try not to use the same word to communicate a different aspect of water, but if you must use the same word, make sure the associated action is different.

8. Practice each word and movement phrase until your class is confident performing them.

9. Create an order to the phrases (1. rainfall, 2. river, 3. tsunami, 4. pond) and link all the text and movement phrases together to create a long Water dance and vocal symphony.

10. If your class was able to perform their entire water symphony and there is time remaining, consider adding their word and movement phrases from the first lesson to the dance.

Grades 2 Through 3 Variation

1. Follow the first five steps listed in the Variation for Kindergarten Through Grade 1 students.

2. Invite your class to return to their small groups.

3. Assign each group a specific water event or environment (waterfall, ocean, stream).

4. Ask your students to create their own word and action phrase inspired by their assigned water event or environment using three or four water words.

5. It's fine if more than one group is doing the same event.

6. Review the Protocol for Collaborative Dance Creation (figure 1.2, page 11).

7. Emphasize the importance of working constructively.

8. Remind your students that it's okay if they don't like all the ideas their group creates. Group members are expected to support the ideas of others, not just their own.

9. Visit the groups while they're working to see how things are progressing.

10. When all the groups are ready, invite each group to present their word and action phrases.

11. After all the groups have presented, ask the groups to return to their working areas and be ready to present again one after each other.

12. Create an order for the groups (1. waterfall, 2. ocean, 3. stream, and so on) and see if they can perform their pieces one after another without pausing.

13. If your class was able to perform their water symphony and there is time remaining, consider ways to add their original word and movement phrases from the first lesson to the dance.

Discussion for Kindergarten Through Grade 3

- "Were the word and movement phrases able to communicate specific water events and environments?"

- "Were some of the water events and environments harder to communicate than others? If yes, explain what aspects of water were challenging and why?"

- "How did it feel when the phrases were spoken and performed together?"

Journal Entry for Kindergarten Through Grade 3

"Write, map out, or draw your group's new water phrase."

Grades 4 Through 6 Variation 1

Recommended Music

Track 5

Instructions

- If you're doing this variation at the beginning of your second lesson (as listed in the Lesson Plan Suggestions), give the quartets time to review and practice their word and movement phrases using their journal notes.

- After your students have reviewed their word and movement phrases, invite the class to participate in a structured improvisation.

- The improvisation will use selected sections from each group's text and movement phrases. Each quartet will need to select the following:

  · One or two words from their text to speak softly—their quiet words

  · One or two words to speak loudly—their strong words

  · A soft, calm, or flowing movement phrase that can be repeated multiple times without stopping—this is a gentle, repetitive movement

· A strong action or action combination with a finishing shape that can be held, then slowly melts

- Let the groups know that the words and phrases they select and practice should be performed by all members of their group in unison.

    1. Allow students 3 or 4 minutes to make their selections and practice.

    2. Ask students to sit with their quartets throughout the performance area.

    3. Assign a number to each quartet.

    4. At the start of the water symphony, quartets will work in the order assigned to them.

    5. Let everyone know that after the first few minutes of the symphony, the order will not always be followed.

    6. You'll be conducting, pointing to each group when it's their time to vocalize or move.

    7. Sometimes a group will work on their own. At other times, groups may be asked to work at the same time.

    8. Play track 5 at a low level.

    9. Start with the quiet words.

    10. Signal group 1. Have them repeat their quiet word or words 2 or 3 times. Allow for a moment without voices—only the music is heard.

    11. Signal group 2 to speak their quiet words. Rest for a moment, then signal group 3, then group 4, and so on.

    12. After all groups have spoken their quiet words, signal the first group to do their strong word.

    13. Alternate group 1's strong word with group 2's quiet words, and keep alternating the groups until every group has vocalized a second time.

    14. Signal group 1 to do their gentle repetitive movement phrase while groups 2, then 3, and then 4 speak their quiet words.

    15. Signal group 2 to do the repetitive movement phrase while groups 3, then 4, and then 5 speak their quiet words.

    16. Continue inviting each group to do their repetitive movement phrase accompanied by three groups' quiet words until every group has moved.

    17. Signal all groups to perform their strong action and call out their strong word at the same time. Let the sound of their words fade as their held shapes melt or ripple away.

    18. Repeat, having all groups perform their strong action and call out their strong word at the same time. Let the sound of their words fade as their held shapes melt or ripple away.

    19. One by one, signal for each quartet to perform their strong action without words and slowly melt or ripple to the ground.

    20. When the last group melts down, slowly fade the music while everyone remains in stillness.

Discussion

- Identify which sections were successful (and why) and the sections that were less successful (and why).

- When using this type of choreographic structure, there's no way of knowing what the end result will be. How did you feel while you were conductor?
- Ask your students if they would lead the choreography differently if they were the conductors. If yes, how?

Grades 4 Through 6 Variation 2

Instructions

Ask each group to assign their members a number from 1 to 4.

1. Ask all the ones to form a new group, all the twos to form a new group, and the threes and fours to form their own groups.
2. Each newly formed group has representatives from the original smaller groups.
3. The four large groups have all the words and actions used in the last exercise at their disposal to create a large water symphony.
4. No additional choreography or words may be added.
5. The first step for this assignment is for group members to share their words and movements.
6. Once all the words and movements have been shared, group members will decide how they wish to use it.
7. Not all words and movements need to be used.
8. Group members may work in unison and have solos, duets, and trios.
9. Words and movements may overlap.
10. Remind the class that water isn't one-dimensional. Like water, their choreography can be layered.

> **Important note regarding lesson planning:** This is the most complex choreographic assignment to date. An additional lesson may be required for students to complete their choreography. Make sure there is time for everyone to write down their dances in their journals before the second class comes to a close.

Optional third class:

1. Allow time for groups to review their notes and practice their pieces with full vocalizations before bringing everyone together for the presentations.
2. After all the groups have presented, discuss the presentations.

Discussion

- Every group had the same words and movement vocabulary to work with. Did their choreography look and sound the same? Highlight some of the differences.
- Highlight one or two of the most successful moments in each groups' choreography and identify why it was so successful.

Journal Entry Grades 4 Through 6

"Create a poem or drawing inspired by three water words. The words you chose don't have to be words you used in your dance."

EXERCISE 4.2   WAVES

This exercise is all about waves. Some explorations are performed on-the-spot while others require open space as your students create wave-inspired dances using a variety of patterns and pathways. If there's no large open space available indoors, this is a great exercise to take outdoors.

In the foundation exercise 1.1, the idea of using the term *still water* instead of parallel position was introduced. If you haven't referred to parallel position as *still water*, do so in this exercise and throughout this chapter. You can remind your class that the grade 3 student who suggested the term said that still water is calm but alive with possibilities.

Lesson Plan Suggestions

Kindergarten Through Grade 3

First lesson: Teach steps 1, 2, and 3 with all grade-level variations (videos: Water Study, the first 4:00, and Water, 3:01)

Second lesson: Warm up with one or two of your students' favorite wave variations from lesson 1; if your class hasn't watched the recommended videos, do so now; then introduce steps 4 and5; journal entry

Grades 4 Through 6

First lesson: Teach steps 1, 2, and 3 with all grade-level variations (videos: Water Study, the first 4:00, and Water, 3:01)

Second lesson: Warm up with one or two of your students' favorite wave variations from lesson 1; if your class hasn't watched the recommended videos, do so now, then do step 4 and begin step 5

Third lesson: Warm up with one or two wave variations from lesson 1, then step 6 to finalize and present the dances and reflect on the process; journal

Recommended Music: Track 5 or 10

Step 1: What We Know About Waves

The word list your class compiled in exercise 4.1 may contain a dozen words that describe waves: ripple, curl, rough, choppy, and sway, to name a few. Review the word list and highlight the words that relate to waves. After this exercise, your students will probably have new words to add.

Take a moment to discuss different types of wave activity: huge tsunami tidal waves, strong waves that wash organic and inorganic matter onto the shore, gentle waves that bob up and down, big waves to surf on, churning waves and swirling currents in white-water rapid runs, and calming waves that lull you to sleep. All these waves move up-down, up-down, up-down.

Step 2: The Stadium Wave

The first step of this exercise is similar to step 4 of exercise 1.1, when your students stood in a circle and performed a turn and freeze, one after another. In that exercise, everyone was invited to present their own turns and create original frozen shapes. In this exercise, your class will perform an up-down wave action, just as they would if they were in the stadium cheering on their favorite team. The exercise is performed without music, but it's important to establish a beat for your students to count silently.

Instructions

1. Ask your class to form a circle and stand in parallel or still water position.
2. Review the up-down arm action of the stadium wave with your students: Arms reach up for 2 beats and then lower for 2 beats.
3. Pick a leader, identify the direction the wave will travel in, and see if your class can do the up-down arm action around the circle 3 times, maintaining a steady beat without stops or hesitations.
4. Remind your class that whenever they're not performing the action, they should be in parallel or still water position.
5. After 3 repetitions, stop the wave action by signaling the leader to stop when the action comes to the end of the circle.

Repeat the process 2 or 3 more times with new leaders and using the following 2-beat actions to make the wave more dynamic.

- Try a big jump with the arms reaching up and the body landing in a low crouch.
- Or kick forward with the arms reaching inward, then bring the feet together.

Next Wave Challenge for All Grades

Instructions

Try sending two waves around the circle. Start with this simple combination:

1. Jump with the arms reaching up; land and lower the arms.
2. Pick a new leader.
3. Explain that the exercise will start the same way they've been practicing, but when the action has traveled halfway around the circle, the leader will send the same action around the circle so two waves are traveling at the same time.
4. Let both jump wave actions travel around the circle 2 times before signaling the leader to stay still when the action comes to them.
5. When the leader stops passing the wave action on, both waves will eventually die out.

Next Wave Challenge for Grades 1 and Up

Instructions

- If your class was able to maintain the equal distance between the two waves as the actions traveled around the circle, try the variation one more time using different actions for the different waves.
  - First wave: jump and reach up
  - Second wave: kick forward with the arms reaching inward
- Both wave actions should use the same number of beats so the distance between them as they travel around the circle stays equal. (If one action takes longer to perform, the other action will catch up to it.)
- See if your class can maintain the two different actions with equal distancing.

- If your class found the variation challenging, identify why (having two different actions to follow) and devise strategies to help your students succeed. (If having two different actions is confusing, practice sending the same action around the circle a number of times before trying different actions.)

Next Wave Challenge for All Classes That Succeeded at Variation 1

Instructions

Add more actions to travel around the circle.

1. Create a third wave action.
2. The new action should use the same number of beats as the others.
3. Practice the three different wave actions collectively.
4. Pick a new leader and identify the direction the action will travel.
5. Signal the leader to begin.
6. When the first action has traveled a third of the way around the circle, signal the leader to introduce the second action.
7. When the second action has traveled a third of the way around the circle, signal the leader to introduce the third action.
8. The three actions should remain evenly spaced as they travel around the circle.
9. Let the actions travel around the circle 2 or 3 times, then signal the leader to stop.

Congratulate your class if they succeeded at keeping three actions going around the circle. This exercise is a great way to warm up. Try using it in the gym and outdoors and see how many actions you can add to the wave.

Step 3: Waves on the Shore

This step uses a similar structure to the one introduced in step 2 of exercise 1.2.

Recommended Music

Track 5

Instructions

1. Ask your class to form two parallel lines on either side of the performance area.
2. The line on the right side is line A, and the line on the left side is line B.
3. Ask both lines to take 4 steps forward, toward the center of the room, and 4 steps backward.
4. There should be space in the center of the room between the lines to ensure that the two lines stay apart.

Now try the following wave patterns:

All Grades Variation 1

1. Ask everyone in line A to walk forward for 4 beats and walk backward for 4 beats.
2. Ask everyone in line B to walk forward for 4 beats and walk backward for 4 beats.

3. Ask both lines A and B to walk forward for 4 beats and backward for 4 beats twice without stopping.

4. When walking, the lines should remain straight as they travel forward and back. No one should lag behind or race out in front.

5. Remind your class to use their peripheral vision so they can stay connected with the people in their line.

All Grades Variation 2

- Once the A, B, A, B pattern has been established, try adding movement dynamics. Ask everyone to lift their heels and reach their arms up when they come to the center and ripple their arms when they walk backward.

- Make it more dynamic: Try running for 2 beats into the center. Jump up high on 3, land softly on 4, and then walk backward for 4 beats with arms rippling low.

All Grades Variation 3

Perform the run-jump-walk back pattern introduced in variation 2 two at a time.

1. Ask only the two students at the top of lines A and B to run forward-jump-walk backward with rippling arms pattern at the same time.

2. When they have returned, the next two students will perform the same movement phrase, then the next two students, and the next, until the pattern has traveled down the lines. If there is an uneven number of students, ask the final three students to move together at the end.

Grades 2 Through 6 Variation 4

Use the pattern from variation 3 but ask the second pair to start running inward while the first pair are traveling backward.

Grades 2 Through 6 Variation 5

1. Ask the students at the top and bottom ends of lines A and B to do the run-jump-walk back pattern at the same time.

2. When the two outside pairs have returned to the lines, the next two pairs will perform the phrase, then the next and the next.

3. As the wave action moves inward, the wave appears to grow stronger.

4. Ask the final four (the center) to perform the pattern twice before reversing the order of the wave action outward down the lines.

5. The pattern will come to an end with the outermost four students.

Watch two contrasting choreographic pieces inspired by water.

- Watch the first 4 minutes of Water Study (8:48 total) from the list of video links in HK*Propel*. Created in 1928 by modern dance pioneer Doris Humphrey (1895–1958), Water Study conveys the gentle ebb and flow of waves on the shore.

- Watch the Water video (3:01) from the list of video links in HK*Propel*. It is a contemporary work that used a different approach to wave and water motions.

Discussion

- Did you see some of the wave patterns your class explored in their dances? If yes, identify the movement patterns and describe how the choreographers made the patterns more dynamic (use of different actions, levels, tempos).

- "Water manifests in many ways, and the two dances were quite different. Did one more effectively create the idea of water, or were both interpretations valid?"

Step 4: Exploring Low- and Mid-Level Waves

Both dance videos combined low-, mid-, and high-level actions to create exciting waves.

- "Can you remember any of the multileveled shapes and actions the choreographers had the dancers perform?"

- Compile a list of low- and mid-level movements your class can explore, including rolling, rising up and down on ones' knees, stretching out low on the ground, rippling the fingers on the ground, going into plank position, and rippling the torso.

- "The choreographers created a number of other exciting wave-inspired pathways. Do you have new ideas for wave actions?"

Students creating waves.

© Janice Pomer

Step 5: Create Your Own Wave Dances

Using ideas generated by the videos and post-video discussion, create original dances inspired by waves.

Kindergarten Through Grade 3 Variation

Explore the low- and mid-level wave actions.

Recommended Music

Track 5

Instructions

1. Ask your students to spread throughout the room at least two arm's-lengths apart.

2. Let them know that you'll be calling out different movement ideas from the list of low- and mid-level wave-inspired actions they saw in the videos.

3. Allow enough time between movement ideas for everyone to try numerous approaches to the action. Use prompts to support their work: "Try rolling on the floor like waves." "Can you roll your shoulders, your head, or your hips?" "Try rippling your fingers on the ground and along your arms." "What arm positions look like waves?"

4. After exploring, invite them to select their favorite low wave action and practice it on their own.

5. After a minute of practicing, invite half the class to share while the other half watches. Repeat so everyone shares and observes.

6. Tell your students to remember the low-level wave action they performed.

7. Now invite your students to select their favorite mid-level wave action (reaching forward on one knee, walking in deep lunges with wavey arms) and practice on their own.

8. After a minute of practicing, invite half the class to share while the other half watches. Repeat so everyone shares and observes.

9. Once again, ask everyone to remember their mid-level wave action.

10. Use the low- and mid-level wave actions to review the line formation and pattern from lesson one.

11. Instead of walking forward and back, students can use their new wave actions.

12. Their new actions need not travel the same distance: 4 beats of log rolls will travel farther than 4 beats of fingers rippling on the ground, but together they create a beautiful picture of multilayered moving waves.

13. After working low-level forward and back actions, try the mid-level actions, and try combining them.

14. Now, instead of working in two lines facing inward, create new formations: moving outward and inward in circles, V shapes, or zigzag lines.

15. Afterward, ask your class to select their three favorite formations.

16. Use one formation for low-level wave movements, another formation for mid-level wave movements, and the final formation for high-level movements.

17. After practicing the three formations separately, create a water traveling action to move from the low-, mid-, and high-level formations. Try reversing the sequence so it shows the waves decreasing in power.

Discussion

- "Are there any other wave actions or formations you think should be added to your Wave dance?" If yes, share the ideas with the class, and if time allows, incorporate it into the dance.

- If there are numerous ideas, extend the exercise into a third lesson and add them to the dance.

Grades 4 Through 6 Variation

Recommended Music

Track 5 or 10

Instructions

Work in groups of five to seven students and create dances inspired by the way waves increase and decrease in strength. All dances should contain the following elements:

- A unison section where everyone is doing the same thing at the same time

- A section where half the dancers are working at one level and half at another level

- A section where half the dancers are working at one speed and half at another speed

- A variety of traveling patterns and formations introduced in the first class and new ones inspired by the dance videos

Find ways to communicate waves increasing and decreasing in power, speed, and size. There is no time limit, but don't make the dance so long that memorizing the dance becomes an issue.

Your class will likely need an additional lesson to complete this dance creation assignment. Let your class know the following:

1. This lesson is for brainstorming ideas, exploring, creating, and recording the dances in their journals.

2. These dances take longer than usual because there are so many ideas to sift through, and they'll need to be very focused choreographing the sections to weave the different timings and levels together.

3. The groups will want to include traveling patterns and spatial relationships, which may be an issue if you're working in a classroom.

4. If outdoors or the gymnasium isn't an option, there may be space in the hallway or nearby alcove where one or two of the groups can work quietly. Otherwise, ask students to practice some movements on-the-spot, knowing that when performing, they'll be able to travel freely.

5. Ask everyone to use the last 5 minutes of the second class to record their dances.

Step 6: Finalize the Wave Dances

Grades 4 Through 6

Instructions

- Solidify the dances created in step 5.
- Allow time for your students to do the following:
  - Review their choreographic notes
  - Practice their dances
  - Present them to each other
- After every group has presented, reflect on the process.

Discussion

- Were there any patterns or formations that every group used? If yes, ask each group to explain why they chose to use it. Did every group have the same reason?
- Did every group create a unique pattern?
- Ask everyone to identify a section they saw another group perform that they felt effectively communicated waves.
- "Did watching the two dance videos influence your choreographic decisions? If yes, explain."

Journal Entry for All Grades

"Imagine you're a wave traveling across the Atlantic Ocean from the shores of Africa or Europe to the shores of North or South America. How do you feel? Who or what would you meet? What would happen when you arrived? Write or draw your response."

EXERCISE 4.3   FROST AND SNOW

One of my favorite memories from childhood is waking up on winter mornings to discover exquisite feathery leaves of frost had grown across my window. The frost pattern created a magical glow in morning light, giving the illusion of warmth to the chilly winter landscape.

Lesson Plan Suggestions

Kindergarten Through Grade 3

First lesson: Teach steps 1, 2, 3 (videos: Time-Lapse Frost, 1:58; Géométrie Variable, Tutting, 1:36; and Sadek Waff, 2:47 [5:40 total]), and 4 (follow the grade-appropriate variations)

Second lesson: Warm up by reviewing step 4 and do steps 5 (video: National Ballet of Canada, Snow Scene from the Nutcracker, 2:53) and 6 (follow the grade-appropriate variation)

Grades 4 Through 6

First lesson: Teach steps 1, 2, 3, (videos: Time-Lapse Frost, 1:58; Géométrie Variable, Tutting, 1:36; and Sadek Waff, 2:47 [5:40 total]), and 4 (follow grade-appropriate variations)

Second lesson: Warm up by reviewing step 4 and finish the second variation if there wasn't enough time in the first lesson; go on to steps 5 (video: National Ballet of Canada, Snow Scene from the Nutcracker, 2:53) and 6 (follow grade-appropriate variation)

Recommended Music: Track 7

Step 1: What Happens When We Get Cold

Instructions

- Water and humans have similar reactions to cold weather.
- Lead this visualization with students standing or sitting.
- Ask your students to close their eyes.
- Remind your class to keep their bodies calm and still while they internally experience the images you present.
- After reading each line aloud, allow your class several moments to process the image and feel their internal responses before reading the next line.
- The visualization is as follows:
    1. "Imagine it's a warm sunny day."
    2. "You've been outside playing or walking or maybe riding your bike."
    3. "How does your body feel?"
    4. "How do your muscles feel?"
    5. "Are they relaxed and loose?"

6. "Do you feel stretched out and limber?"
7. "Imagine you're lying down on the grass or sand."
8. "What position are you lying in?"
9. "Are you able to relax and breathe deeply?"
10. "Now imagine it's a cold, wintery day."
11. "You've been waiting and waiting for the bus."
12. "How does your body feel?"
13. "Are your muscles relaxed and loose, or are they tight and contracted?"
14. "Are your arms and legs straight, or are your elbows and knees bent?"
15. "Are you standing tall, or are you hunched over?"
16. "Are your toes relaxed, or have they tightened up?"
17. "You see the bus—it stops, and you get inside."
18. "You find a seat, and it's close to a heating vent."
19. "The warm air relaxes your legs and arms."
20. "The warm air relaxes your shoulders."
21. "You can move your fingers and toes."
22. "Your spine lengthens."
23. "You can breathe deeply again."
24. "Soon, the bus comes to your stop."
25. "You step out and are hit by a blast of cold air."
26. "How does your body react?"

- Allow a moment of silence before asking your class to open their eyes.

Discussion

- Do a survey of how your class felt at the start of the visualization (warm, relaxed, loose).
- Do a survey of how your class felt when they were waiting for the bus (tight and contracted).
- What happened when they entered the bus and started to warm up?
- What happened when they left the bus and returned to the cold?

Our bodies contract in the cold and expand in the heat. When we're cold, we tend to be more angular: our knees, elbows, and torso bend inward, trying to contain heat. In the summer, our bodies expand, the muscles loosen, and we sleep in open positions to disperse heat. In the visualization, you may have felt your body become tighter, more angular and contracted when you were cold. Just like people, water responds to temperature changes; water contracts when it cools, but unlike people, when water reaches 39 degrees Fahrenheit (4 C), it starts to slowly expand and continues to expand when it freezes. Use the visualization experience to inform your students' movements in this warm-up inspired by frost.

Step 2: Frost-Inspired Warm-Up

Recommended Music

Track 7

Instructions

1. Ask your students to spread throughout the room and stand in parallel or still water position.

2. Invite your class to use this exploratory warm-up to discover new angular shapes and actions inspired by the image of frost creeping up a windowpane, forming over a pond, or covering grass and trees.

3. Students may work on-the-spot or travel as long as their traveling steps contain angular elements (a zigzag pathway; the feet turn in and out) and don't interfere with others in the room.

4. The exercise is a freeze game. When you call out, "Freeze," everyone freezes.

5. When you call out, "Frost," that's the signal to move.

6. As always, the purpose of exploratory exercises is discovery and to take chances and try new shapes and ways to travel.

7. Encourage your class with prompts: "Can you create shapes containing three or more angles?" "How about five or more angles?" "Have you tried exploring angular pathways at high and low levels?"

8. After several minutes of exploratory movement, sit down and discuss the lesson.

Students explore movements using bent knees and elbows.

© Janice Pomer

Discussion

- "Were some parts of your body easier to create angles with? If yes, identify them."

- "Did you spend most of your time working on-the-spot? If yes, why?"

- "Did you discover angular ways to travel?" If yes, ask students to share some of their angular traveling patterns.

Step 3: Watch Videos

Share these three short videos with your class from the list of video links in HK*Propel*.

1. Watch a fascinating time-lapse video of frost forming (1:58). After seeing frost form, your class will have a clear sense of how important geometric shapes will be for their Frost and Snow dances.

2. Tutting is a dance style that emphasizes geometric arm movements. Watch Géométrie Variable perform mesmerizing tutting choreography in this clip (1:36).

3. The third performance to watch was choreographed by Sadeck Waff, Géométrie Variable's founder. He leads 126 dancers with mixed abilities in this inspiring video (2:47).

Step 4: Create Choreography Inspired by Frost and Snow Using Tutting Techniques

Kindergarten Through Grade 3 Variation 1

Lead your class in a group mirroring exercise.

1. Stand at the front of the room and move very slowly as you create angular arm shapes for your students to follow.

2. You can slowly change levels by bending your knees or stepping out to the side, but don't go too low. Keep working at levels 5 and up.

3. After a minute of quiet mirroring work, stop.

4. Invite one of your students to lead.

5. After 30 seconds, ask the leader to stop and find another leader.

6. Encourage student leaders to focus on arm shapes and to move slowly and smoothly.

7. Allow 2 or 3 more students to lead before inviting your class work in partners.

8. Once everyone is partnered up, they should stand face-to-face arm's-width apart.

9. Remind your class that most of the movements they saw in the dance video were performed smoothly, slowly, and steadily.

10. The dancers in the video created strong angles and diagonal lines using their arms, elbows, wrists, and fingers.

11. Let students decide who will lead first and who will lead second.

12. Once that's decided, they should stand face to face without talking.

13. Put on the music and ask those who are leading first to begin.

14. After 20 to 30 seconds, ask everyone to freeze. Then ask those who are leading second to begin.

15. Keep changing the lead every 20 to 30 seconds.

16. Support students' work with gentle prompts to remind leaders to work slowly and smoothly and focus on creating angular shapes.

17. Remind your class that's it's not a matter of how many shapes they can think of. What's important right now is controlling their speed and having a smooth movement quality.

Kindergarten Through Grade 3 Variation 2

Your class will now be working in groups of four.

1. Ask two pairs to stand facing each other arm's-width apart in a diamond shape.
2. Each person in the group will have an opportunity to lead.
3. Decide the order of leadership.
4. Put on the music and ask those who are first to begin.
5. After 20 seconds, call out, "Freeze." Then ask those who are second to begin.
6. Continue with the structure until everyone has had a turn leading.

Grades 4 Through 6 Variation 1

- Invite your class to create short duets inspired by the videos. The required elements for the duets are the following:

  - They should stay on-the-spot.
  - They may face each other for the first 4 beats but must be facing the front for the final 8 beats.
  - All movements should be symmetrical and follow the same beats.
  - Stand upright (no floor work, use levels 5 and up).
  - Duets should be 12 beats long and must be repeatable so that the first shape or action can be performed immediately after the last shape or action without or pause or additional beats.

- Allow time for your students to create their 12-beat phrases.

- Once they have created the phrases, ask them to practice repeating it 3 times without stopping.

Symmetry.

© Barry Prophet

- When everyone is comfortable repeating their phrases, ask your class to present them, two or three pairs at a time.

Grades 4 Through 6 Variation 2

Instructions

- Ask three duets to volunteer and demonstrate this variation.
- They will perform their 12-beat duets 3 times without stopping. The dancers will start and finish at the same time.
- Ask the volunteers to stand in a hexagonal formation with partners standing across from each other as shown in figure 4.1.
  - Staying true to their choreography, they may face inward for the first 4

beats, but after that they should face outward (some will be able to look straight ahead; others may find themselves facing stage left or stage right).

- · After they've performed the pattern once, invite them to very slowly and smoothly travel a yard (meter) outward (see figure 4.2) while they're performing the pattern a second and third time.

- After the volunteer group has presented, ask them to share their insights about the challenges of performing their duets in formation.

- Get viewer feedback by asking the following questions:
  - · "Were the performers able to maintain the hexagonal shape as they moved outward?"
  - · "Were individual partners able to maintain their synchronicity?"
  - · "Did the three original duets combine well? Identify any eye-catching moments."

- Invite your class to go into groups of six and try the variation.

- If there are too many or not enough duets for all the duets to work in sixes, there can be one or two smaller groups of four.

- Allow everyone time to practice, then present one group at a time.

A

B   **C**

C   **B**

A

Figure 4.1   Hexagonal formation.

Discussion

- "In the video, the dancers were confident in their actions and never lost their focus. When you were presenting, were you able to stay focused, or was it difficult working with the others duets and traveling outward?"

- "Did any interesting relationships between the duets occur?" If yes, identify the group and ask them to present that section again.

Combining the duets may not accurately represent a snowflake's symmetrical formation, but it acknowledges the multitude of snowflake variations and creates a contrast for the second section of the dance in step 5.

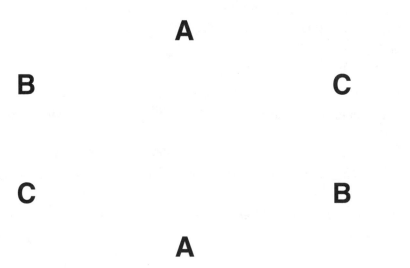

Figure 4.2   Expanded hexagonal formation.

© Barry Prophet

Exploring snowflake-inspired shapes in small groups.

Step 5: Snowfall

 Watch The Snow Scene video (2:53) from the list of video links in HK*Propel* to see the beauty of ice and snow come to life. The video is a scene from *The Nutcracker*, one of the most popular ballets in the world.

For All Grades

There are many types of snow, so those who live in snowy regions understandably have a wider vocabulary of snow words than those who interact with snow less frequently. Compile a list of words to describe what snow looks like when it falls and how it feels when you play in it. The list may include to float, swirl, drift, feathery, delicate, soft, icy, stings, stormy, flurries, wild, and billowy.

Instructions

1. Explore the list words collectively.
2. Start with everyone standing throughout the room in parallel position.
3. Your students may want to move throughout the room as they blow, drift, float, and swirl.
4. Remind them to work in their own bubbles and to not interfere with others.
5. Play track 7. Call out the first word and let everyone begin to explore.
6. Alternate strong, fast words with slow, gentle words.
7. After several minutes, finish with a quiet word. Then bring the exploration to a close.

Step 6: Create a Falling Snow Dance

Kindergarten Through Grade 3 Variation

Instructions

- Ask students to share their favorite words and movement patterns from the exploration.
- After everyone has shared, create your class Falling Snow dance.
    1. Pick five or six contrasting movements from those your students shared.
    2. Identify specific spatial relationships for the beginning and end of the dance.
    3. You may want some movements to be in a circle, with other actions traveling from side to side or randomly throughout the room.
    4. Find a finishing position, something low to show that all the snow has finished falling.
    5. Practice performing the choreography several times.
- Review the step 4, variation 2 quartet dances.
    1. Use the symmetrical quartet exploration from lesson 1 at the beginning of the Falling Snow dance. Ask students to go into groups of 4, facing inward to create a diamond shape, standing arm's-length apart.
    2. Create an order for each student to lead.
    3. Practice leading and following slow, smooth, and angular movements.
- Combine the two dances.
    1. Ask your students to start in their diamond formation, and each leader will get the same amount of time to lead. Call out when to change.
    2. When the fourth leader has finished leading, ask everyone to perform their favorite snow movement for 20 seconds throughout the room.
    3. Call your class into the opening formation of the Falling Snow dance.
    4. Perform the Falling Snow dance together.
    5. Students should freeze in the final position until the music stops.

Discussion

"When you were performing the Falling Snow dance, did you feel like you were the snow, or did you also feel a person traveling through the snow?"

Grades 4 Through 6 Variation

Instructions

- Allow students 3 to 4 minutes to return to their groups of six and review their dance phrases from lesson 1, step 4 variation 2, then begin work on the next section of their snow-inspired dance. Ask each group to:
    1. Create a 16-beat movement phrase inspired by three or four of the words from the falling snow list.
    2. The phrase should travel and use different levels and directions.
    3. The movement phrase will be performed immediately after their tutting-inspired snowflake dance phrases.

4. The new falling snow phrase should move students out of their hexagonal positions *and* return them to their hexagonal positions.

5. Provide time for your students to create and practice their new 16-beat falling snow phrases.

6. Once everyone is confident performing the falling snow phrase, connect it with the hexagonal, on-the-spot snowflake phrase.

7. Perform the 12-beat on-the-spot snowflake phrase once.

8. Travel outward, through the room, and back into hexagonal formation with the 16-beat falling snow phrase.

9. Perform the 12 beat on-the-spot snowflake phrase once more.

10. Freeze in the final shape.

11. Invite one group to present at a time.

12. After each group has presented on their own, try having two groups present.

13. Invite one group to work on stage left and the other stage right. One group should be slightly upstage and the other downstage.

14. Both groups will start in their hexagonal positions.

15. Ask the group on stage left to start with their 16-beat falling snow phrase and the group on stage right to start with their 12-beat on-the-spot snowflake phrase.

16. Give dancers a minute to mark through their dances. They may have to modify their falling snow phrases so they don't interfere with the group performing the snowflake phrase.

17. Once everyone has presented using the second structure, sit down and discuss it.

Discussion

- "When you watched individual groups performing, did the snowflake phrase and the falling snow phrase provide two different perspectives of snow? If yes, explain how."

- "Was it effective when two groups juxtaposed the two sections? If yes, explain how."

Journal Entry for All Grades

"Draw a picture or write a poem or short paragraph that highlights the two perspectives of a single snowflake and a heavy snowfall. Is the snowflake eager to grow and join the others? Do snowflakes fall haphazardly, colliding into each other, or is there a pattern to the descent? How do they feel once they've landed? How do they feel as other snowflakes fall upon them?"

EXERCISE 4.4   RAIN

I can think of more than a dozen songs about rain: "Singin' in the Rain;" "It's Raining, It's Pouring;" "Raindrops Keep Fallin' on My Head;" "Rainy Days;" "Rainy Day Blues;" "Rainy Days and Mondays;" "Rainy Night in Georgia;" "I Can't Stand the Rain;" not to be confused with "I Can't Stop the Rain" or "You Can't Stop the Rain" or simply "Can't Stop the Rain." And that's not to mention all the songs about rain that don't contain the word *rain* in the title, such as the "Inky Dinky Spider." Why are there so many songs about rain? Do we feel differently when it rains? Does rain change the way we look at the world, ourselves, and others?

Lesson Plan Suggestions

Kindergarten Through Grade 3

First lesson: Teach steps 1, 2, 3 (video: Tap Dance Showdown, 2:36), and 4 (follow grade-appropriate variations for every step)

Second lesson: Warm up with some of the rhythmic patterns from step 2 and do step 5 (follow the grade-appropriate variation)

Grades 4 Through 6

First lesson: Teach steps 1, 2, 3 (video: Tap Dance Showdown, 2:36), and 4 (follow grade-appropriate variations for every step)

Second lesson: Warm up with some of the rhythmic patterns from step 2, and do step 5 (follow the grade-appropriate variation)

Step 1: What We Know and How We Feel About Rain

With your class, compile two lists. The first list will contain words to describe the sounds and actions of falling rain. The list may include drops, drips, pours, drizzles, taps, pitter-patters, and drums. The second list should contain words and phrases describing how rain makes you feel and why. The list may include anxious (to walk quickly and not get wet), disappointed (can't play outside), tired (the sky is gray), wet and chilled (didn't have an umbrella and got soaked), excited (to splash in puddles), happy (trees and gardens always look brighter after it rains), relief (if there was a dry spell or drought), and concerned (if it rains too heavily for too many days).

Step 2: Rhythmic Rain Variations

Snow falls silently, but rain can be a sonic event. Step 2 focuses on the sound of rain and rhythmic patterns using body percussion exercises introduced in exercise 1.3 and new variations.

Instructions

- Sitting in a circle, warm up with the following simple rhythmic pattern. It will become more challenging in the variations to come.

1. Tap your thighs 4 times with both hands simultaneously. Make sure your students are kind to their hands. Their taps and claps should be light and gentle. The emphasis is on the lift off, not the downward attack.
2. Clap your hands 4 times.
3. Tap your shoulders 4 times with both hands simultaneously.
4. Clap your hands 4 times.
5. Set a steady tempo and count everyone in (and keep counting for kindergarten and grade 1)

- After performing the pattern 1 or 2 times, try it using alternating the taps.

All Grades Variation 1

- Thigh taps will now be right hand, left hand, right hand, left hand.
- Claps stay the same.
- Shoulder taps will now be right hand, left hand, right hand, left hand.
- Claps stay the same.

All Grades Variation 2

Change the number of taps and claps by doing only 2 beats in each position 4 times through: the first time at a slow speed, the second at a moderate tempo, the third faster, and the fourth fastest.

- Thigh taps will now be right hand, left hand.
- Clap your hands 2 times.
- Shoulder taps will now be right hand, left hand.
- Clap your hands 2 times.

All Grades Variation 3

Alternate the location of the taps:

- The first set of taps will be right thigh, left shoulder, right thigh, left shoulder.
- Clap your hands 4 times.
- The second set of taps will be right shoulder, left thigh, right shoulder, left thigh.
- Clap your hands 4 times.

Practice variation 3 using 2 beats and alternating locations 4 times through—the first time at a slow speed, the second time at a moderate tempo, the third faster, and the fourth fastest.

- The first set of taps will be right thigh, left shoulder.
- Clap your hands 2 times.
- The second set of taps will be right shoulder, left thigh.
- Clap your hands 2 times.

All Grades Variation 4

- Work standing up. You may need to slow the tempo down a bit so there is sonic clarity between each footstep and jump.

- Walk on-the-spot for 4 beats. Start with the right foot.
- Jump on-the-spot for 4 beats.
- Repeat those two 4-beat phrases twice.
- Walk on-the-spot for 2 beats. Start with the right foot.
- Jump on-the-spot for 2 beats.
- Repeat the 2-beat phrases 4 times.
- The footsteps and jumps need to be in unison for the individual beats to be heard clearly.
- Ask your class to imagine they're playing a giant drum or piano and each step is a note on the keyboard. Each jump is the *dom, dom* on the drum. Land the jumps softly. The trick to creating a strong solitary beat is to jump in unison.

All Grades Variation 5 (kindergarten and grade 1 keep walking on-the-spot)

Start this at a slow tempo.

- Start with the 4-beat phrases.
- Step forward with the right foot, then the left; step back with the right foot, then the left.
- Land jumps with wide legs, parallel legs, wide legs, parallel legs.
- Repeat 2 or 3 times.
- Then do these 2-beat phrases.
- Step forward with the right foot, then the left.
- Land one jump with wide legs and one with parallel legs.
- Step back with the right foot, then the left.
- Land one jump with wide legs, one with parallel legs.
- Repeat 2 or 3 times.

All Grades Variation 6 (kindergarten and grade 1 keep walking on-the-spot)

Try a call-and-response structure using the Variation 5 phrase.

- Divide the class into two groups.
  - Group A performs the phrase with 4 beats for each action.
  - Group B performs the phrase with 4 beats for each action.
  - Group A performs the phrase with 2 beats for each action.
  - Group B performs the phrase with 2 beats for each action.

All Grades Variation 7

Combine all the elements of the thigh-clap-shoulder phrase with the walking and jumping phrase into an original pattern. Kindergarten and grade 1 work collectively.

Variation 8 for Grades 2 Through 6

Instructions

Work in groups of four to create an original unison phrase that contains all the elements from the two rhythmic phrases. Make it challenging. "Can you walk and jump while clapping and tapping?" "Can people's walking paths intersect?" "How precisely can you perform the sounds?"

Discussion

- "Were you always able to keep a steady beat? If not, what happened? When or why did you speed up or slow down?"

- "Were you able to perform the sound of taps, claps, steps, and jumps clearly? If yes, how were you able to accomplish that?"

- "Landing jumps at the same time can be difficult. Come up with strategies for jumping and landing in unison."

Raindrop fingers.

© Janice Pomer

Step 3: All Grades

Instructions

1. Watch the Tap Dance Showdown video (2:36) from the list of video links in HK*Propel.* Having just explored rhythmic variations, your class will appreciate this video of a dazzling young tap dancer battling it out on stage with his teacher.

2. After watching the video, bring your chairs into a circle and try some fancy rhythmic footwork.

Step 4: Footwork

Instructions

- Warm up the feet and ankles by flexing and pointing.
  - Straighten the right leg so it extends a few inches off the ground.
  - Flex and point the right foot for 8 beats. Lower the foot to the ground.
  - Flex and point the left foot for 8 beats. Lower the foot to the ground.

- Make sure your students are sitting up tall. Anyone having difficulty maintaining an upright spine may press their hands gently down on the chair with straight elbows to provide stability.

- Repeat the point and flex stretch a second time. Besides warming up the feet and ankles, this exercise is also good for stretching out the calf muscles and strengthening the back.

All Grades Variation 1

- Tap the toes of the right foot on the floor once (the foot gently points).

- Tap the toes of the left foot the floor once (the foot gently points).

- Tap the heel of the right foot the floor once (the foot gently flexes).
- Tap the heel of the left foot the floor once (the foot gently flexes).

Repeat the pattern 4 times, focusing on sonic clarity.

All Grades Variation 2

- Lift the feet a few inches off the floor and clap them together on beat 1.
- Place them down on the floor in parallel position on beat 2.
- Lift the feet a few inches off the floor and clap them together on beat 3.
- Place them down on the floor in parallel position on beat 4.

Repeat 3 to 4 times, focusing on maintaining a steady beat.

All Grades Variation 3

- Combine the two patterns and create your own.
  - Alternate toe and heel taps for 4 beats.
  - Alternate foot claps and apart for 4 beats.
  - Improvise your own 8-beat foot dance.
- Repeat the sequence 4 times, alternating between the unison phrase and the improvisational section.

Step 5: Create Your Own Rain Dance

Instructions

- If you are doing step 5 at the beginning of a class, you may want to watch the video from step 3 again. The quick feet, rhythms, and level and direction changes should get everyone ready to create their original rhythmic rain-inspired dance.
- Kindergarten through grade 3 work collaboratively. (Some grade 3 classes may prefer to follow the grades 4 through 6 variation.)
- All classes will have the following elements:
  - Original rhythmic phrases that can vary in volume and sonic intensity
  - Original movement phrases using ideas from the second list of "responding to rain" created in step 1

Kindergarten Through Grade 3 Variation

- Collaboratively work with your class to explore ideas and images from the second list of "responding to rain" they compiled from step 1.
- Ask everyone to spread throughout the room and stand in parallel position.
- Call out ideas from the second list, such as the following:
  - "You feel the first drops of rain."
  - "Oh no, I don't have an umbrella! Run for cover."
  - "I have an umbrella, but my new shoes are getting wet."
  - "Puddles don't bother me. I'm wearing waterproof boots!"
  - "Jumping in puddles is one of my favorite things!"
  - "I'm looking out my window, wishing it was sunny."

- Once you have explored ideas, work collaboratively to do the following:
  1. Select three contrasting ideas (feeling rain fall, running for cover, splashing in the puddles).
  2. Explore different ways to interpret those ideas.
  3. Solidify which movement ideas will be used in your dance.
  4. Practice the ideas 2 times.
  5. Don't put them in performance order yet.
- Create a rhythmic pattern. Use all the ideas explored in the first lesson and other sonic ideas your students suggest.
  - The rhythmic pattern can be 8 to 16 beats.
  - Don't make the pattern too complicated. You want to maintain a steady beat and sonic clarity.
- Practice the rhythmic pattern 2 or 3 times.
- Combine the two sections.
- Use the rhythmic pattern as a chorus and repeat it at the beginning, middle, and end of the dance.
  1. Establish an order to connect the ideas together, with the following as an example:
  2. Perform the rhythmic rain pattern followed by the "feeling the first drops of rain" phrase.
  3. Perform the rhythmic rain pattern followed by the "run for cover" phrase.
  4. Perform the rhythmic rain pattern followed by the "I love splashing in puddles" phrase.
  5. Practice your dance together 2 or 3 times.
  6. If there's time remaining, divide the class in half.
  7. Lead group A as they perform for group B.
  8. Lead group B as they perform for group A.

Discussion

- "Could you feel the rain when you were performing sections of the dance?"
- "What do you feel was the most effective part of the dance? Explain why."

Grades 4 Through 6 Variation

- Review the ideas from the second list (that focuses on how rain makes us feel) compiled in step 1.
- Ask your students to work in groups of four to six.
- The choreography must contain at least two ideas from the second list and two rhythmic sections (12 or 16 beats each), and each rhythmic phrase should be repeated at least twice.
- An example of the elements in this rain-inspired dance may include the following:
  - Rhythmic hand and finger taps, claps, and snaps
  - People feeling the first drops and looking at the sky
  - Rhythmic foot taps and jumps

- People moving quickly, running to find cover
- Rhythmic foot taps and jumps
- Jumping and splashing in the puddles and playing in the rain
- Rhythmic hand and finger taps, claps, and snaps
- Tempo and movement changes as the rain starts and stops

- In this example, the rhythmic patterns communicate the strength of the rain: light at the beginning, strong midway, and light at the end. The dances don't have to follow that structure, but make sure there is a relationship between the sections.
- There isn't a beat limit for this assignment.
- Allow time for your class to create, practice, and present one group at a time.

Discussion

- Ask each group which ideas they used for their nonrhythmic sections and to explain their reasons for selecting them.
- Did any group keep performing the rhythmic phrases from start to finish with one, two, or three students or everyone performing it?

Journal Entry for All Grades

"Write a poem or draw a picture that conveys how you might feel on a rainy day."

EXERCISE 4.5   WATER CYCLE

The water cycle is one of nature's perpetual motion machines. Water falls in the form of rain and snow; accumulates in rivers, lakes, oceans, and soil; evaporates; and condenses, forming clouds from which rain and snow fall. This seemingly never-ending process replenishes Earth's most precious resource.

Lesson Plan Suggestions

Kindergarten Through Grade 3

First lesson: Teach step 1 (video: Water Cycle, 3:16) to introduce younger students to the water cycle; do steps 2 and 3 (follow grade-appropriate variations)

Grades 4 Through 6

First lesson: Teach steps 1, 2, and 3 (follow grade-appropriate variations)

Recommended Music: Track 5

Step 1: Introduce the Water Cycle

You may only need a minute or two to review the water cycle with older students, but for any class that isn't familiar with the water cycle, this fun dance-music video will teach them everything they need to know.

Watch the Water Cycle video (3:16) from the list of video links in HK*Propel* to see an energetic dance-music video introducing students to the five stages of the water cycle. It's great to learn about transpiration (when plants and trees release water, which then evaporates), but our water cycle choreography focuses on these four stages of the water cycle:

1. Precipitation: when water in the form of rain, snow, hail, or sleet falls from the clouds
2. Accumulation: when precipitation collects in the streams, rivers, lakes, oceans, and the earth
3. Evaporation: when the heat of the sun turns water into vapor
4. Condensation: when water vapor in the air cools, becomes water droplets, and forms clouds

Step 2: Warm Up With Movement Inspired by the Water Cycle for All Grades

Recommended Music

Track 5

Instructions

1. Ask your students to spread throughout the room, two arm's-lengths apart.
2. Let them know that they'll be exploring the four water cycle steps.
3. Play the music and call out, "Precipitation." Give your class 30 to 60 seconds

to explore precipitation. The previous two exercises focused on rain, ice, and snow, so they should have a large vocabulary to draw from. Use prompts if needed.

4. Call out, "Accumulation." Let students work for 30 to 60 seconds and call out prompts as needed: "River levels rise and fall due to melting snow and heavy precipitation." "How can you show water traveling through soil?" "What happens when there's too much rain?"

5. Call out, "Evaporation." Let students work for 30 to 60 seconds. The movement dynamics between accumulation and evaporation are very different. "Does evaporation happen quickly or slowly?" "Is it gentle or forceful?" "Can we see it or touch it?" "How can you become something that can't be seen?" "What direction does it travel in?"

6. Call out, "Condensation." Let students work for 30 to 60 seconds as they transform into clouds. "Can you slowly transform yourself into a big, billowy cloud?" "What happens to your cloud shape when a gentle breeze passes by?" "Does it remain the same, or does it shift into a new shape?"

At the end of the exploration, sit together for a brief reflection.

Discussion

"Was it easy to find actions for all the water cycle stages, or were some more challenging than others?" Identify the most challenging ones and brainstorm movement ideas.

Step 3: Create a Water Cycle Dance

Kindergarten Through Grade 3 Variation 1

Recommended Music

Track 5

Instructions

1. Ask your class to spread throughout the room.

2. Let them know that you will be calling out the four stages of the water cycle again, but this time students will only have 16 beats for each stage.

3. Put the music on and establish the beat.

4. Call out, "Precipitation." Count the 16 beats aloud while your class moves as rain, snow, or hail.

5. Call out, "Accumulation." Count the 16 beats aloud while your class seeps and spreads into the ground, lakes, and fast-moving rivers.

6. Call out, "Evaporation." Count the 16 beats aloud while your class slowly floats upward.

7. Call out, "Condensation." Count the 16 beats aloud while your class slowly transforms into clouds.

8. Repeat the pattern a second time with only 8 beats per section.

Kindergarten Through Grade 3 Variation 2

Instructions

• Create a simple on-the-spot Water Cycle dance using the arms and upper body.

- This variation is something your class can perform while they're sitting, standing on-the-spot, or walking in a line or circle.

- For example, for Precipitation, start with the arms raised overhead. Slowly lower them and wiggle your fingers. For Accumulation, let the arms ripple forward and out to either side. For Evaporation, the arms rise up, and for Condensation, they create cloud shapes overhead.

1. Every stage of the water cycle will have 4 beats.

2. The movement will focus on the arms and torso.

3. Ask your class for movement suggestions that can be performed in unison.

4. The actions should be simple and easy to repeat.

5. Once your class has created the four actions, go into a large circle and practice the phrase twice while standing on-the-spot.

6. Water cycle activity is a global event. Tell students to imagine the circle they're standing in is planet Earth.

7. Invite your class to perform the pattern while slowly walking in a circle.

8. Repeat the pattern 2 to 4 times without stopping.

- Afterward, sit together and brainstorm ways to connect their unison water cycle pattern with their more expressive creative movement ideas from the first variation; perhaps some students perform one aspect of the water cycle throughout the room while others stand at the sides performing the unison arm patterns, or try performing the unison arm pattern at different levels and in different formations. Try the structure presented in Variation 3 or create your own.

Dancers show water flowing and spreading.

Kindergarten Through Grade 3 Variation 3
Instructions
You can suggest this structure or create your own.

1. Start with everyone standing in a circle.

2. Perform the on-the-spot unison pattern once facing inward.

3. Perform the pattern once again with everyone walking around the circle.

4. Let everyone move out of the circle to perform their own Precipitation dance for 8 beats.

5. Let your students continue performing their own interpretations for Accumulation and Evaporation, allowing 8 beats for each stage.

6. After Condensation, ask your class to stay where they are and perform the unison water cycle pattern one last time on-the-spot.

Water cycle walk.

Grades 4 Through 6 Variation 1

Instructions

- Divide your class into four groups.

- Ask each group to create their own Water Cycle dance using these requirements:

  · Create four different 16-beat unison phrases—one for each water cycle stage, following the order established in the warm-up.

  · Each phrase should stay relatively on-the-spot. Keep traveling distances limited to 3 to 4 steps in any direction.

  · The phrases needn't be complex but should employ different timings, levels, and gestures to communicate the individual stages.

  · The final step or action of each phrase should lead into the first step or action of the next phrase so that each phrase transitions smoothly into the next, and the cycle can be performed over and over again.

- Allow enough time for your students to create and practice their dances, then ask each group to present.

Discussion

All the dances communicated the water cycle. Did all the groups use the same movements, or did each group create unique moves? Identify the unique actions and ask groups how they came up with their unique ideas.

Grades 4 Through 6 Variation 2

The water cycle is always active, but different regions of the planet experience different stages of the cycle at different times. What would that look like if we apply that idea to your students' Water Cycle dances?

Instructions

- Divide the performance space into quarters.

- Ask each ensemble to divide themselves into two groups: A and B.
- Invite all the A's to come into the performance area.
- Give each group of A's their own stage area to work in.
- Assign a number from 1 to 4 to each group.
- Group 1 will begin their dance with Precipitation.
- Group 2 will begin their dance with Accumulation.
- Group 3 will start with Evaporation.
- Group 4 will start with Condensation.
- Group 1 will freeze after it performs Condensation.
- Group 2 will freeze after it performs Precipitation.
- Group 3 will freeze after it performs Accumulation.
- Group 4 will freeze after it performs Evaporation.
- Ask all the groups to hold their final shapes for 4 beats.

After the A's have presented, invite the B's to present.

Discussion

- "Did the structure illustrate how water activity is different around the world?"
- "What would happen if the number of people in each group was uneven? For example, if nine people performed the same stage of the cycle while only one, two, or three people performed the other stages, would that illustrate events of severe drought or flooding?"

Journal Entry

"Draw a picture or write a poem or short descriptive paragraph about water as it transforms from one stage in the water cycle to another."

EXERCISE 4.6   DROUGHT

In the previous chapter, students' Water Cycle dances gave equal beats for each stage of the cycle. Some communities receive balanced amounts of precipitation, but many do not. Floods and storms can devastate communities and habitats, and so can drought.

Lesson Plan Suggestions

Kindergarten Through Grade 3

First lesson: Teach steps 1, 2, 3, and 4 (follow the grade-appropriate variations)

Second Lesson: Optional for classes who wish to create a Flood dance; journal

Grades 4 Through 6

First lesson: Teach step 1, 2, 3, and 4 (you can choose between option A or B; option A will require a second lesson)

Second lesson: For classes using option A, warm up quickly, review choreographic notes, finish the dances, practice them, and present them or use the second lesson for classes doing an additional flood dance; journal

Recommended Music: Track 10

Step 1: When There's Too Much or Too Little Water

In your Water Cycle dances, every stage was allotted the same number of beats, but that doesn't always happen in nature.

Instructions

Ask students to take a minute or two to reflect on your local weather.

- "What types of precipitation does your community experience? Have there been any significant weather events (rain, snow, hailstorm, drought)?"

- "Did you receive more precipitation this year compared to last year? If yes, how has the amount of precipitation affected you and your community? If no, how might an excess of rainfall affect yours or other communities?"

- "Was it drier than last year? If yes, how has the lack of precipitation affected you and your community? If no, how might lack of rainfall affect yours or other communities?"

Step 2: Drought

The definition of drought is "the continued absence of rain."

Instructions

1. Ask your class how they feel after they've run a long race. "Tired and thirsty" will be the most common answer.

2. Tell students, "At school, students are able to drink some water after the race, but imagine feeling tired and thirsty and not having any water to drink. Not

after a race, not after being at school all day. It's hard to work when you're thirsty. It's hard to sleep when you're thirsty. Drought affects all living things."

3. Compile a list of words and movement phrases associated with the way people respond to droughts, including tired, dried up, wilted, crumbling, listless, weak, dust-covered, worried, frightened, hungry, thirsty, searching for water, and looking up at the sky for rain.

Step 3: Explore Your Word List

Throughout this chapter, your class has been embodying water in its various forms. Now they'll explore how living things feel when there is not enough water.

Instructions

1. Ask your class to spread out in the performance area two arm's-lengths apart.

2. One by one, call out the words and images in your class list.

3. Use prompts to help your students silently navigate the emotions associated with drought.

When the exploration has concluded, sit together and reflect.

Discussion

• How did you feel throughout the exploration?

It's common for students to feel real thirst after they explore drought words. If that's true for your class, give them a short water break with the following conditions:

1. "Don't get distracted and talk to each other."

2. "Focus on how you feel as you get your water bottle or line up at the fountain."

3. "How does the first swallow of water feel?"

4. Let them know that they'll be sharing a word or phrase to describe how that first swallow felt once everyone has returned and is sitting together. Here are some examples of student comments from classes I've taught: "Water never tasted so good." "It's like a magic potion." "I feel like me again." "A gulp of life."

Step 4: Create a Dance Inspired by Their Drought Exploration

The structure for this dance will be the same for all grades.

1. Part 1: Searching for water

2. Part 2: How you feel without water

3. Part 3: Rain begins to fall

4. Part 4: How you feel during and after the rain

Brainstorm ideas for each section. Here are a few suggestions to get your class going:

• Part 1: Students can look up to the sky, dig to find underground water sources, walk miles to distant wells and streams, and carry buckets and bottles back home.

• Part 2: Students can look tired and worried and protect the little water and food they have, being frightened and suspicious that others will try to take it away.

- Part 3: Let the rain start slowly. Who notices it first? Try to catch each drop as it falls. Students can cup their hands and open their mouths. The rainfall increases; they can fill up buckets and bowls.

- Part 4: Students can show disbelief and joy; they can share water with others and celebrate.

Kindergarten Through Grade 3 Variation
Recommended Music
Track 10
Instructions

- Explore the suggested ideas and your students' ideas together.

- Start with the first section.

  - Play the music softly, call out an idea, let your class respond to it, call out the next idea, and continue until all the ideas for part 1 have been explored.

  - Come together and reflect on the exploration. Identify 3 or 4 of your students' favorite movement ideas. Write them down, then move to the second section.

  - Continue exploring and reflecting on ideas for all sections.

  - Are there actions or parts where everyone should do the same thing at the same time? For example, in part 4, could you create a short celebration movement phrase everyone can perform at the end?

  - Are there actions or parts where everyone should do their own interpretation of the idea? For example, for part 2, everyone could be tired, frightened, and fearful in their own way.

- Consolidate the decisions your class has made and perform them together.

- If time allows, divide your class into two groups and perform it for each other.

Discussion

- "How did you feel while you were performing the dance?"

- "Did this dance exploration deepen your appreciation of water? If yes, explain."

- "Can you create another dance to show how and why communities get flooded (heavy rains, melting snow and winter run off, hurricanes and monsoons)? Try starting the dance with the arrival of rain/water being welcomed by people, plants, and animals, then show how the water becomes destructive and makes the land uninhabitable."

Grades 4 Through 6 Variation
Instructions

There are two ways to approach this dance assignment:

- Option A: Divide your class into small groups of five or six students and ask each group to choreograph a work that contains all four sections. This option requires longer creation, practice, and presentation time and may require an additional lesson to complete.

- Option B: Divide your class into four groups and assign one section to each group. This option requires less creation, practice, and presentation time.

Note for using option B:

- Ask the students who are choreographing part 4 to create a 16-beat "celebration of water" phrase for the end of the dance that everyone can learn and join.

- After all the groups are ready to share their choreography, invite each group to present in sequential order.

- Ask students to consider performing parts 1 and 2 in silence and use the music only for parts 3 and 4 to help magnify the feelings between the two halves of the dance.

- Afterward, invite part 4 dancers to teach the class the final 16-beat celebration of water movement phrase so everyone can join in at the end.

- Ask all the groups to perform their dances again, and when part 4 draws to a close, everyone can join in for the final 16 beats.

Note for using option A:

- This option requires more time than option B.

- Allow time for your class to record ideas about their choreography in their journals before their class ends.

- In the following lesson, lead them through a quick warm-up, then let them work in their groups to finish their dances, practice, and present to each other.

Discussion for Options A and B

- "Did this dance exploration draw your attention to the value of water? If yes, explain how."

- "Could these dances be used to communicate the importance of water to others?" If yes, expand the idea: "Where can the dances be performed? Who should see the dances?"

- "Climate change has brought drought to some communities and flooding to others. Can you create a dance about rising water levels and weather events (heavy rains, melting snow and winter run off, hurricanes and monsoons), and how an excess of water can be destructive, destroy communities, and make the land uninhabitable?" If your class agrees, continue work on their Flood dance in their next lesson.

Journal Entry for All Grades

"Come up with a catch phrase, such as 'Water is life!' or 'Where would we be without water?' and create a poster to illustrate the importance of water."

EXERCISE 4.7   WATER POLLUTION (GRADES 4 THROUGH 6)

Water pollution is not an isolated event. It affects all life forms on the planet. In this exercise, students investigate the ways water pollution affects communities, wildlife, and habitats.

Lesson Plan Suggestions

Grades 4 Through 6 Only

First lesson: Steps 1a-c, 2 (videos: The Gulf Oil Spill, 2:36, and How Big the Great Pacific Garbage Patch Really Is, 3:18, [total 5:53]), and all of the explorations in step 3

Second lesson: Steps 4, 5, and 6

Third lesson (optional): Depending on the length and complexity of the choreography, some classes may require a third lesson; journal

Step 1 is in three parts. Have multiple flip charts available to record your students' ideas. Additional charts will be required for steps 2 and 3.

Step 1a: How Do Freshwater Sources Get Polluted?

Compile a list of reasons that freshwater lakes, rivers, and underground water sources are polluted. The list may include chemicals and waste from factories and mines going directly into the water, agricultural waste from industrial farms seeping into land near a water source, lack of proper infrastructure to deal with human waste, lack of recycling programs to prevent plastic and other synthetic waste from going into lakes and rivers, or individual actions (buying overpackaged products, not recycling).

Step 1b: What Do We Know About Ocean Pollution?

Compile a list of actions that pollute seas and oceans. The list may include oil spills from tankers and oil platforms; factory runoff that has chemicals and waste; and plastic, and other synthetic waste from cargo ships, fishing ships, ocean liners, and oceanfront communities.

Step 1c: What Life Forms Suffer When Water Is Polluted?

Compile a list identifying the life forms affected by water pollution, including waterfowl, water mammals, fish, mollusks, coral reefs, water vegetation, animals, and humans. All life forms rely on water, and polluted water affects everyone.

Step 2: Videos

- Watch The Gulf Oil Spill (2:36) and How Big the Great Pacific Garbage Patch Really Is videos (3:18; total time 5:53) about ongoing catastrophic water polluting events in or adjacent to North America from the list of video links in HK*Propel*.

- After the Gulf Oil Spill video, get feedback from the students by asking them:
  - "How did the video make you feel?"
  - Write down the first response and ask the student who contributed the word to explain why he or she feels that way.
  - Keep asking the class for their responses and reasons for feeling that way.
- Draw a line under your students' responses to the first video.
- Watch the second video.
- Repeat the same process of gathering students' responses.
- Keep the lists available so students can refer to them while creating their dances.

Step 3: Review Lists and Explore Choreographic Possibilities

- Explore the different forms of pollutants featured in the videos and find ways to translate them into movement.
- After each movement exploration, return to the flip charts if students have new words and ideas to contribute.

First Exploration Related to the First Video

Ask students: "How did the pollutant enter the water system?" Explore on-the-spot actions, traveling patterns and pathways, timings, and spatial relationships that relate to the first video. For example: the oil rig exploded and burned; it gushed, poured, and spewed oil.

Second Exploration Related to the Second Video

Explore movement ideas related to the second video about the Pacific garbage patch. For example: Plastics were dumped, discarded, and slowly accumulated, and as the patch floats with the currents, it continues to collect more garbage and grow.

Third Exploration Related to Both Videos

Ask students: "Are the pollutants different in shape and texture?" Remember exploring the soft petals and sharp thorns in exercise 2.2? Texture will play a strong role in shaping the movements of these dances. The garbage patch is a tangled mass of industrial fishing nets, large hard containers, and all sizes of plastic bags and discarded objects, while oil is thick, sticky, and viscous. It adhered to waterfowl and marine life and solidified into toxic clumps capable of destroying islands and important nesting ground habitats.

Remember, after each movement exploration, return to the flip charts and list new words and ideas.

Fourth Exploration Related to First Video

Ask students: "What is the impact on water, wildlife, humans, and neighboring ecosystems?" For the Gulf Oil Spill video, after the oil rig explosion, there was loss of human lives; catastrophic loss of waterfowl, marine reptiles, fish, and shellfish; loss of habitat; loss of employment for fishery and tourism workers; and the destruction of the nesting grounds, which means the possible demise of some bird species.

Fifth Exploration Related to Second Video

Plastics ensnare and kill marine mammals, fish, and reptiles. It also poisons them when they ingest pieces of plastic. Microplastics become part of the food chain, killing or poisoning any living creature, including humans, that consume them.

Sixth Exploration Related to Both Videos

Review the list of feelings students had after watching the videos. The most common student feelings and responses include the following:

- Sadness over the death and suffering of wildlife and habitats and for people who lost their lives and livelihoods
- Confusion and disbelief that oil spills have such a long-lasting impact and that discarded garbage accumulates and forms huge, destructive entities throughout our oceans
- Frustration and anger that water wildlife and ecosystems around the world are struggling to survive
- Hopeful because there are people who are trying to correct the damage and make things better
- Inspired to become part of the solution

Finish the first lesson on a positive note.

Seventh and Final Exploration

Ask students: "How does water move before being polluted?" Select one or two fun water-inspired movement phrases from previous exercises to review. Keep the lists of students' responses for the second lesson.

Water pollution.

© Janice Pomer

Step 4: Create Dances to Show Water Before and After Being Polluted

Divide your class into four groups. Ask two of the groups to create a movement piece about the Gulf oil spill and the other two groups to create a movement piece about the great Pacific garbage patch. Both groups can use the following structure:

- Create an approximately 24-beat movement phrase showing water in its un-polluted state. Use a variety of levels, speeds, and pathways. Half the dancers in each group perform the Water dance. This will be the first section of the dance.

- Create an approximately 24-beat movement phrase showing oil or plastic. Refer to the lists compiled in the previous class for ideas. Half the dancers in each group will perform it. This will be the second section of the dance.

- Once the two phrases have been created, students need to find a way for the pollutant to enter at the end of the clean water dance section (plastic could slowly infiltrate along the sides, while the oil could erupt from within the water).

- Those performing water movements should continue moving but will need to modify their movements as the pollutants overwhelm them.

Step 5: What Comes Next?

- Write the following questions on the board or flip chart:
  - Do you want to show what happens to marine life caught in the pollution?
  - Do you want to leave the dance with the pollution overwhelming the water?
  - Is there a more positive way to resolve the situation?
  - Is there a way to combine a number of ideas or outcomes?

- Bring everyone's attention to the questions. Ask each group to discuss possible endings for their dance.

- Allow time for groups to create the final section of their dances. Most classes will require an additional lesson to complete the choreographic assignment.

Step 6: Final Presentation

Ask each group to present their dances. Afterward, ask a representative from each group to explain why they chose the ending they presented.

Journal Entry

- "Do you think your dance can help others understand some of the issues regarding water pollution?"

- Here are two journal entries from students after they presented their dances about water pollution:

"We chose oil spills because we thought it would be powerful to show how animals suffer and die because of oil spills. When Jackson and I pulled Ben and Lochlann, it was like we were the oil spill sucking the animals down."

"I think we successfully showed the topic of pollution when Anna stepped over us at the end. It shows that right now humans are stepping on water and ruining it."

If the subject of water pollution resonates with your class, consider planning a school event where they can share their dances to celebrate International Water Day (in the latter part of March) and International Ocean Week (in early June).

EXERCISE 4.8   WETLAND HABITATS

Wetlands are unique ecosystems that support diverse wildlife: mammals, reptiles, birds, fish, plants, and insects. Wetlands also prevent floods and land erosion and help in water conservation. This culminating exercise is an opportunity for your students to bring together movement ideas from chapters 2, 3, and 4 to create dances inspired by wetland habitats.

Lesson Plan Suggestions

Kindergarten Through Grade 3

First lesson: Steps 1 (video: explaining the importance of wetlands 2:07), 2 (video: Pond, 1:16), and 3, and if time allows, begin exploring ideas for step 4 (follow the grade-appropriate variation)

Second lesson: Warm up by reviewing some of the movement explorations from step 3, then go to step 4 (follow the grade-appropriate variation) to plan, create, and perform your Pond dance; journal

Grades 4 Through 6

First lesson: Steps 1 including video explaining the importance of wetlands (2:07 minutes), 2 (video: Pond, 1:16), and 3, and introduce the structure for step 4 (follow the grade-appropriate variation)

Second lesson: Warm up by reviewing some of the movement explorations from step 3 and then go to step 4 (follow the grade-appropriate variation); if there's not enough time for students to share their dances, make sure there's time for them to record their choreography before the second lesson ends

Third lesson (optional): Lead a general class warm-up, then ask students to go into their working groups to review, practice, and present their dances; journal

Recommended Music: Track 11

Step 1: What We Know About Wetland Habitats

All Grades

There are many different types of wetlands: ponds, swamps, marshes, bogs, lagoons, mangroves, everglades, and floodplains. They are all vitally important to the planet's ecosystem.

Watch the first video (2:07) from the list of video links in HK*Propel* to learn why wetlands are invaluable to maintaining a healthy planet. The video's information is simple to understand and is imparted through short text blocks. Teachers for younger grades will need to read the text aloud for their classes.

Kindergarten Through Grade 3

After watching the first video, go directly to step 2 and watch the next video. The section of choreography shown in the second video displays how wonderfully dance can re-create images of pond life: lily pads, frogs leaping, insects flying over and lying on the surface of the water.

Grades 4 Through 6

- Can your class cite the differences between seasonal, permanent, saltwater, fresh water, tidal, tropical or boreal, and wetlands?

- Start brainstorming by asking your class they know about freshwater ponds. Ask them the following:

  · "How would you describe the water?" (still, murky, filed with vegetation)

  · "What animals live there?" (waterfowl, frogs, turtles, dragonflies, otters)

  · "What plants grow there?" (lily pads, bull rushes, algae, willow trees)

- Depending on where you live, your students will be familiar with different types of wetlands.

- See if your class can articulate some of the differences between freshwater ponds and one or two other wetlands on the list. Then move on to the next step.

Step 2: Pond

Watch the Pond video (1:17) from the list of video links in HK*Propel*. This short dance excerpt brilliantly portrays a murky pond at dusk. The lighting for the dance is purposefully dim to create twilight—when frogs and insects are active. The dancers use low rolling platforms and appear to float across the stage, sometimes forming exquisite lily pads. With most of the dance performed at a low level, their frog leaps appear incredibly dynamic and powerful.

Step 3: Can We Dance a Wetland?

All Grades

Recommended Music

Track 11

Instructions

After watching the second video, you may want to revisit your word list for ponds, then collectively explore movement ideas for each word or image.

1. Ask your class to spread out, standing in still water or parallel position.

2. Put on the music. Ask everyone to close their eyes and listen to it for 30 to 45 seconds. The composition features outdoor field recordings of water, birds, and insects.

3. The environmental sounds are soft and calm, but the sounds don't necessarily reflect the speeds of the birds and insects at all times. For example, like water, animal actions ebb and flow.

4. Share the image of a crane swooping down, landing in the wetland, and then standing as still as a statue while searching for food. Suddenly its head plunges down, and when it raises it up, there's a fish floundering in its beak.

5. Share another image of a frog sitting as still as a stone before it shoots its tongue; the frog has captured and swallows a water bug.

6. Invite your students to try shifting between short bursts of speed followed by a slow and sustained movement.

7. If *still* is one of the words for water, what kind of small, subtle movements can you create to show water reacting to the activity on its surface and below? (soft pulses, ripples, the occasional splash)

8. Try exploring mid- and low-level water actions, and use the higher movements for insects and birds.

9. Use prompts to encourage your class to try new ideas. Bug actions can use the full body or arm and hand movements as they skim over the surface of the pond. Ducks and swans fly, float, glide, paddle, waddle, shake, and plunge their heads down or lift their heads up as they shake and elongate their necks.

10. "How do the bullrushes and surface plants differ from the underwater vegetation, and how do they respond to the activity around them?" Use different levels to indicate above and below water. "Are underwater plants softer, more flowing? Do fish and other creatures hide in them?"

Use flip charts to record favorite actions, images, and movement ideas to be referred to in step 4.

Water grasses.

Step 4: Pond Dance

Kindergarten Through Grade 3 Variation

Recommended Music

Track 11

Instructions

After the explorations, sit together to share favorite movements and start strategizing ways to create a dance that combines all the elements of a pond habitat. Here's one structure to try or create your own:

- Create a simple water phrase that's easy to repeat for everyone to learn and practice.

- Divide your class into three groups. Each group will be responsible for two different forms of pond life:

  · Group A will do insects and herons and cranes.

- Group B will do ducks and swans and tall grasses.
- Group C will do underwater vegetation and frogs, turtles, and fish.

- The entire class will create the pond.

    1. Start with everyone performing the repeatable water phrase.
    2. After repeating their Water dance twice, the different groups will perform their individual sections in the following manner (while the other groups do very gentle water movements).
    3. Ask group A to improvise insect-inspired movements throughout the pond area.
    4. After 30 seconds, ask group B to improvise duck and swan movements and group A to return to doing gentle water movements.
    5. After 30 seconds, ask group C to improvise underwater vegetation as group B returns to gentle water movements.
    6. Repeat the structure with each group doing their second movement assignment.
    7. Finish with everyone returning to water and performing the water phrase one last time.

Discussion

- "Was it hard to stay focused when other groups were doing different actions?"
- "Did everyone remember to find moments of quiet stillness in their improvised movements (frog watching for bugs)?"
- "Did having people do different movements create the feeling of being at a pond? If yes, explain. If no, what could be done to show pond life more clearly?"
- "How did the music help to create the feeling of being at a pond?"

Journal Entry for Kindergarten Through Grade 3

"Write about or draw a picture of your favorite movement moment in the Pond dance."

Grades 4 Through 6 Variation

Instructions

Introduce your class to the structure outlined for kindergarten through grade 3 classes.

1. Divide your class into four groups.
2. Invite your class to adapt the structure for their own pond-inspired dance.
3. If there is a wetland in your community, province, or state, or if your class has been studying a wetland in current events (recent flooding or habitat loss) or in history (the annual flooding of the Nile was of great importance to the ancient Egyptians), you can ask students to focus on that wetland for their dance.

All groups should have seven to nine students, enough to ensure that the element of water will always be present in their dance and that there will be two or three small ensembles within each group. Whichever wetland they choose to be inspired by, follow these guidelines:

- The dances should have a set vocabulary for water that everyone will learn.
- They should have three small ensembles of two or three students.

- Assign different flora and fauna to small ensembles within the larger group.
- Make sure each ensemble has contrasting plants and animals to perform (no ensemble should do only plants).
- Layer the choreography so that when one ensemble is performing flora or fauna, the others are doing gentle water movements.
- The water movements can be choreographed to highlight an animal action; if geese land on the water, the water should respond.
- The water movers can change position, face different directions, create ripples, and play with timing changes while the other members in their group present animals or vegetation.

Unlike the kindergarten through grade 3 dance, older students will have time to plan and rehearse. There's no time limit on the choreography, but your class should be able to rough out and notate their dances in their journals during their second lesson and then review, practice, present, and reflect in their third lesson.

Discussion

- Were these dances the longest pieces your students have choreographed?
- "The music was atmospheric. Did it help create the wetland environment? If yes, explain. If no, what type of soundtrack would have been more helpful?"
- "Was it challenging to choreograph to music that has no beat?"
- "Since there were no beats or significant sound cues, how did each group make smooth transitions between the different ensembles?"
- Identify a unique image or movement phrase from each group and ask how they came up with the idea.

Journal Entry for Grades 4 Through 6

Play the composition while students are writing. Invite your class to close their eyes and listen to the composition for a minute, then write a poem or descriptive paragraph from the perspective of water in a wetland. Use these prompts: "What changes occur to the water and the life forms around and within it?"

SUMMARY

In this final exercise, your class combined movement ideas from chapters 2, 3, and 4. They layered movement phrases, timing changes, and spatial relationships, and each student was required to perform three roles: water and two contrasting flora or fauna roles to bring a wetland habitat to life. In the upcoming chapter, your students will be challenged even further as they explore some of the surface terrains and internal forces of Earth.

World Wetlands Day is February 2. Can your students plan an event to inform the school community about the importance of wetlands?

Go to HK*Propel* to find audio files, reproducible forms, and a list of video links corresponding to chapter exercises.

© Janice Pomer

CHAPTER 5

Earth

All the nature-themed exercises are connected to Earth, but the exercises in this chapter focus specifically on Earth itself: soil, rocks, and sand; the push and pull of invisible forces made visible by the mountains and valleys they cut and carve; and elemental magma from beneath Earth's crust.

In a classroom several years ago, while the students and I were compiling our word database to inspire Earth movements, someone suggested the word *bleed*. Another student asked, "How does the earth bleed?" The first student said that magma was the earth's blood, and when a volcano erupts, the flowing magma is the earth bleeding.

That idea led to a discussion about our planet being a living organism, which then led to a discussion on the duality of volcanic activity. One student said that an eruption is a catastrophic event that destroys living things, while another pointed out that volcanoes create islands where new life eventually grows.

Plants, animals, water, and people are multidimensional, and so, too, is Earth. Our planet supports life, and it can also be destructive. Earth is a wonder we must cherish and respect.

EXERCISE 5.1   EARTH WORDS

In exercise 4.1, your class compiled water words and used them to create word and movement phrases. In this exercise, you'll use the same template to create word and movement phrases inspired by the earth.

Lesson Plan Suggestions

Kindergarten Through Grade 3

First lesson: Teach steps 1, 2, and 3 (follow the grade-appropriate variation)

Second lesson: Warm up quickly with a few action words from step 2, review the word and movement phrases created in step 3, and explore steps 4 and 5; journal

Grades 4 Through 6

First lesson: Teach steps 1, 2, and 3 (follow the grade-appropriate variation)

Second lesson: Warm up quickly with a few action words from step 2, review the word and movement phrases from step 3, and explore steps 4 and 5; journal

Recommended Music: Track 12

Step 1: How Earth Moves

- Compile a list of words that describe the many ways the earth moves, including pushes, pulls, cracks, crumbles, rises, falls, erodes, shifts, heaves, erupts, quakes, shakes, collapses, slides, nourishes, feeds, grows, protects, dries, absorbs, rests, sleeps, spins, rotates, and orbits.

- Start a second list for words describing different Earth surfaces, including sand, soil, mud, clay, pebbles, stones, rocks, cliffs, canyons, hills, ground, mountains, and valleys.

- Start a third list for Earth textures, including firm, rough, sharp, hard, jagged, bumpy, soft, smooth, slick, sticky, porous, and solid.

- Keep these word charts readily available over the time your class is working on the exercises in this chapter, and invite everyone to add new words to the list each day.

Step 2: Warming Up With Earth Words

Recommended Music

Track 12

Instructions

Some of the actions on the Earth word list, such as falls, spins, and freezes, appear on your water word list and have been used in choreography in previous exercises. Remind your students that the focus of this warm-up is to explore these words as they pertain to Earth. A spinning planet isn't the same as a whirlpool; a landslide falling isn't the same as a waterfall.

Follow the improvisational template established in previous exercises:

1. Ask everyone to start in parallel position.

2. During the movement exploration, they're to stay in their personal bubbles and not interfere with other people's work.

3. Play music to support the exploration.

4. Use Earth words from all three lists.

5. Let students know that some exploration will be to create shapes for tableaux; other explorations require full-body movements.

6. Create word phrases, such as *hard, jagged rocks*, to inspire a series of frozen shapes or tableaux.

7. To move out of tableaux, use words such as *crumble* and *erode*.

8. Other word phrases, such as *soft, shifting sand* or *ground quakes and shakes* are inspirations for continual movement.

9. Give your class 30 to 60 seconds (depending on age) to explore each combination using full actions and smaller isolations (arms, torso) before you call out the next word or phrase.

10. Use additional prompts: "Can you make the movement smaller or larger?" "Can you repeat an action at different levels?" Encourage your class to think about timing. "When Earth dries up and cracks, does it happen all at once, or does it crack bit by bit?"

11. Remind students to use isolations as well as full-body movements: "Can your shoulders rise and fall to create rolling hills?" or "Can you press your elbows, knees, and thighs together like two land masses pushing against each other?"

12. After several minutes, bring the exploration to a close. Finish with a restful combination, perhaps *soft soil sleeping*, then invite students to sit down.

Discussion

- "Did you have a favorite action or phrase? If yes, what was it and why?"

- "Were there any words that were hard to communicate through movement?" If there are a number of words your class had difficulty translating into movement, brainstorm ideas for making them easier.

- Did anyone think of other words to add to the lists while they were moving? If yes, add them to the list.

Step 3: Creating Earth Word Movement Phrases

Kindergarten Through Grade 3 Variation

Instructions

Compose four contrasting Earth word phrases. Start by introducing students to these two suggestions, then create your own, such as these:

- Towering mountains pierce the sky.

- Earth spins as it orbits the sun.

Start the exercise by asking your class to work in groups of two (though kindergarten teachers may wish to keep students working collectively).

1. Allow time for the duets to explore ideas for the word and movement phrases. (Kindergarten and grade 1 teachers may choose to assign one movement phrase at a time.)

2. The structure for the word or movement phrase will be the following:
   - Say the words.
   - Perform the movement inspired by the word phrase.
   - Freeze in a tableau inspired by the word phrase.

3. There can be up to 8 beats of action followed by a tableau that should be held in stillness for 4 to 8 beats. Encourage your class to fill their freezes with Earth energy.

Invite two students to demonstrate the assignment using "towering mountains pierce the sky" and "Earth spins as it orbits the sun." Invite them to do this:

- Start frozen in a low crouch arm's-length apart.
- Instruct them to stay frozen until you've said, "Towering mountains pierce the sky."
- Then they can begin to move slowly, watching each other as they move in unison, rising up, standing, reaching their arms up and toward each other so their fingertips touch to create a pointed mountain top. To increase the mountain shape, they can move one leg behind them to create a wide base to contrast the pointed top.
- Ask them to freeze in their mountain shape for 4 beats.

Invite two new students to demonstrate, saying, "Earth spins as it orbits the sun."

- Invite one student to be the sun, stepping into a wide A stance while reaching their arms out in all directions to show the sun emanating light.
- Invite the other mover be Earth, slowly spinning and circling the sun.
- After 8 beats of spinning, ask the movers to freeze.

After the demonstrations, do this:

- Collectively create additional spoken Earth phrases for your class to use (you can use the two from this book and two new ones).
- Establish an order for the Earth phrases to be performed.
- Review the following process for working with others:
  · Remind your students to talk quietly while planning their actions and freezes.
  · Share ideas and listen to each other.
  · If there is a disagreement, don't let it escalate. Ask for assistance.
- Allow time for your students to create their movement phrases and practice them.
- Divide the class into two groups: half the duets will be group A and the other half group B.
- Group A will share their movement phrases first. Invite group A into the performance area and ask them to wait in their opening positions in silence and stillness.

- Invite group B to pay close attention to the different ways group A duets have interpreted the four phrases.
- The presentation of the duets does not require music.
    1. Call out the first phrase and watch the duets move and freeze.
    2. After everyone has held the final shape for at least 4 beats, call out the next phrase. Repeat the process until all four phrases have been presented.
- After the final freeze, invite group B into the performance area while group A watches.
- Afterward, sit together and discuss the performance.

Discussion

- "Which action or freeze was your favorite to do? Explain why."
- "Which action or freeze was the most eye-catching to watch? Explain why."
- "Does anyone have additional ideas for Earth word phrases for movement inspiration?" If yes, add them to the list.

If there isn't time to create new movement phrases to go with the new word phrases, save them until the next lesson.

Journal Entry for Grades 1 Through 3

"Notate your word and action phrases. They'll be used next lesson."

Grades 4 Through 6 Variation

Instructions

Ask your students to work in groups of three or four and compose four contrasting Earth word phrases to inspire movement. You can use these two phrases as example:

- Towering mountains pierce the sky.
- Earth spins as it orbits around the sun.

Students can use any of the Earth words from the charts or words they've just thought of that haven't been added to the charts. Once a group has used an Earth word in a phrase, it shouldn't be used in any of their other phrases.

The structure for combining words and movement is the following:

1. Establish an opening shape.
2. Speak the phrase.
3. Perform an 8- or 12-beat movement phrase inspired by the word phrase.
4. Finish in a freeze and hold it for 4 or 8 beats.
5. While still frozen in the first shape, speak the second phrase.
6. Perform an 8- or 12-beat movement phrase inspired by the word phrase.
7. Finish in a freeze and hold it for 4 or 8 beats.
8. Continue working with this pattern through all four phrases.

Play the music at low volume during the creation process. Give your class time to work on the text and movement. During the final few minutes of work time, encourage everyone to practice their text at full volume, then invite groups to present their creations one by one.

Discussion

- Did every group present four contrasting phrases?

- Were any Earth actions or images used by a number of groups? If yes, what were they, and why were they so popular?
- Was there an Earth action or image used by only one group? If yes, what was it? Ask the group why they selected it.

Journal Entry

"Notate your word and action phrases. They'll be used next lesson."

Use incremental levels to create a sense of movement in tableau.

Step 4: Combining Solos and Duets or Groups

Kindergarten Through Grade 3 Variation

Instructions

Review the Earth word movement phrases from step 3.

1. If your class worked collaboratively, review the phrases together. If they worked in duets, give them time to review their phrases on their own.
2. Review the order of the word phrases. Examples are the following:
   - Mountain phrase
   - Earth orbit phrase
   - Sand phrase
   - Cave phrase
3. Find a place in the room to work with partners.
4. During this review, the teacher will be the only one speaking the text.
5. Call out the first word phrase, and let the movers respond and freeze.
6. Call out the second word phrase, and let the movers respond and freeze.

7. Continue in that fashion until all the phrases have been performed.

8. Divide the class (or duets) into three groups: A, B, C.

9. Assign duets a number. If the groups contain 4 or 5 duets, assign each duet in every group a number 1 through 5.

10. If your students are working collaboratively, divide your class into groups of seven or eight students and assign individual students a number. It's fine if the groups aren't even in number.

11. Ask the duets in group A to enter the performance area and go into their starting positions for the first word phrase.

12. Play track 12 softly to support movement work.

13. Say the first word phrase, then signal duet (or student) 1 to perform.

14. When the first duet (or student) freezes, the second duet (or student) performs their phrase. Then the next pair performs, and so on.

15. When everyone has finished the first phrase and everyone is frozen in their final positions, repeat the same process with the second and subsequent phrases.

16. After group A has presented, invite the other groups to present.

Discussion

- "Mountain ranges stretch across continents, and Earth spins around and around. Did repeating the movement phrases one after another make the mountain ranges seem bigger or Earth's orbit longer?"

- Ask the same question for the other images and actions.

Grades 4 Through 6 Variation

- Ask two groups to work together and combine their movement phrases using this structure:

  · Both groups start in stillness in their opening positions.

  · Their spatial relationships can be close or far apart, and they can change as the movement progresses.

  · Group A speaks and performs their first movement phrase and freezes.

  · After group A freezes, group B speaks and performs their first movement phrase and freezes.

  · Group A speaks and performs their second movement phrase and freezes.

  · Group B speaks and performs their second movement phrase and freezes.

  · Continue with this pattern until the final phrase has been performed and everyone is frozen.

- The groups don't need to learn the other's phrases, but they'll need to familiarize themselves with each other's spacing and final positions of each phrase.

- Groups can imagine that they are creating an ever-changing view of mountains, valleys, caves, and deserts.

- They can juxtapose their phrases: A become mountains; B, a desert; A, caves; and B, orbit.

- They can explore ways to spread their phrases across the performance area and at times overlap while performing so that group A's frozen shapes become part of the landscape for group B's movement.

- Play track 12 softly to support the movement work.
- After they present their collaborations, discuss them.

Discussion

- "Did this presentation variation provide a wider range of Earth movements?"
- "Did the frozen shapes add to the presentations? If yes, explain."

Step 5: Creating a Unison Earth Section

Kindergarten Through Grade 3 Variation

Recommended Music

Track 12

Instructions

1. Create a movement phrase to be performed by everyone in a circle.
2. Brainstorm Earth movements with your class to create a unison phrase inspired by six or more Earth actions.
3. Select contrasting actions such as: push, pull; erupt, crumble; and smash, protect.
4. Practice the phrase standing in a circle. The actions can move in and out and around the circle.
5. The music is atmospheric and slow. Establish a moderate tempo and practice the dance first in silence. Then add the music.
6. This new phrase can be performed on its own or added to the phrases established in step 4.

Discussion

- "Was it difficult to move from fast to slow with atmospheric music? If yes, explain why."
- "Did your movements and the music's slowness help communicate how Earth (and all that dwell on it) move at different speeds?"

Journal Entry for Kindergarten Through Grade 3

"Illustrate your favorite Earth phrase."

Variation for Grades 4 Through 6

Instructions

Ask your class to stay in their combined groups and create a final Earth phrase for both groups to perform.

- The final phrase can be 16 to 24 beats.
- Encourage the groups to use Earth actions they haven't used in their individual phrases.
- The final unison phrase should finish in a spatial configuration that they feel communicates Earth.
- The movement phrase should contain contrasting Earth elements (erupt, crumble, protect, smash), traveling patterns, levels, and tempos.
- They'll be using the same slow, atmospheric music that supports their word and movement phrase. They should establish a moderate tempo for their unison phrase, practice it in silence, and then add the music.

Allow time for creating the new choreography and practicing the transition between their word and movement freezes from step 4 into the new unison phrase. Then ask the groups to present.

Discussion

- "Was it easy to find new Earth actions after you'd used so many for the word or movement phrases?"

- Ask each group to explain how they selected the final shape of dance (a circle represented the planet, and an inverted V represented a large mountain).

- "Was it difficult performing the unison phrase to slow and atmospheric music? If yes, explain why."

- "Did the contrast of quick movements and the music's slowness help communicate how Earth and all that dwell on it move at different speeds?"

Journal Entry for Grades 4 Through 6

"Write a poem or descriptive paragraph to describe how you would feel if you were in one of the landscapes your group explored through movement."

EXERCISE 5.2   TERRAINS

In step 2 of exercise 1.5 in chapter 1, your class traveled through different environments: a jungle, a haunted house, a snowstorm, and floating in space. We're going to revisit that exercise but this time focus on how different natural surfaces feel under our feet.

Lesson Plan Suggestions

Kindergarten Through Grade 3

First lesson: Teach steps 1, 2, and 3 (follow the grade-appropriate variation)

Grades 4 Through 6

First lesson: Teach steps 1, 2, and 3 (follow the grade-appropriate variation)

Recommended Music: Track 8

Step 1: What's Under Our Feet

All Grades

Instructions

Ask students to stand in three or four horizontal lines, with six to eight students per line. One line is behind the other at one end of the room.

1. Tell your class that you'll be calling out different surfaces for them to walk on.
2. Their job will be to notice how their feet (and their bodies) respond to each surface as they walk from one end of the room to the other.
3. When the first line gets halfway across the room, ask the second line to begin.
4. When a line gets to the far side, they should walk quietly along the perimeter of the room so they don't interfere with the students who are still traveling across the open space.
5. Once everyone has returned to the starting area and are standing in their lines, give them a new terrain to travel on.
6. Introduce each surface so everyone has a clear idea of what they're walking on and how it might affect the way they move.
7. When your students were introduced to this exercise in chapter 1, they were encouraged to respond with dramatic movements and facial expressions.
8. In this exercise, the outward movements will be much more subtle.
9. The main purpose of the exercise is to deepen your students' connection to their feet and to notice how their feet (and legs and spine) respond as they walk over dry, moist, stable, mobile, soft, and rugged terrain.
10. Suggest to your students that they silently compare the surfaces using a Goldilocks analogy: "That terrain was soft and comfortable, the one before was too hard, the other one was too slippery."

Feel free to add to the list of surfaces after your class has explored the following:

1. The sidewalk: This is a neutral walk for urban dwellers.

2. Grass: Use the front yard or park grass, not tall, wild grasses; grass adds a little bounce to one's step.

3. Gravel: Use small, crushed stone used for pathways and driveways; gravel isn't completely flat or stable.

4. Packed soil: Use hard, packed soil with no vegetation to separate your feet from the earth. Ask students: "Is there a difference between it and sidewalk concrete?"

5. Forest path: Tell them it has tree roots and other undergrowth. Ask students: "Can you walk without looking down?"

6. Rocky terrain: Include boulders and midsized rocks to climb and clamber over.

7. Dry sand: Their feet will sink or slide when they step.

8. Mud: It is squishy, it sticks, and it offers resistance each time you lift your feet.

Students imagine different terrains beneath their feet.

Discussion

- Ask your class to describe how it felt to travel on each surface.

- Compile a word list based on their comments. The list should include easy, firm, smooth, gentle, tiring, slippery, uneven, rough, unstable, gooey, and messy.

- "Did you leave footprints on the surface of the terrains you walked on? If yes, list which ones had the footprints."

- "Were there terrains where your footsteps left no impression? If yes, list which ones had no footprints."

Step 2: Being Walked Upon

All Grades

Let's look at our footsteps from a different perspective and explore how different terrains respond when we walk over them. This visualization requires focus and a willingness to suspend disbelief.

> Special Note for Kindergarten Through Grade 3 Teachers: Some primary classes love doing visualizations, but others get fidgety and find it difficult to concentrate. If your class finds it difficult to stay still, it's better to read the first few images, then move for a minute, refocus and read a few more images, then move again until they've experienced all the images.

Instructions

On-the-Spot Visualization

1. Ask your class to sit or lie down on the floor or sit at their desks. Regardless of their position, they should close their eyes (and they can rest their head on their desks).

2. Remind everyone that the visualization is experienced in silence and that there'll be time to talk afterward.

3. Remember to leave a moment of silence between each image or idea.

Start the visualization.

1. "Imagine you are a grassy field in a park; the surface of your body is covered in grass, and underneath the grass, you are soil."

2. "Someone is walking on you. Every blade of grass that's stepped on feels the weight of each footstep."

3. "But the blades of grass manage to bounce back up without experiencing too much discomfort."

4. "A game of Extreme Frisbee has started! People are running, jumping, falling, and sliding all over you."

5. "How does it feel when someone slides heavily into the ground? Does it hurt? Have clumps of grass been torn from the soil? Will they survive?"

6. Let your class focus on this for 5 to 10 seconds, then move on to the next image.

7. "From being a grassy field, let yourself become firmly packed soil."

8. "Someone with running shoes is jogging on you, but the soil is firm, and the jogger is treading lightly."

9. "It's not digging into you, but you feel mild pressure."

10. "Now imagine someone with high-heeled pumps is walking on you."

11. "Does that feel like you're being poked with pins and needles?"

12. Allow 5 to 10 seconds for students to focus on that image.

13. Ask everyone imagine themselves as large, rounded rocks.

14. "A large group of hikers come by. They walk and climb over you. Does it bother you?"

15. Allow 5 to 10 seconds for students to focus on that image.

16. "Now allow your rock image to become a sand dune in a desert."

17. "You can feel a gentle breeze lightly blow, and a few grains of sand move, but the breeze doesn't disturb the rest of you."

18. "You feel quite comfortable until a group of travelers walk on you."

19. "Their steps sink down into you."

20. "When they lift their feet, you try to fill in the holes their feet have made, but you can't return all the grains of sand back to where they had been."

21. Allow 5 to 10 seconds to focus on that image.

22. "Imagine being a large mud puddle."

23. "Someone walks on you, and you feel the pressure of their footsteps. The parts of you that are pressed down squish you outward."

24. "Bits of you cling to the boot as it's pulled away. More people pass by, and you keep being squished down. Their boots get covered in mud, and they walk away, carrying bits of you home."

25. Allow 5 to 10 seconds to focus on that image.

Let everyone rest for a moment in stillness and silence.

Discussion

- "Have you ever considered that the ground has feelings?"
- "Which surface did you most enjoy being? Explain why."
- "Which surface was the most uncomfortable to be? Explain why."

Step 3: Create a Travelers and Terrains Dance

Use the explorations from steps 1 and 2 as the foundation for a dance where you are both the travelers and the terrains.

Kindergarten Through Grade 3 Variation

Recommended Music

Track 8

Instructions

- When your students were walking over the terrains in step 1, which were the most memorable and offered the most contrast in movements?
- Select two terrains.
- Brainstorm ideas for ways to travel (besides walking) over the terrains.
- Then start working with the music. Ask your class to spread throughout the room.
- Call out: "Traveling over rocks." (Use another terrain if your students didn't select rocks.)
- Encourage your students to explore ways of pulling themselves up onto rocks or leaping from rock to rock.
- Use prompts: "Be careful. You don't want to get your feet caught between rocks." "When you get to the top of a tall rock, take a moment to look around." "Are some of the rocks too smooth or slippery to climb up?"
- After 1 or 2 minutes of exploring ways to travel over rocks, call out the next terrain your students suggested.
- Explore ideas for traveling over grass or mud. They're a good contrast to rocks.
- After exploring ways to travel over the selected terrains, invite your students to demonstrate some of their favorite moves.
- Select ideas to represent traveling over each terrain.
- Practice the movements and create pathways for each. The following are examples:
  - Travel in diagonal zigzags while climbing over rocks.
  - Travel in a square (4 squishy steps forward, twist and squish a quarter turn to the right, 4 squishy steps, another twist and squish a quarter turn to the right) all around the circumference of a big mud puddle.

- Create two movement phrases based on your students' experience of *being* terrains.

- Create movement phrases for the same terrains your students selected to travel over.

- If your class created a "traveling over big rocks" pattern, they'll need to create a "how it feels to be rocks" movement phrase.

- The movement phrase for rocks may be more of a tableau than full action, and that's fine. Their phrases for the other terrain they're traveling over (mud) will provide a contrast.

- Explore ideas and work together to create the "how the terrain feels" movement phrases.

- How can your class silently show they're being squished and that pieces of mud are being splashed afar and stuck on boots and carried away?

- Once all patterns and phrases have been created, put them in the following order:
  - Traveling pattern for first terrain
  - Movement phrase showing how the first terrain feels
  - Traveling pattern for second terrain
  - Movement phrases showing how the second terrain feels

- You can have the entire class do all the dance or divide the class into two groups and ask one group to do the traveling patterns and the other to perform the "how the terrain feels" phrases.

- Try an additional presentation variation and ask travelers and terrains to perform their dances side by side at the same time.

Discussion

"Did the 'how terrain feels' movement phrases communicate what you imagined rocks, mud, grass, and sand experienced in the visualization?"

Grades 4 Through 6 Variation

Instructions

Ask your students to work in groups of five or six and create a Traveler and Terrain dance using the following requirements:

- Select two contrasting terrains.

- Create a 16- to 20-beat traveling phrase for each terrain.

- The traveling phrases should highlight the different ways we travel over each terrain—for example, jump, run, and roll over the grass while playing Extreme Frisbee; sink, slip, and slide through sand.

- Create a 16- to 20-beat "how it feels" phrase for each terrain.

- These phrases are from the imagined perspective of the terrain; the grass may try to lean away as it tries to protect itself, while sand grains may be reaching out to each other as individual grains helplessly roll away from each other.

- Connect the phrases using the following order:
  - First traveling phrase, then the "how it feels" phrase for that terrain
  - Second traveling phrase, then the "how it feels" phrase or that terrain

Discussion

- "Did the 'how terrain feels' movement phrases communicate what you imagined rocks, mud, grass, and sand experienced in the visualization?"

- "Could the relationship between the 'traveling over' and 'how it felt' phrases symbolize human relationships?"

Journal Entry for All Grades

"Soil is alive. A single tablespoon of soil contains 50 billion cellular organisms, and these microscopic life forms nourish and enrich the earth. Plants require nutrient-rich soil to grow. Everything is connected. Write or draw a picture about what it would be like if you were one of those cellular beings living in the soil."

EXERCISE 5.3   ROCKS AND SAND

This exercise builds on the previous exercise, further exploring the three different types of rocks and the relationship between rocks and sand.

Lesson Plan Suggestions

Kindergarten Through Grade 3

First lesson: Teach steps 1, 2, 3, (grades 2 to 3 watch 4:12 video), and 4 (follow the grade-appropriate variation)

Grades 4 Through 6

First lesson: Teach steps 1, 2, 3, (watch 4:12 video), and 4 (follow the grade-appropriate variation)

Recommended Music: Tracks 12 and 9

Step 1: Taking a Closer Look at Rocks

Introduce the three rock groups. Rocks are divided into three general groupings: igneous, sedimentary, and metamorphic. For classes that haven't studied rocks, those words may sound intimidating, but most everyone will be familiar with what rocks look like.

1. "Sedimentary rocks have layers, like a sandwich. The layers contain a mix of sand, shells, smaller rocks, and other particles. These small pieces are called sediment, and as the layers of sediment accumulate, they solidify and harden into rock. But you'll still see bits of sediment in the layers. Sedimentary rocks are soft and can break apart. Fossils are most often found in sedimentary rock."

2. "Igneous rocks are formed when magma (molten rock from deep within the earth) cools inside the earth or when lava (magma that rises to the surface from volcanic eruptions) cools and solidifies. When lava cools quickly, the rock looks shiny (obsidian rock). Sometimes gas bubbles are trapped inside the lava, and that creates holes in the rock."

3. "The word *metamorphosis* means change. A metamorphic rock has experienced change. Metamorphic rocks created inside the earth have been pushed, heated, and squeezed by powerful Earth forces. When this occurs, you can see thin, ribbony layers that ripple through the rock. Marble is a metaphoric rock."

Step 2: Exploring Rocks

All Grades

Recommended Music

Track 12

Instructions

Sedimentary rock.   Invite your students to work in pairs and find a spot to work. Let them know that when the music is turned on, it's the signal to start, and turning it off signals them to freeze.

1. Sedimentary rocks are created over a long time. All the movement will be in slow motion.

2. When the music comes on, ask your students to work silently as they slowly create a horizontally layered shape with their partners. (See photo.) At no time should anyone put their weight or pressure on their partner.

3. Play music for 20 to 30 seconds, then stop the music.

4. Everyone should freeze.

5. Walk around the room to view all the horizontally layered shapes.

6. Repeat the process.

7. Ask everyone to create a second shape inspired by sedimentary rock.

8. Pause the music when it looks like everyone is in a new sedimentary shape.

9. Take a moment to view all the shapes.

10. Ask students to maintain their shapes but to imagine there is a strong force pushing upward from underneath at the center of their rock shapes.

11. Students should slowly allow the center section of their rock shapes to move upward.

12. Now ask them to imagine pressure from above on the shape's outer edges.

13. Slowly let the outer areas of the shape lower. The sedimentary rock has now transformed and become metamorphic.

14. Ask students to release their shapes and return to standing.

Sedimentary rock.

Igneous rocks   Working on your own.

1. "Step away from your partner to find a spot on your own."

2. Play track 12.

3. "Start by moving slowly as hot, thick magma." Students may travel slowly from their starting spots.

4. Prompt your class with images of being hot, thick honey or molasses. If your class is studying viscosity in science, encourage them to explore the concept through movement.

5. After 10 to 15 seconds, tell everyone to slowly form themselves into a rounded rock shape.

6. Pause the music.

7. Walk around to view the shapes, then repeat the process of being hot magma, forming into a rounded shape, and cooling one more time.

8. Pause the music when your class has created their second igneous rock shape.

9. Ask students to maintain their shape but to imagine a strong focus pushing from above at the center of their shape.

10. A small section of the shape will move slightly downward.

11. Now feel pressure against the right side.

12. Slowly let the rock shapes respond by pushing out through the left.

13. The igneous rock has transformed and become metamorphic.

Discussion

- "Could you feel yourself being reshaped according to the outside pressure?"

- "Did you try to resist?"

- "How did being pushed in one direction affect the parts of your body that weren't being pushed?"

Step 3: Taking a Closer Look at Sand

All Grades

Recommended Music

Track 9

Instructions

- Lead a brief discussion about sand.

- "Sand is made up of tiny particles of rocks that have been eroded by wind and water. Deserts weren't always deserts. Many inland deserts were once green and fertile agricultural land." (Remind them about learning about floodplains in chapter 4 and how some places, like the land around the Nile, were once fertile agricultural land.)

- "*Desertification* describes once-fertile lands that become arid. Desertification is happening right now in many places around the world. The Gobi Desert in China and Mongolia is increasing in size by more than 1,000 square miles (over 1,600 sq km) every year."

- Ask everyone to find a spot in the room and remind them to stay within their bubbles.

- Music: Track 9

  1. Your students can move throughout the room but shouldn't come within arm's-length of each other.

  2. Softly play the music as your lead them through this exploration.

  3. "Imagine the room is filled with dry desert sand."

  4. "Pick up a handful of sand and let it fall through your fingers."

  5. "Pick up another handful of sand and slowly pour it into your other hand."

6. "Slowly pour the sand back and forth between your hands."

7. "Some granules may stick to your palms, just like water droplets."

8. "Move your hand along the surface of the sand."

9. "Imagine how the surface changes as your hand moves across it."

10. "Slowly draw a design in the sand and watch how the granules respond."

11. "The grains of sand roll over each other smoothly."

12. "Unlike rock, sand appears to move effortlessly."

13. "Imagine being sand being moved by the wind."

14. "Feel yourself shift, roll and settle, shift, roll and settle."

15. "You can roll on the ground or work at mid and high levels, rolling your torso, shoulders, and hips."

• Let your class explore sand moving and settling for 1 to 2 minutes, then bring the exploration to a close.

Step 4: Create a Dance Inspired by the Rocks and Sand of the Sahara Desert

Grades 2 and up watch the How Many Grains of Sand Are in the Sahara? (4:12) video from the list of video links in HK*Propel*. This mathematically mind-boggling video answers the question of how many grains of sand are in the Sahara Desert and provides beautiful footage of rock and sand desert landscape to inspire your students' choreography.

Kindergarten Through Grade 3 Variation

Recommended Music

Track 9

Instructions

1. Your class explored rocks and sand in the previous exercise, so it should just take a moment to identify the contrasting dynamics between the two terrains.

2. Ask your students if they had a favorite rock shape in step 2 of this exercise.

3. "Can you create several large rock formations with 10 or more students using everyone's favorite rock shape?"

4. Ask your class what their favorite sand movements were and whether they can suggest ways to create a movement pattern of shifting sand dunes that are blown across the performance area.

5. Explore your students' suggestions and create a movement piece combining large, still rock formations and soft, shifting sand.

Sand dunes.

Grades 4 Through 6 Variation

Instructions

Ask your class to work in groups of seven or eight students to create pieces that highlight the contrasting dynamics between rock and sand. The choreography should meet the following criteria:

- It should contain rock formation(s) with a variety of levels and shapes.
- It should have sand dunes and shifting sand movement phrases.
- Keep in mind that when sand moves, we don't see the individual grains. Sand can appear like a thin veil or almost liquid. Movement phrases for sand can include body ripples, log rolls, and wave-like motions to convey connectivity between movers.
- No one should be frozen throughout the entire choreography.
- It should employ different tempos and pathways; the rocks erode slowly, while sand, when blown, moves quickly and can travel distances.
- Use either track 9 or 12 for the choreography. Track 12 is atmospheric. Keep the dance approximately 30 seconds (28 to 32 beats).

Invite each group to present.

Discussion

"Knowing that sand is eroded rock, did you sometimes feel as if the rock formations were wondering when they will also become sand?"

Journal Entry for All Grades

"Draw a picture or write a poem or paragraph examining the relationship between rocks and sand."

EXERCISE 5.4 TECTONIC PLATES

This exercise explores the push-pull force of tectonic plates. Like giant jigsaw pieces, the plates slowly shift and slide, separating Earth's original land mass into continents; forming mountain ranges and deep gorges; and causing catastrophic earthquakes, volcanoes, and tsunamis.

Lesson Plan Suggestions

Kindergarten Through Grade 3

First lesson: Teach steps 1, 2, 3, 4, and 5 (video: Tectonic Plates and Earthquakes, 2:06)

Second lesson: Warm up quickly with one or two variations from step 3 or 4, do step 6 (video: Backbone by Red Sky Performance, 1:12), and create the dance

Grades 4 Through 6

First lesson: Teach steps 1, 2, 3 (follow grade-appropriate variations), 4, and 5 (video: Tectonic Plates and Earthquakes, 2:06)

Second lesson: Warm up quickly with one or two variations from step 3 or 4, do step 6 (video: Backbone by Red Sky Performance, 1:12; follow the grade-appropriate variation), and create the dances

Third Lesson (optional): May be required if your class created long dances in step 6

Recommended Music: Track 19

Step 1: Push and Pull

For All Grades

Instructions

Use the walking-across-the-floor structure from exercise 5.2 to do the initial push-and-pull exploration.

1. Ask your class to create three or four horizontal lines, with six to eight students per line. One line is behind the other at one end of the room.

2. Instead of focusing on terrains as they did in exercise 5.2, invite your students to imagine that there's a large, heavy object (car, refrigerator, grand piano, boulder) that they must push all the way to the other side.

3. Each student will push their imagined object without using an imagined aid to assist them. They can push with their hands, back, sides, and feet. At no time should they let the object be damaged—it must get to the far side unscathed.

4. Put on the music and signal the first line to start.

5. When the first line has pushed their objects halfway across the room, signal the second line to start. When they've reached the halfway point, ask the next line to start.

6. When a line reaches the far end, students should quietly walk along the outsides of the room in single file to the starting point, without disturbing those who are still working.

7. When the last line has traveled across the room, ask the first line to repeat the journey, this time pulling a heavy object. The heavy object may be the same or different from the one they pushed. In the pulling action, they can include an imaginary manual aid such as a rope.

8. They must drag and pull the object across the room without it being damaged.

After everyone has completed the second task, let everyone rest.

Discussion

- "How did you feel while you were pushing and pulling the object?"
- "Could you feel the object you were pushing?"
- "Did you feel the rope or cord you were pulling with?"

Step 2: Tug-of-War

All Grades

Instructions

Divide your classroom through the center. Invite half your students to stand on one side and half on the other side.

1. Ask everyone to face the center of the room and make eye contact with someone standing on the far side so they have a partner to work with. Those teaching younger grades may want to assign partners and position them close to each other.

2. Without touching or speaking, your students will have a tug-of-war contest with their partners.

3. In many ways, this is harder than pulling an object across the room. Students have to constantly watch their partners and respond appropriately to their partner's actions.

Pull.

© Janice Pomer

4. Your students may travel forward and back as they pull, but no one should cross the center line.

5. If the room is too crowded for everyone to work at the same time, ask half the pairings to watch. After two minutes, the ones working should watch and the watchers should work.

Discussion

- "Even though there was no rope connecting you, could you feel the tension on the rope?"

- "Were you able to stay connected with your partner's movement at all times, or were there moments when you misread your partner's actions?"

Step 3: Push Foundation Movement Phrase

Recommended Music

Track 19

Instructions

When your students were pushing their objects, they may have used forward lunge positions as they traveled across the room. Take a moment to review on-the-spot lunges that shift from side to side.

1. Stand with the legs apart and the feet turned out slightly to the sides, in an A stance.
2. Bend the right knee and keep the left leg straight.
3. Straighten the right knee, returning to an A stance.
4. Bend the left knee and keep the right leg straight.
5. Repeat going from side to side
6. Now lunge from side to side without stopping midway at the A stance, 8 times.

Teach the following movement phrase to your class.

1. Stand with the legs apart in an A stance.
2. Slowly bend the right knee, turn the torso to the right, press both hands and arms to the right, and keep the left leg straight for 4 beats.
3. Slowly bend the left knee, turn the torso to the left, press both hands and arms to the left, and keep the right leg straight for 4 beats.
4. Step the right leg forward, slowly bend the right knee, press both hands and arms forward, and keep the left leg straight for 4 beats.
5. Step the left leg forward, slowly bend the left knee, press both hands and arms forward, and keep the right leg straight for 4 beats.
6. Step into the A stance, look up, push both hands and arms up to the ceiling for 4 beats.
7. Bend both knees, look down, lower the hands and arms, and press downward for 4 beats.
8. Step the right leg backward, slowly bend the right knee, press both hands and arms backward, and keep the left leg straight for 4 beats.

9. Step the left leg backward, slowly bend the left knee, press both hands and arms backward, and keep the right leg straight for 4 beats.

10. Repeat the sequence, starting to the left.

Once your class is confident performing the combination, try the phrase using the following variations:

Kindergarten through grade 1 teachers should read through the variations and select one or two ideas to share with their class.

Grades 2 Through 6 Variation 1

Redraw the imaginary center line in the room to divide the class into two groups.

- Group A is on the right, and group B is on the left.
- Both groups face the center of the room.
- Everyone starts lunging and reaching to the right.
- The groups will push to opposite sides of the room.
- One group's first push will be to the front of the room and the other to the back.
- Both groups' forward lunges will be toward the center of the room.
- Both groups' backward lunges will move away from the center of the room.

Tectonic plates.

© Janice Pomer

Grades 2 Through 6 Variation 2

- Follow the first variation, but ask group A to push backward and away from the center for actions 4 and 5 while group B pushes forward and toward center for those actions.
- Ask group B to push backward and away from center for actions 8 and 9 while group A pushes forward and toward center for those actions.

Grades 2 Through 6 Variation 3

Instead of working in groups, ask everyone to find a partner.

- Students should face their partners and stand arm's-length apart.
- Repeat variation 2.
- Tell students that at no time during the forward or back pushing should they touch their partners.

Grades 2 Through 6 Variation 4

Work in groups of three to five students to explore the following:

- Some movers do up and down pushes while others do side-to-side pushes.
- Some movers do forward and back pushes while others do side-to-side pushes.
- Explore other ways to make the simple lunge and push vocabulary interactive.

After 2 to 3 minutes, ask each group to show one of their interpretations of the new configurations.

Step 5: Tectonic Plates

All Grades

Instructions

Watch the Tectonic Plates and Earthquakes video (2:06) from the list of video links in HK*Propel*. The video provides a basic understanding of tectonic plates: what they are, how they move, and how those movements have sculpted the surface of the earth.

Discussion

In the previous step, your class explored the three examples of tectonic plate movement shown in the video.

- "Did you realize that the push and pull actions you performed in step 3 were inspired by the activity of tectonic plates?"
- "When working on your own, did any of the groups create a phrase that contained all the examples of tectonic plate activity shown in the video?"

Step 6: Mountain Creation Dance

All Grades

Instructions

Watch the Backbone by Red Sky Performance video (1:12) from the list of video links in HK*Propel*. This action-packed dance clip shows Earth forces powerfully pressing upward. The dance was inspired by the creation of the Rocky Mountains; you can feel the dancers straining to crack the earth's crust; then they break through, rise, and propel their movements upward. (So much action happens in this short clip that most classes want to watch it a second or third time.)

Discussion

Take a moment to reflect on the video. Identify the moments that resonated the most with students and discuss the importance of unison work in the choreography.

Kindergarten Through Grade 3 Variation

Instructions

- Explore the following movement ideas collaboratively with your class:
  - Tectonic plate actions from step 3
  - Slow, low, and mid-level upward pushing or pressing actions
  - An energized upward movement phrase (other than slow pushing or pressing)
  - Mid- to high-level mountain range formations using A stances and other shapes
- Grades 2 and 3 classes may wish to work in groups of four or five students, while younger grades can work together to create a dance that contains their favorite pushing and pressing elements.
- If your students are working in small groups, allow them time to create and practice. Then invite them to share their dances.
- Classes that have been working collaboratively should practice their dance several times, then divide into two groups and present the dance for each other.

Discussion

"Did any of the movements you performed make you feel like a mountain? If yes, which movement was it, and what does mountain energy feel like to you?"

Grades 4 Through 6 Variation

Instructions

- To conclude your post-video discussion, compile a list of words that describe the actions and movement qualities incorporated in the dance.
- Encourage your students to apply those actions and concepts in their own Mountain Creation choreography.
- Invite your students to work in groups of four to six students.
- Their dances should include the following elements:
  - Slow, low, and mid-level upward pushing and pressing actions (use isolations and full-body movements)
  - An energized upward movement phrase containing actions other than slow pushing or pressing
  - Mid- to high-level phrase as energy burst upward and ultimately creating a mountain range
  - Perform some of the phrases in unison.
  - Perform at least one phrase where forces collide.
- There's no time limit on the piece. Before you begin, survey the class to see if they're inspired to create something long or short. If they choose to work on a longer piece, let them know they'll be able to record their half-finished dances in their journals and continue to work and present them in the next class.
- After each group has presented their dances, sit together and discuss them.

Discussion

- Did all the groups incorporate different levels and speeds? If yes, identify the most effective use of level and speed changes in each piece.

- Was every group able to create phrases to convey the difference between below-the-surface and above-the-surface activity?

Journal Entry for All Grades

"Draw a picture or write a short poem or paragraph about the birth of a mountain. Are you the mountain or a witness?"

EXERCISE 5.5   VOLCANOES

In the previous exercise, your students created dances inspired by tectonic plate activity and the creation of mountain ranges. Volcanoes, another product of tectonic plate activity, are the focus of this exercise.

Lesson Plan Suggestions

Kindergarten Through Grade 3

First lesson: Teach steps 1 (including introductory video: Volcanoes 101, 4:58), 2, 3, and 4 (follow the grade-appropriate variation)

Grades 4 Through 6

First lesson: Teach steps 1 (including introductory video: Volcanoes 101, 4:58), 2, and 3 and rough out the assignment from step 4 (follow the grade-appropriate variation)

Second lesson (optional): Warm up quickly, return to groups, review the dances from step 4, do step 5 practice, and present the dances

Recommended Music: Tracks 12 and 19

Step 1: What We Know About Volcanoes

Ask your class what they know about volcanoes. Older classes will have studied volcanoes and younger grades should have a general idea about how volcanoes are formed, thanks to the video on tectonic plates seen in the previous exercise.

Tectonic plates are responsible for volcanic activity and the creation of volcanic islands. Magma works its way up to the surface and erupts in the form of lava. When volcanoes erupt, rocks and huge amounts of toxic ash explode into the air and cover the surface of the surrounding area. The toxic ash can be more deadly than the lava. In recent years, there has been violent, sometimes deadly, volcano activity in Iceland, Hawaii, and the Canary Islands, providing the world with stunning footage of these catastrophic events.

Volcanic activity also occurs on the ocean floor. Over time, the layers of lava build up on the ocean floor, layer upon layer, until a mountain of hardened lava rises above the sea's surface in the form of an island.

 Watch the video about volcanoes (4:58) from the list of video links in *HKPropel*. This powerful video features incredible footage of exploding magma and flowing lava to give your students a rare glimpse into what lies below the earth's mantle.

Step 2: Comparing Active and Dormant Volcanic States

- Compile a list of words to describe a volcano when it's active. The list will include violent, fiery, fuming, uncontrollable, powerful, destructive, explosive, smoldering, deadly, raging, and angry.
- Compile a list of words to describe a volcano when it's inactive or dormant. The list will include calm, resting, asleep, peaceful, still, patient, and waiting.

Step 3: Explore the Volcano's Duality

Instructions

1. Ask your students to spread throughout the room and stand in parallel position.

2. Play track 12 to support your students as they explore words on the inactive volcano list.

3. Call out a word and allow time for students to explore ways to convey concepts such as "patient" and "calm" through movement.

4. The idea isn't to just stand still in a mountain shape but to find movements that embody the concept of patience or peacefulness. They may use small isolations while the rest of their body is still, shift slowly from side to side, and create shapes that slowly expand and contract (as if inhaling and exhaling).

5. Call out prompts such as "Is peaceful different from resting or sleeping?" "How can you convey watchfulness?" "Are you looking for someone out in the world or looking inward?"

6. After two to three minutes of exploration, turn off the music and ask everyone to return to parallel position.

7. Use track 19 to support students' exploration of words used to describe an active volcano.

8. Many of the active volcano words are forceful and aggressive. While moving, your students must be attentive and make sure their actions don't interfere with others. Remind your class to stay in their personal bubbles while working.

9. Call out prompts such as "How would the magma move as it smolders within a confined space?" "When it erupts, do you use your whole body in a big jump or can it erupt through your hands, feet, or top of your head?" "How many different ways can you move as a river of burning lava?"

10. After two or three minutes of exploring active volcano words, lower the volume and use a few words from the inactive list to help your students cool down after all the fiery movement.

Discussion

- "Was it difficult to find different movements for some of the inactive volcano words such as 'asleep,' 'resting', and 'calm'? If you were successful at finding multiple movement ideas, explain your strategy." (Using different levels, shapes, and body isolations.)

- "Were you able to find movements to convey the idea of having something burning inside of you?"

- "Did any nonvolcanic images help you move as burning lava? If yes, what were they?" (Snakes, serpents and dragons, forest fires, burning coals.)

Step 4: Creating a Volcano-Inspired Dance

Kindergarten Through Grade 3 Variation

Instructions

Your class has explored a wide vocabulary of movements to work with to use in a volcano-inspired dance. This suggested structure requires little planning time and allows movers to use their own movement ideas and apply the push-pull explorations from the previous exercise.

Use this structure to perform a Volcano dance, or create a structure of your own with input from your class.

1. Start with your students scattered throughout the room.
2. Identify an area in the center of the room for students to direct their pushing and pressing actions.
3. Perform peaceful, calm on-the-spot movement for 8 to 12 beats.
4. Moderate pushing: Perform on-the-spot movements directed toward the center of the room for 8 to 12 beats.
5. Resting: Stay on-the-spot; this can be a freeze or calm action for 8 to 12 beats.
6. Stronger pushing: Movers travel a yard (a meter) toward the center with their pushing actions for 8 to 12 beats.
7. Resting on-the-spot: This can be a freeze or calm action for 8 to 12 beats.
8. Stronger pushing: Those at the center of the room can begin to push outward toward the movers that are pushing in toward them for 8 to12 beats.
9. Resting on-the-spot: This can be a freeze or calm action for 8 to 12 beats.
10. Strongest pushing: The force of arms, backs, and possibly feet pressing toward (but not touching) has those in the center feeling more compressed while the students on the outside lean inward and upward creating a / \ shape around the inner group of students for 8 to 12 beats.
11. Heating up: The inner students explore bubbling and boiling actions while the outer students start to tremble and shake on-the-spot for 16 beats.
12. Erupt: Inner students start jumping.
13. Outer students shake tremendously, then begin to melt 8 to 12 beats.
14. Lava flows: Everyone moves as ribbons of lava flowing throughout the classroom. Use level changes to show the terrain the lava flows over. Your students can use their own flowing actions or follow someone else's actions to create rivers of lava. Keep moving for 24 to 32 beats.
15. Cooling: Lava flow slows down, and some of the movers who formed the outer mountain shape may slowly move back into that shape. The others stay cooling on-the-spot for 12 to 16 beats.
16. Peace and rest: The mountain sleeps, and the lava has cooled. Hold in stillness for 4 to 8 beats.

Discussion

- "Did you use any of the pushing movements you created from the previous exercise in this dance, or did you create new pushing actions? If you created new actions, share them with the class."
- "If you were part of the inside group bubbling and boiling, was it a relief to finally erupt and move outward?"
- "If you were part of the outside group, how did you feel when you melted and became flowing lava?"

If time allows, divide the class into two groups and invite each group to perform while the other groups watch.

- As a viewer, did the dance convey the contrasting dynamics of active and inactive volcano?
- What was the most exciting section to watch? Explain why.

Journal Entry for Kindergarten Through Grade 3

"Draw a picture or write about the section of the Volcano dance that you most enjoyed. Was it feeling calm and majestic, erupting, or being part of a river of lava?"

Grades 4 Through 6

Instructions

Work in groups of four or five to create volcano-inspired dances containing the following requirements:

- An opening tableau that alludes to the outward shape of a volcano
- A slow, peaceful, calm movement phrase
- Slowly the calm movements start to rumble as forceful pressure builds up beneath the surface
- A series of strong quakes building to a single or series of eruptions
- A burning, raging movement phrase representing lava spreading outward
- Movements that calm down, cool, and slowly stop in a tableau that is similar but not the same as the opening tableau

© Janice Pomer

Earth energy.

There are no time limits to this movement assignment. If your class decides to create short dances, there should be enough time for them to create and present in one lesson. If your class decides to create long choreography, make sure they have time to record their work in their journals before the end of the first lesson.

Step 5: If a Second Lesson Is Required

Grades 4 Through 6 Only

Instructions

1. After doing a short warm-up, ask your students to go into their groups and review the dance notes in their journals.

2. Let them know they have 15 to 20 minutes to finalize and practice their dances.

3. Invite the groups to share their choreography with their classmates.

Discussion

- Did every group use a similar opening and closing tableaux? If there were some unique tableaux, ask those groups to explain why they decided on the shape.

- Did all the sections in the dances last the same amount of time? Were some much shorter or longer than the others? Ask groups that varied the lengths of their sections to explain why some were short and others long.

- Were there moments in the choreography when the dance could have been conveying human emotions? If yes, discuss when human behavior is similar to that of a volcano.

Journal Entry for Grades 4 Through 6

"Do people ever feel like volcanoes? Write a short paragraph depicting how a person might feel like a volcano: burning up inside and ready to erupt."

EXERCISE 5.6   MAPPING THE LAND

Several years ago, on my third visit to a classroom, I noticed that a large map made by students had been taped on the wall. The class had been studying Canada's provinces and territories and created their own topographic map of the country. After our warm-up, I asked the class to tell me about the map. It was connected with a study assignment; groups of students had been given a province or territory to learn about and then share with the class. Afterward, they created the map with each group responsible for the area they'd been studying. I asked the class if they thought we could use the map as foundation for dance creation.

The students said yes, and after collectively exploring movement ideas for mountains, forests, coastlines, and icebergs, the class divided into the following work groups: the Atlantic Provinces, Central Canada, the Prairie Provinces, the West Coast, and the Northern Territories. Before they began to work on their choreography, I asked them to consider the following:

- Ways in which the Rocky Mountains and the Laurentian Mountains are different
- Ways in which the Prairies and Arctic tundra are different
- Ways in which the Atlantic, Pacific, and Arctic coastlines are different
- Ways in which ocean waters and shorelines are different from the waters and shoreline of the Great Lakes
- Ways in which boreal forests and temperate forests are different

The students used those questions to plot movement ideas inspired by specific aspects of shorelines, mountains, forestation, and terrains that were unique to their province or territory. The class worked on this dance assignment for two lessons. They presented dances that were focused and thoughtful, and they were able to articulate the differences I'd asked them to consider. The Atlantic coastline was rocky, and the waters were very rough; the Pacific coastline was forested and less aggressive, and the Arctic shoreline was even calmer and featured broken ice flows. The pieces demonstrated the students' ability to articulate what they knew about the multifaceted topography of the country and translate the information into movement. The classroom teacher was impressed by her students' commitment to the movement assignment and how well the choreography communicated the landscape.

Invite your students to assist you in determining what area of land will inspire their culminating exercise for chapter 5. It could be a state, province, or country they've been studying, or it could be their own community.

Lesson Plan Suggestions

Kindergarten Through Grade 3

First lesson: Teach steps 1, 2, and 3, and start step 4 (follow the grade-appropriate variations)

Second lesson: Warm up by reviewing the movement ideas selected for step 4, and create the sections and the transition phrases

Grades 4 Through 6

First lesson: Teach steps 1 and 2, and start working on the step 3 assignment (follow the grade-appropriate variation)

Second lesson: Warm up quickly, return to groups, review the completed sections from step 3, create additional sections including traveling phrases, practice the dance, and present

Third lesson (optional): If extra time is needed

Recommended Music: Your choice

Play several pieces during the creation process and ask students which composition they want to use in their Topographic dance.

Step 1: Map Making

- In your Mapping the Land dances, students will use maps and their knowledge of a geographical area (state, province, county, country, or community) and bring it to life through dance.

- Familiarize your students with maps depicting surface features, including mountains, lowlands, forests, lakes, and waterways.

- Bring their attention to the legends at the bottom corner of the maps, where the symbols used on the map are listed and explained. The legend will also clarify the scale of the map. For example, an inch can equal 10, 50, 100, or 500 miles.

- Older students will have experience making and reading maps with legends. For younger students, take a moment to introduce them to some of the more common symbols.

Step 2: Warm-Up With Earth, Plants, and Water

All Grades

Recommended Music

Your choice

Instructions

1. Select warm-up exercises from chapters 2 and 4 to provide your class with a 10- to 15-minute refresher of plant and water movements.

2. Make sure the exercises have contrasting dynamics.

3. The suggested exercises are Trees (exercise 2.1), Tall Grasses (exercise 2.5), Water Words (exercise 4.1), or Waves (exercise 4.2).

Step 3: Choosing Locations

Kindergarten Through Grade 3 Variation

Use this exercise to reinforce your students' knowledge of their local community or to engage them in a state, province, or country they are studying.

1. Ask your class to identify natural landmarks in their town, city, or county (or state, province, or country they're studying).

2. Make a list of large or small landmarks or features, such as parks, hills and flat terrains, ponds, farmland, forests, and lakes.

3. Identify which movement exercises from the previous chapters could be used to help communicate those natural features.

4. Review those exercises to see if they can be adapted for your dance and explore additional ideas your students suggest.

Grades 4 Through 6 Variation

Instructions

- Discuss the following with your class:
- Indicate which state, province, country, or continent they'd like to dance.
- If choosing a country or continent, the class can be divided into small groups and create choreography inspired by different regions of the country.
- How can students use online or classroom maps to help plot their choreography?
- Once you've established whether students' dances will be inspired by the same location or if each group can work on a different locale, do the following:
  1. Divide your class into groups of five to seven or seven to nine.
  2. Familiarize them with the chapter introduction and the process used to help students highlight unique aspects of the geography.
- Each dance should highlight four topographical features (or more if you want the exercise to extend into a third lesson) and use levels, directions, tempo, texture, shape, spatial relationships, and energy to articulate different aspects of the topography.
  - Look for unique topographical elements to highlight.
  - Not all forests, fields, valleys, and shorelines are alike. Encourage students to think about what makes them unique.
  - Consider the distance between features and create traveling or transition phrases. These phrases can reflect the terrain that is being traversed from one area to the next (water, ice fields, desert, rock cliffs).
  - There's no time limit to the dance, but try to have most of the ideas roughed out by the end of the first lesson (unless you plan to let students continue for a third lesson).
- Allow students time to notate their work in their journals at the end of the first lesson.
- At the start of the second class, do a 5-minute warm-up. Then ask your students to review and practice their pieces and present them to each other.

Discussion

- Ask each group to explain what two features they enjoyed translating into dance the most and why.
- "What feature was the most challenging? Why?"
- "How did the transitional traveling phrases work? Were there any unique approaches to that aspect of the dance?"
- "Do you think these dances would be effective if they were performed outdoors in various locations? If yes, explain why, and as a class consider ways you might be able to perform and video your dances outdoors."

Step 4: Dancing Landmarks and Unique Features

Kindergarten Through Grade 3

Instructions

- Not all parks, farms, forests, and shorelines are alike. Try to identify each area's unique feature.
- List the natural features near your community.
  - "Is your community close to a shoreline; is it a river, lake, or ocean?"
  - "Is your community close to foothills or a mountain range?"
  - "Is your community close to a valley or prairie?"

Rolling foothills.

Mountains.

- There may be a number of parks in your community. Ask students to consider the following:
  - Are the parks all the same size?
  - Are there any features that differentiate one from the other? Perhaps one park has a pond and wetland area, another has extensive flower beds, and another has a hilly section that's great for tobogganing.
- There may be a number of farms in your community. Ask students to consider the following:

- Do all the farms grow the same crop? And what crops grow? (tall corn, bending wheat, low-lying melons, cucumbers, strawberries, or root vegetables)
- Do some of the farms have trees or hardwood vines? (fruit orchards, grape vines)
- Do some of the farms have grazing lands for livestock?

- Analyze the natural features your class has listed and explore movement ideas together.

    1. After exploring ideas, invite your students to share their favorite ones.
    2. Work together to finalize movement phrases for each natural landmarks.
    3. Teachers may wish to assign a landmark or unique element to individual groups.
    4. Determine a performance order for the different sections.
    5. Practice the sections individually, then create tableaux or short movement phrases to transition from one feature to the next.
    6. You can use the distance between features to determine the length of transition phrase. If you're dancing a park and there is a pond in a park, a tableau might be all you need to change from parkland to pond, but if the pond isn't close to the park, use a transition phrase to represent the distance and terrain that must be traveled.
    7. Combine all the movement sections in the order your class has selected.
    8. If possible, video the dance and add text to video that identifies the landmarks students are dancing.

Discussion

- "Did you learn things about the land, water, and vegetation in your community?" If yes, ask students to share those insights with the class.
- "Do you think you could perform and video this dance outdoors on the school grounds or perhaps in some of the locations featured in your dance? If yes, discuss what preparations need to be done?" (Field trip requests or permits may be needed if dancing in public spaces.)

Journal Entry for All Grades

"Draw a picture or write a short paragraph or poem inspired by the landscape you danced."

SUMMARY

This culminating exercise highlights your students' expanded abilities, their movement confidence and choreography skills, their ability to observe the world around them, and their ability to translate what they see and learn into dance. In this exercise, your students applied skills, ideas, and images explored in chapters 2, 4, and 5 to create dances inspired by the landscapes of the world.

April 22 is international Earth Day. The event started in 1970, and now billions of people around the globe participate. Can your class adapt one of their dances from this chapter or create a new Earth-inspired dance to celebrate Earth Day? Can drawings and writing from their journals be compiled into a bound or digital book? What can your class do to help inform the school community about the earth?

Go to HK*Propel* to find audio files, reproducible forms, and a list of video links corresponding to chapter exercises.

© Janice Pomer

CHAPTER 6

Sky

Was there a time when human beings did not study the sky, the sun's daily journey, the moon and stars at night, the ever-changing clouds, bolts of lightning, majestic rainbows, and dancing auroras? Nowadays, urban dwellers see fewer and fewer stars as city lights overpower night's natural starlight, and some cities with high levels of air pollution are unable to clearly see the sun. The exercises in this chapter invite your students to look up and rediscover the beauty of the world above us.

EXERCISE 6.1   CLOUDS

While organizing the exercises for this book, I had to decide whether the cloud exercise should be in chapter 4 with the water exercises or placed in chapter 6 with sky and space. Your students will have created some cloud-inspired shapes and movement phrases as part of their Water Cycle dance in exercise 4.5, but I felt that an in-depth cloud exercise was important and that placing it at the beginning of chapter 6 was the perfect way to refocus your students' gaze from the earth to the sky.

Lesson Plan Suggestions

Kindergarten Through Grade 3

First lesson: Teach steps 1, 2, 3, and 4 (follow the grade-appropriate variations)

Second lesson: Warm up with step 4, do step 5 (video: 20 Amazing Cloud Formations, 3:49), and do step 6 (follow the grade-appropriate variations)

Grades 4 Through 6

First lesson: Teach step 1, 2, 3, and 4 (follow the grade-appropriate variations)

Second lesson: Warm up with step 4, do step 5 (video: 20 Amazing Cloud Formations, 3:49), and do step 6 (follow the grade-appropriate variations)

Recommended Music: Track 6

Step 1: Cloud Watching

No matter how scientific one's knowledge of clouds is, their beauty and variety never cease to be a source of wonder. Compile a list of words your students associate with clouds. This word list can contain scientific terms (we'll be reviewing those in step 2) and descriptive words, including cotton puffs, pillows, feathery, magical, transforming, rolling, angry, concealing, foggy, ribbony, looming, majestic, and mysterious.

Step 2: Introduce or Review These Four Cloud Formations

Cirrus Clouds

Cirrus clouds appear high in the sky like wispy strands, ribbons, or streamers of clouds that have gently pulled, lengthened, and floated away from a larger formation. The Latin word *cirro* means "curly" or "fibrous."

Cumulus Clouds

Cumulus clouds are big, multilayered puffball clouds. These clouds regularly amaze sky gazers as they majestically transform in an endless array of billowing shapes. The Latin word *cumuo* means "heaped" or "piled."

Stratus Clouds

Stratus clouds are the lowest-lying clouds. They can appear like a blanket across the sky. Stratus clouds are thick with moisture and can accompany fog or mist. The Latin word *strato* means "layers" or "sheets."

Nimbus Clouds

Nimbus clouds are gray and bring rain or snow. Nimbus clouds can be divided into two main subsets: cumulonimbus, which are huge, voluminous rain clouds, and nimbostratus, which is a thick blanket of rain. In Latin, the word *nimbus* means "precipitation."

Step 3: Exploring the Four Cloud Forms Through Movement

Recommended Music

Track 6

Instructions

Older students are welcome to apply their knowledge of cloud subsets to their movement work, but the four types of clouds listed above contain all the information your students will need for the exercise.

Invite your class to spread through the room and stand in parallel position.

1. Let your class know that for this exercise, you'll be playing slow, atmospheric music and that you'd like everyone to work slowly, even when exploring movement ideas for storm clouds.

2. Working slowly will allow students to move safely through the room during the exploration. That doesn't mean everyone has to travel from their spot, but they have the option to do so.

3. Play the music.

4. Call out, "Cirrus clouds." These clouds appear like ribbons high up in the sky.

5. Suggest everyone start by moving their fingers, hands, and arms overhead. Call out prompts, such as: "Are your ribbony clouds hovering or are they rippling through the sky?" "Can you extend your torso to become part of the ribbon?" "How can you make your body even longer, more ribbon-like?" "Can you balance on one foot to create a long ribbon by extending your lifted leg and reaching with your arms?"

6. Allow 1 to 2 minutes for students to explore cirrus clouds.

7. Call out, "Cumulus clouds." These are the huge, puffy clouds that transform into magical shapes.

8. The previous clouds were long and thin. Suggest that students start this exploration by going into a wide stance and puff themselves up.

9. Cumulus clouds are like cotton candy or puffballs.

10. Once everyone's puffed up, suggest that a very gentle breeze is moving them through the room as they ever so slowly shift from shape to shape.

11. Allow 1 to 2 minutes for students to explore cumulus clouds.

12. Call out, "Stratus clouds." These are the thick clouds that cover the sky like a blanket.

13. From the puffed, rounded shapes of cumulus clouds, students will need to rearrange themselves. Suggest that they imagine they're wearing huge capes or veils.

14. Can they slowly cover the sky with their capes? Or draw a curtain across the sky?

15. Stratus clouds are heavy with moisture. They don't float as high as cirrus and cumulus clouds. Try taking wider and heavier steps.

16. Allow 1 to 2 minutes for students to explore stratus clouds.

17. Call out, "Nimbus clouds." These are the storm clouds filled with rain or snow.

18. Nimbus clouds can appear as huge, round cumulus clouds or thick, heavy stratus clouds, but regardless of the shape, nimbus clouds are active with precipitation.

19. These clouds can rumble and shake.

20. Allow 1 to 2 minutes for students to explore nimbus clouds.

Afterward, invite everyone to rest and reflect on the exploration.

Discussion

- "Which type of cloud did you enjoy exploring most? Explain why."
- "Which type of cloud did you find most difficult to interpret through movement? Explain why."

Step 4: Creating Group Clouds

Recommended Music

Track 6

Kindergarten Through Grade 3 Variation

Instructions

Practice mirroring. Younger grades will benefit by reviewing the simple mirroring rules introduced in exercise 4.3, step 4.

1. Ask your class to stand in parallel position, facing front.
2. You can start by being the leader, then later invite students to lead.
3. Play track 6.
4. Let your class know that you will be using the cloud movements explored in step 3.
5. All your movements will be slow and smooth.
6. Ask everyone to follow your actions and perform them with the same slow and sustained qualities.
7. After you've led for 30 to 45 seconds, invite a student volunteer to lead for 20 to 30 seconds.
8. Remind the new leader that the movements they share with the class should be inspired by the different cloud types.
9. After 20 to 30 seconds, invite another volunteer to lead, and continue the process with three or four more student leaders.

Practice mirroring in pairs using cloud-inspired movements.

10. Partners start by standing in parallel position facing each other about 3 feet (1 m) apart.
11. Partners should decide who will be the first to lead.
12. Let your class know that you'll be asking them to change leaders several times during the exercise.

13. When they hear the instruction "Change leader," partners should freeze in their cloud shapes for a moment and then begin to move from that shape with the new leader in charge.

14. Imagine that for a moment the cloud is still, and then a new air current starts it moving again.

15. Start the exercise by inviting the first leaders to slowly move while their partners follow.

16. After 20 seconds, ask them to change leaders.

Mirroring cloud shapes.

17. Remember to call out prompts to remind students to use all the ideas the explored in step 3.

18. After several minutes of mirroring, invite half the pairs keep working while the other half watches. After a minute or two, invite the groups to switch places so that everyone gets to watch and present.

Discussion

- "What was challenging about the exercise? Following the leader? Remembering the different types of clouds? Moving slowly?"

- Students often comment that cumulus clouds are the easiest to make because cumulus clouds can look like almost anything.

Grades 4 Through 6 Variation

Instructions

Instead of working in partners or small groups, the entire class will be working together, following one leader at a time. Over the course of the exercise, the leader will change. Those who are following may need to shift slightly to follow but shouldn't move away from the spot they're working on.

1. Start off by reviewing basic mirroring skills.

2. Ask your class to stand in parallel position, facing front.

3. You can lead or invite a volunteer to take the lead.

4. The leader will use movements that are slow and cloudlike.

5. Everyone will follow the leader's actions and perform them using a slow and sustained quality.

6. Besides trying to create a massive cloud, one of the other objectives of this exercise is to create the illusion that everyone is working in unison—no one is leading, and no one is following.

7. There should be no sudden movements. Everyone's actions should flow smoothly together.

8. Leaders should use actions that the rest of the class can follow.

9. Let your class know that over the course of the exercise, different people will become the leader, and the leaders will be in different areas of the room.

10. You or the volunteer can begin to move slowly, using cloud vocabulary for approximately 30 seconds.

11. Before the leader has come to a stop, invite a student near the back to become the leader.

12. Instruct the class to stay on their spots and use the first leader's last movement to slowly turn to face the back of the room.

13. If any student has difficulty seeing the new leader, they can simply follow a student who can see the leader.

14. After 30 to 40 seconds, invite the leader to very slowly turn to the right.

15. Remind the rest of the class that as the leader turns, they should, too.

16. As the class slowly rotates to the right, call out the name of a student in the far right of the room and let the class know that that person will be their new leader.

17. There's no need for the new leader to face the class. All the new leader needs to do to slowly present new cloud-inspired movements.

18. Quietly call prompts if leaders seem to be repeating themselves. "Are you using all the levels available?" "Cumulus clouds take on thousands of forms. They can look like giant real and mythical animals in the sky."

19. After 30 to 40 seconds, ask everyone to slowly face inward, into the center of the room. Some students won't need to rotate, but others will.

20. Identify a student in the center of the group to be the new leader.

21. Some students will watch the leader's movements from behind and others from the front. It doesn't matter. If any student has difficulty seeing the leader, all they need to do is follow someone who can see the leader.

22. After 30 to 40 seconds, identify another student in the center of the room.

23. Everyone will be able to see the leader without moving.

24. After 30 to 40 seconds, invite everyone to return to parallel position and sit down for a brief discussion.

Discussion

- Students were mirroring while facing the leader's front and back and working from random directions. "Was that challenging? If so, why?"

- Was everyone able to maintain the slow and smooth movement qualities throughout the exercise? "List words or images to describe the way you were moving." (Pouring thick honey or molasses; being weightless or floating in outer space.)

Grades 4 to 6 Variation

Instructions

Invite half your class to repeat the exercise while the other half watches.

1. Ask for a volunteer from the first group to start as the leader.

2. Invite the leader to stand in the front, back, side, or center of the group.

3. Put on the music and let the group begin.

4. Every 20 to 30 seconds, announce a new leader.

5. If at any time leaders are having difficulty creating shapes, gently offer some prompts.

6. The leaders should be from different locations within the group so students may have to carefully reorient themselves in order to follow.

7. After four or five people have led, invite the presenting group to sit down and the viewers to present.

8. Repeat the process with the second group presenting.

Discussion

Did the presenting groups have moments when everyone was moving in unison? If yes, did that convey any images or feelings? Was there a sense of calm, lightness, or peace?

Step 5: Slideshow of Incredible Clouds

All Grades

Instructions

Watch the 20 Amazing Cloud Formations (3:49) video, a slideshow containing photographs of amazing cloud formations, from the list of video links in HK*Propel*. How long you spend viewing the slideshow is up to you.

1. Watch the slideshow once in its entirety.

2. Students will want to talk about the photos while the slideshow is in progress. Let them know they'll be seeing the slideshow a second time and that they'll be able to share their ideas during the second viewing.

3. Before you watch the slideshow for second time, turn the sound off.

4. When the first image comes up, freeze the slideshow.

5. Ask your class to think about a title for the photo.

6. The titles can be scientific, descriptive, or poetic.

7. Remind your class that there are 20 distinctly different photographic cloud images.

8. Here's a small sampling of title suggestions from grades 1 through 6: Mirrored Mountain, Heaven's Boot, Blazing Popcorn, Dawn of the Beginning, and Screaming Sky.

9. Divide your class into two groups. Those sitting on the right side of the room are group A, and those to the left are group B.

10. Pick five or six students from group A to make title suggestions for the first photograph and five or six students from group B to suggest titles for the second photograph. Keep alternating throughout the slideshow.

11. Kindergarten through grade 3 teachers should record student suggestions.

Discussion

"Did the pictures give you new ideas for cloud formations? If it did, that's great. You'll need them for step 6."

Step 6: Create New Cloud Formations

Kindergarten to Grade 3 Variation

1. Read out the titles your students suggested

2. Pick one of the titles and ask your class if they can create a group cloud shape based on the title. If they say yes, put a star beside it on the flip chart.

3. Pick out a contrasting title and again consult with your class. Do they think they can create a group cloud shape based on that title? If they say yes, place a star beside it on the flip chart. If they say no, suggest another title.

4. Work collaboratively to create the first cloud shape. Identify two qualities you want to highlight (a specific shape, emotion, spatial relationship).

5. Work collaboratively to create the second, contrasting cloud shape.

6. Highlight the differences between the two clouds to make sure the shapes are at different levels and spatial relationships; perhaps one cloud shape has everyone stretched out long and the other close and clumped together.

7. Play track 6 and slowly ask your class to move into shape one.

8. Hold the position for 6 to 8 seconds, then move slowly into shape two.

9. Hold the second shape for 6 to 8 seconds, then rest.

10. Create two more contrasting cloud shapes using the same process.

11. Create a faster, storm-like movement transition between the two shapes.

12. Play the music and perform the two new cloud shapes using a fast movement transition.

13. Ask half the class to perform the first two shapes (with the slow transition movements) and the other half to perform the second two shapes (with the stormy transition movements).

Ask your class if they have other ideas for cloud shapes. Invite them to work in smaller groups and create their own cloud shapes to share with each other.

Grades 4 to 6 Variation

Invite your students to work in groups of four or five to create three still cloud shapes using the following structure:

- Shapes can reflect scientific knowledge of clouds or be purely imaginative.

- Use different levels, shapes, and spatial relationships to make each cloud unique.

- After creating and practicing the three cloud shapes, choreograph three different ways of moving from one cloud formation to another.

- To make each transition unique, think about the direction of the wind (up, down, side to side, swirling), the amount of moisture in the cloud (is it heavy or light?), and whether it's high or low.

- One of the transitions can be stormy and move quickly. Otherwise, the movements from one cloud to another should be slow and sustained.

- Each group should decide on a starting position that is not one of their cloud formations. It can be off or on stage.

- To prepare for presentation, practice moving from the starting position into the first cloud shape. Hold the shape for 6 to 8 seconds, transition into the second cloud shape, hold it, transition into the third shape, and hold the final shape to finish.

- Finally, create titles for each cloud shape. The titles should be spoken (by individuals or the group) when the group is frozen in each cloud shape.

- Practice moving into the cloud shapes, holding, speaking, and moving.

Allow 10 minutes for your class to complete the entire assignment, then invite groups to present one at a time.

Discussion for All Grades

- "Did watching the slide show help you create a greater variety of cloud shapes? If yes, describe one cloud shape that inspired you."

- Did any group create distinctly unique choreography between shapes? If yes, identify them and ask the group to explain their creation process.

Journal Entry All Grades

"Draw a picture or write a descriptive poem or paragraph about what it might feel like to be either a majestic cumulus cloud or a storming nimbostratus."

EXERCISE 6.2   THUNDER AND LIGHTNING

Lightning storms can be magnificent and terrifying. When I watch them from the safety of my home, I'm awestruck by their power and majesty, but being caught outdoors during a violent lightning storm is frightening. No wonder thunder and lightning has been associated with the powerful sky dwellers and ancient gods.

Lesson Plan Suggestions

Kindergarten Through Grade 3

First lesson: Teach steps 1, 2, 3, and 4 (video: Jumps, 0:56)

Second lesson: Warm up by reviewing step 2 and 3, introduce step 5, and finish with step 6 (follow the grade-appropriate variations)

Grades 4 Through 6

First lesson: Teach steps 1, 2, 3, 4 (video: Jumps, 0:56)

Second lesson: Warm up by reviewing step 2 and 3, introduce step 5, and finish with step 6 (follow the grade-appropriate variations)

Recommended Music: Track 14

Step 1: Warm Up With Storm Clouds

Warm up with this structured improvisation

1. Ask your class to find a spot in the room arm's-length apart from other students.
2. Invite your students to apply their cloud vocabulary from the previous exercise to conjure up the gathering storm.

© Barry Prophet

Lightning.

3. Let them know that when you call out, "Lightning!" they should freeze in angular position inspired by lightning.

4. They should hold the shape until you call out, "Storm clouds!" Then they can move throughout the room as gathering storm clouds.

5. Change the duration between storm clouds and lightning as the warm-up evolves.

6. Encourage students to find a wide range of angular shapes: balance on one foot, change the shape of the lifted leg, try alternating between symmetrical and asymmetrical arms, tilt the torso in different directions, and find ways to incorporate the head.

Step 2: Lightning Jumps

Recommended Music

Track 14

Instructions

Apply the lightning shapes from the warm-up to on-the-spot jumps and traveling leaps.

Review landing jumps safely:

1. Wake up the feet. Ask everyone to stand in parallel position, then lift their heels off the floor for 2 beats and lower the heels while keeping the legs straight for 2 beats. Repeat 4 times.

2. Repeat 4 more times, but bend the knees as the heels lower.

3. Make sure the torso remains upright to develop awareness of back alignment and abdominal muscle engagement.

4. Now review the importance of landing jumps quietly through the toes, balls of the feet, and heels.

5. For the jumps, divide the class in half. Everyone on the right side of the room is group A and everyone on the left side group B.

6. Group A will do a jump in parallel position, then group B will do a jump in parallel position.

7. Let the groups alternate 3 or 4 times.

8. Encourage groups to land as quietly as they can while jumping as high as they can.

9. After group B finishes their fourth jump, take a moment to rest.

10. Resume jumping, but now ask students to create angular lightning shapes while they're in the air. Ask everyone to try to use some of the lightning shapes they created in the warm-up in their jumps. Use the same structure of group A doing their first lightning jump, then Group B doing their first lightning jump.

11. After group B finishes their fourth lightning jump, sit down and discuss.

Discussion

- "Were you able to apply the angular shapes from the warm-up to your jumps?"

- If several students had trouble creating angular shapes in the air, brainstorm strategies with you class. Perhaps their lightning shapes were too complex. Can they simplify them?

- Try lightning jumps again.
- Survey the class to see if they were more successful performing lightning jumps after brainstorming strategies.
- Now transition your jumping skills into leaps.

Step 3: Lightning Leaps

> Note to kindergarten through grade 1 teachers: Leaping from one leg onto the other can be very challenging for younger children. Putting something small, soft, and low on the floor for your students to first step over and then leap over can be helpful.

All Grades Variation 1

In these leaps, your students will travel like an arrow: taking off on one leg upward, forward, and then gently down, landing on the other leg. To get your class leaping, invite your class to practice the following simple traveling pattern:

1. Step forward with the right foot, then the left foot. Then take a giant step forward with the right leg. You can imagine there's a big puddle that you have to step over and you don't want to get your shoes wet.
2. Step forward with the left foot, then the right foot. Then take a giant step forward with the left leg.
3. Practice this alternating pattern for a minute.
4. Once everyone is comfortable with the "step, step, giant step" pattern, ask your students to turn the giant step into a leap and the small steps can become gentle running steps.
5. The leaping leg should be stretched forward in the air as it stretches over the puddle.
6. Ask your class to practice the leap phrase for 1 minute. Remind them to land safely and quietly.

All Grades Variation 2

Younger students can run, run, big jump if they're unable to leap. To perform big leaps safely, you'll need to create as much open space in the center of the room as you can.

Instructions

1. Ask group A to move along the right side of the room and group B to move to the left.
2. Ask for a volunteer from each group to stand in their upstage (farthest) corner.
3. Ask for two more volunteers (one from each group) to stand behind the first person in their group.
4. The other members of each group can line up one behind the other along their side of the room.
5. Ask the volunteers to imagine that there is a large puddle in the center area that they have to leap over.
6. The traveling pattern is run, run, leap.
7. They'll have two runs before the leap and then run to the far corner.

8. The first student in group A will run, run, leap diagonally from their starting position (upstage right) to the front corner at the opposite side of the room (downstage left).

9. Then the first student in group B will run, run, leap diagonally from upstage left to downstage right.

10. The second student from group A travels using run, run, leap diagonally from upstage right to downstage left.

11. And the second student from group B will run, run, leap diagonally from upstage left to downstage right.

12. After the four volunteers have demonstrated, check to see if your class has any questions about the run, run, leap pattern or the performance structure.

13. Remind those who are waiting to keep close to the edge of the room.

14. After everyone has had a turn, stop for a moment, clarify any concerns your students may have, and repeat the leap pattern a second time to develop everyone's confidence.

 Watch the Jumps video (0:54) of ballet dancer Jorge Barani from the list of video links in HK*Propel*. You'll see jaw-dropping balletic leaps that reach astonishing heights.

Now Try Lightning Leaps

1. Ask your class to return to their two groups at either side of the room.

2. Let everyone know there will be three rotations through the order to explore lightning leaps.

3. Each time they leap, they should try a different lightning leap idea.

4. Offer the following suggestion or invite students to work with their own ideas:

   1. The first time across the floor, try adding lightning arms to the leaps.

   2. The second time across the floor, try adding lightning legs to create a more complex leap position.

   3. The third time across the floor, try leaping with lightning arms and legs.

Discussion

- "Did you enjoy leaping? If yes, explain why. Was it exhilarating to leap like lightning?"

- "Were you able to incorporate lightning arms and legs to your leaps? If not, what happened when you tried?" Brainstorm ideas to help students who had problems.

- Were some students able to incorporate lightning arms and legs in a single leap? If yes, ask those students to demonstrate their leaps.

Step 4: Storm Soundscape

Clouds build, then thunder and lightning shake the earth and sky.

1. Brainstorm ideas for creating a storm soundtrack using body percussion (you may wish to review ideas from exercise 1.3 in chapter 1).

2. Plot the soundscape by identifying the different stages of a storm.

3. Assign one or two specific sounds to each stage.

You can use this structure of a storm building and decreasing, or your class may have other suggestions:

- Distant rumblings and clouds building: create low rumbling
- Thunder and lightning: clapping hands and stomping feet
- Rainfall and wind: use fast, rhythmic feet; wind wooshes
- Thunder and lightning: return to clapping hands and stomping feet
- Distant rumblings and clouds dispersing: rumbling grows softer and fades

Instructions

1. Divide your class into three groups.
    1. Review conducting signals for start, increase volume, decrease volume, and stop.
    2. Create three new signals: one for rumbling and clouds building and decreasing, one for thunder and lightning, and one for rain and wind.
3. Lead your class through the rise and fall of a storm 3 times.
    - The first time, do the following:
        - Signal group one to do both distant rumblings and clouds building and dispersing.
        - Group 2 should do both thunder and lightning: clapping hands and stomping feet.
        - Group 3 should do rainfall and wind.
    - The second time, do the following:
        - Signal group 2 to do both distant rumblings and clouds building and dispersing.
        - Group 3 should do both thunder and lightning: clapping hands and stomping feet.
        - Group 1 should do rainfall and wind.
    - The third time, do the following:
        - Signal group three to do both distant rumblings and clouds building and dispersing.
        - Group 1 should do both thunder and lightning: clapping hands and stomping feet.
        - Group 2 should do rainfall and wind.
4. Each improvisation will be 20 to 30 seconds long.
5. After the third storm soundscape, take a moment to discuss.

Discussion

- "Were some sounds more successful at depicting the feeling of a storm? Identify the ones that were most effective."
- "Does anyone have other sonic ideas to try?" If yes, explore those sounds.
- "When you were making the windy sounds, were you able to keep your body still, or were you moving?"

Step 5: Dances With Lightning

Create dances with original soundscapes.

Kindergarten Through Grade 3 Variation

Instructions

1. Compile a list of movement elements to use in the dance, including cloud gathering, lightning jumps and leaps, and rain footwork.
2. Collectively review each of those movements.
3. Divide your class into 2 groups.
4. Group A will create the soundscape while group B dances.
5. Group B creates the soundscape while group A dances.
6. Use the same structure that was used in step 4.
7. Conduct the group creating the soundscape so they extend each section long enough for 30- to 45-second movements.
8. The soundscape and the dance should build slowly, come to a crescendo, and then recede.
9. Dancers must listen to and follow the soundscape. When the sounds fade away, dancers should freeze.

Discussion

- "What was your favorite part of the Lightning dance?"
- "When you were creating the soundscape, did you feel that you were in control of the storm?"

Grades 4 Through 6 Variation

Instructions

- Ask your students to work in groups of six or seven to create dances and soundscapes to communicate a storm building and receding.
- The dances should contain the following requirements:
  - Cloud gathering
  - Thunder shakes
  - Lightning leaps and jumps
  - Storm receding
  - Sound to accompany at least two of those movement elements
- Not everyone needs to be doing the same thing at the same time.
- There's no beat limit to the dance.
- While students are working, you can play track 14 softly as a sonic foundation for the dance.
- Allow enough time for the groups to create and practice their dances before sharing.

Discussion

- "Did having to follow the structure of gather, full storm, and then recede make choreographic decisions easy, or did you find it limiting?"

- Ask each group to explain which movements they chose to generate sound for and why they selected them.

Journal Entry for All Grades

"Draw a picture or write a short paragraph describing how it might feel to be in the center of a storm cloud while it rages around you."

EXERCISE 6.3   PAINTING THE SKY

In chapter 1, step 3 of exercise 1.4, your students explored ways to paint the air with movement. This exercise explores some of the ways nature paints the sky: the sunrises, sunsets, rainbows, sun and lunar halos, sundogs, and auroras.

Sunrises and sunsets happen daily, while rainbows occur depending on the level of moisture in the air and are seen after rainfalls or near waterfalls. Sun halos (a rainbow around the sun) are common, while lunar halos (a rainbow around the moon) happen close to or during the full moon. Sundogs, a winter occurrence, look like crystals or prisms in the daytime sky (the scientific term is *parhelia*). Another magical sky event for those living in the far north, or far south in the southern hemisphere, are the auroras (borealis in the north, australis in the south) that pulse and sway across the night sky.

Lesson Plan Suggestions

Kindergarten Through Grade 3

First lesson: Teach steps 1, 2, 3, and 4 (video: Sundogs, 1:02)

Second lesson: Warm up with a quick review of step 2, step 5, (video: Time Lapse of Alaska's Northern Lights, 2:55), and step 6 (follow the grade-appropriate variations)

Grades 4 Through 6

First lesson: Teach steps 1, 2, 3, and 4 (video: Sundogs, 1:02)

Second lesson: Warm up with a quick review of step 2, step 5 (video: Time Lapse of Alaska's Northern Lights, 2:55), and step 6 (follow the grade-appropriate variations)

Third lesson (optional): If groups have created long pieces for step 6, a third class may be needed for them to practice and present their dances

Recommended Music: Tracks 6 and 13

Step 1: Events That Paint the Sky With Color

- What "paint the sky events" are your students familiar with?
- Create a list for each event: one for sunrise and sunset, one for rainbows, one for auroras, and one for sundogs and sun and moon halos (if your students aren't familiar with auroras, sundogs, and halos, wait until steps 4 and 5—the video links will provide a formal introduction).
- "What words could be used to describe sunrise and sunset?"
- Compile a list of words, including rise, awaken, emerge, spread, glow, reach, blush, bleed, melt, fall, descend, fade, rest, and sleep.

Step 2: Sunrise and Sunset

Start with this simple spine stretch. Perform it slowly to atmospheric music. The stretch is inspired by the sun's rise and descent and how the sky slowly changes color.

Recommended Music

Track 6

For All Grades

Instructions

Start standing in parallel position.

1. Start low, knees bent, head down, and hands touching the floor.
2. Roll up through the spine, straightening the knees.
3. Look up and stretch the arms up, reaching the fingers to the ceiling.
4. Open the arms wide and let the torso expand, arching gently through the upper torso.
5. Bring the arms down to the side.
6. Lower the head, bend the knees gently, roll down through the spine, and touch the floor.
7. Repeat a second time.

Take a moment to discuss the stretch.

- "Did the stretching phrase communicate the idea of rise and descend?"
- "Can you think of other movements to add to the stretch to increase the notion of sunrise and sunset?"

Invite your class to do an on-the-spot exploration of other movements inspired by sunrise and sunset. Call out prompts: "What are you emerging from?" "What do you see?" "How do you feel when you're rising up? Do you feel strong and powerful? How do you feel when you're moving downward? Are you tired and sad?"

Working in Groups—All Grades

1. Divide the class by asking groups of four or five students sitting near each other to rise and descend together.
2. Each student will improvise their own sunrise and sunset pattern. See if everyone in the group can finish at approximately the same time.
3. Assign each group of four or five students a number.
4. Ask everyone to find a starting position.
5. When you call out group 1, everyone in that group will begin to slowly rise then descend and freeze in their final position.
6. Call out the remaining groups one by one.
7. When the last group has finished, repeat the sequence a second time but call the group numbers out of sequence: 2, 5, 3, 1, 4.
8. Ask half the students in each group to sit where they are and watch while the others rise and set around them. Repeat so that everyone can watch.

Discussion for All Grades

- "Did having the sunrise and sunset patterns occur one after another give a sense of something happening day after day?"
- "How did you feel while watching the sunrise and sunset patterns around you?"

Painting the sky.

Step 3: What We Know About Rainbows

- Find out what your students know about rainbows, such as their shape and colors, when they appear, and how they occur.

- Ask everyone to spread out and work on-the-spot. Create two (for younger grades) to four (for older grades) rainbow-inspired shapes. Let everyone know that only half the shapes should be full-bodied. The other(s) should be an isolation.

> Safety note: The first shape your students may want to do is a back arch as performed in gymnastics. These arches are normally performed on mats and can be a safety risk when performed in a classroom setting. Instead of back arches, the forward downward dog (as seen in the photograph) is a good alternative.

- After 1 to 2 minutes, ask your students to show you their rainbow shapes.

- Call out, "Shape number 1," and everyone will freeze in their first shape.

- Call out, "Shape number 2" and continue through the remaining shapes.

- Ask your students to work in twos and create a single rainbow with their partner. This should take no more than 1 minute.

- Can several of the two-person rainbows be combined to create a multilayered rainbow?

Rainbow using forward arch.

Step 4: Shapes Inspired by Sundogs

1. Watch the Sundogs video (1:01) from the list of video links in HK*Propel*. If you've never seen sun halos or sundogs, watch this video of the dazzling winter phenomenon. Instead of being arcs or circles, sundogs are individual bursts of color that appear to hang in the sky. Sundogs remind me of crystals in a chandelier, but instead of the chandelier hanging in someone's home, it's outdoors. Sunlight refracts into geometrical rainbow-colored shapes across the sky.

2. Take a moment to explore how geometric shapes work in the following situations:
   - Performing at high levels
   - Standing on one foot (appear to be balancing in the air)
   - Radiating outward like glowing light

3. Allow 1 minute for individual exploration of sundog-inspired shapes.
   1. Ask half your class to stand in the performance area and invite the other half to watch.
   2. Sundogs can pop up at different places across the sky. They'll stay vibrant for different lengths of time before fading out.
   3. With that in mind, ask your students to go into their first shapes. They can stay in that shape for 2 to 5 seconds (their choice), then they should return to parallel position.
   4. Each performer should do three different shapes, appearing and fading at their own time.
   5. After the first group has presented, invite the second group to present.

Step 5: What We Know About the Auroras

Watch the Time Lapse of Alaska's Northern Lights (2:55) video from the list of video links in HK*Propel*. Have you ever seen the evening sky come alive with the aurora borealis (or aurora australis in the southern hemisphere)? If not, this video will give you an idea of how the auroras can transform a cold, dark night into a magical world.

Take a moment to discuss the video. If your students have lots of questions about the science behind the auroras, play the second video on auroras, The Science and Beauty of the Auroras (4:53). The science behind the phenomenon is fascinating but not essential for this exercise.

Exploring Aurora Movement Patterns
Music: Track 13

1. Compile a list of words with your class to describe the aurora. Every display is different, but there are several features that are common to all: pulse, ripple, wavey, undulate, glow, burn, blaze, sizzle, and expand and contract (vertically and horizontally).

2. Look back at some of the wave explorations from chapter 4, exercise 4.2. Ask your class if any of those explorations could be applied to the movement patterns of auroras.

3. If yes, can they think of anything in the exercise they should modify to help emphasize the uniqueness of the auroras?

4. If your class doesn't think any of the exercises can be adapted, can they suggest

Aurora.

another way to explore auroras?

5. Spend a few minutes exploring the rippling, pulsing actions of auroras using either the wave exercises or student-suggested explorations.

Step 6: Creating Your Own Painted Sky Dance

Combine all the movement patterns explored in this exercise to create original dances.

Kindergarten Through Grade 3 Variation

Work together with your class to create a dance that contains these elements:

- Rising and descending (sunrise and sunset)
- Arches (rainbows)
- Geometric on-the-spot shapes (sundogs)
- Rippling, pulsing traveling phrase (auroras)

Once your class has set the movements and order of events, practice it together, then consider the Performance Variations for All Grades that follows.

Grades 4 Through 6 Variation

- Work in groups of five to seven to create a dance combining these elements:
  - Rising and descending phrases (sunrise and sunset).
  - Arches (rainbows).
  - Randomly occurring geometric on-the-spot shapes or jumps, (sundogs).
  - Rippling, pulsing traveling phrase (auroras).
- Mix them and manipulate the elements to create choreography that incorporates changing spatial relationships, levels, textures, and pathways.
- Allow your class time to create and practice their pieces (this may require an additional lesson).

Performance Variations for All Grades

Instructions

After students have performed their choreography, try the following:

- Dimming the lights and projecting the aurora video onto the students while they dance.

- If an old-style overhead projector is available, give your students sheets of acetate to paint. The paintings should be inspired by the images explored in this exercise. Project the images onto the dancers.

- Try overlapping two sheets of painted acetate on the projector and slowly move them in and out or side to side in opposite directions to create pulsing and shifting colors.

Discussion

- "How did it feel to dance with the projected lights?"

- "Did seeing the dance performed with project lights make the dance more dramatic? If yes, what was one of the most effective combinations of dance and light?"

Journal Entry

"Draw a picture or write about how it felt to dance with the projected lights or how you imagine it would feel to be a dancing light in the sky."

EXERCISE 6.4   SUN AND MOON

The sun and moon are our constant sky companions. We couldn't exist without the sun's warmth and light, and what would our nights be like without the moon's silvery glow?

Lesson Plan Suggestions

Kindergarten Through Grade 3

First lesson: Teach steps 1, 2, and 3 (follow the grade-appropriate variation)

Second lesson: Warm up with step 1, do steps 4, 5, 6 (video: Moon Water by Cloud Gate Dance Theatre of Taiwan, 2:47), and 7 (follow the grade-appropriate variation)

Grades 4 Through 6

First lesson: Teach steps 1, 2, and 3 (follow the grade-appropriate variation)

Second lesson: Warm up with step 1, do steps 4, 5, 6 (video: Moon Water by Cloud Gate Dance Theatre of Taiwan, 2:47), and 7 (follow the grade-appropriate variation)

Recommended Music: Tracks 2 and 7

Step 1: Warm Up With a Sun-Inspired Movement Phrase

Recommended Music

Track 2

Instructions

1. Start in a wide A stance (legs apart, arms by the side).
2. Create a big circle with both arms, reaching to the right on beat 1, up on beat 2, left on beat 3, and down on beat 4.
3. Reverse the action: both arms reach to the left on beat 1, up on beat 2, right on beat 3, and down on beat 4.
4. Step forward with the right foot and lift the right arm diagonally upward on beat 1.
5. Step forward with the left foot and lift the left arm diagonally upward on beat 2.
6. Step forward with the right foot and lift the right arm diagonally downward on beat 3.
7. Step forward with the left foot and lift the left arm diagonally downward on beat 4.
8. Jump in a big X on beat 1.
9. Land quietly, arms by your side, on beat 2.

10. Jump in a big X on beat 3.

11. Land quietly, arms by your side, on beat 4.

12. Kick the right leg to the side, arms flame to the right, on beats 1 and 2.

13. Kick the left leg to the side, arms flame to the left, on beats 3 and 4.

14. Bring the arms up overhead into a circle on beats 1, 2, 3, and 4.

15. Keeping the arms in a circular position, lower the arms, head, and spine; deeply bend the knees; and touch the floor on beats 1, 2, 3, 4, 5, 6, 7, and 8.

Practice the combination several times until your students are confident.

Big X jump.

Step 2: What We Know About the Sun

- Create three lists for your students to work with for their Sun dances.

    1. The first list will contain words that describe what the sun looks like the sky, including golden, orb, disc, glowing, and radiant.

    2. The second list will contain words that describe how the sun makes you feel, including warm, comforted, awake, happy, and hot.

    3. The third list will contain scientific information about the sun, including gaseous, boiling surface, and center of our solar system.

- Revisit the Sun Warm-Up.

- Ask your class to consider what sun attributes could have inspired the movements. Here are some possible interpretations.

    · Steps 1 and 2 represent the sun rising and setting.

    · The arms from steps 3, 4, 5, and 6 are the sunrays.

    · The steps from steps 3, 4, 5, and 6 show the sun traveling across the sky.

    · The jumps from steps 7, 8, 9, and 10 represent the sun at its zenith.

- The kicks and flaming arms from steps 13 and 14 represent the heat of the afternoon.
- Step 15 represents the sun setting.

Your students may have interpreted the movements in the sun warm-up differently; the kicks and flaming arms could represent solar flares, and the reaches and forward steps could illustrate the sun's strength and power. Both interpretations are excellent. Dance isn't literal; it welcomes multiple perspectives.

Step 3: Create Your Own Sun Dance

Recommended Music

Track 2

Kindergarten Through Grade 3 Variation

Instructions

Look at the word lists your class compiled.

1. Take approximately 5 minutes to collaboratively explore the words on all the lists.
2. Afterward, ask your class to revisit lists A and B.
3. Work together to create a 12- to 16-beat phrase inspired by the words from list A. Call this phrase A.
4. This phrase will be like the chorus of a song; it will be repeated after each verse.
5. Revisit list B.
6. Create a 12- to 16-beat phrase inspired by two or three similar ideas from list B. For example, the sun can make us feel awake, happy, and warm. Call this phrase B.
7. Create another 12- to 16-beat phrase. This one should be inspired by two or three similar ideas from list B that contrast the phrase created in step 6. For example, the sun can make us feel hot, tired, and thirsty. Call this phrase C.

Try performing all three phrases using this structure:

- Phrase A
- Phrase B
- Phrase A
- Phrase C
- Phrase A

Divide your class into two groups and perform the dance in the following ways:

1. Invite each group to perform the dance for the other group.
2. Ask everyone to return to the performance area and ask one group to perform phrase A while the other group performs phrases B and C.
3. Divide the groups in half and invite half of group A and B to sit and watch while the others perform the dance using the second variation. Then ask the groups to switch places and invite those who'd been watching to perform.

Discussion

- "When you perform the actions for the sun, how did you feel?"

- "Was it easy to show the emotions required for phrases B and C?"

- Look at the third word list your class compiled. Can you create a final Sun dance phrase using words from that list? If there isn't time to create another dance phrase, take a moment to discuss the words from that list you think would be the best to dance.

Grades 4 Through 6 Variation

The sun-inspired warm-up combination used a few of the words on your students' lists, but there's bound to be many words they haven't yet explored.

Instructions

- Divide your students into groups of four to six and invite your class to create their own dances inspired by the sun.

Sun.

© Janice Pomer

1. Their choreography may use one or two ideas from the warm-up but should focus on other ideas from the three lists your class compiled.

2. The warm-up was performed in unison but encourage your students to create dances using a wide range of levels, shapes, spatial relationships, timing, and energy to depict hot, fiery dynamics.

3. The choreography can be 24 to 36 beats long.

4. Allow enough time for your students to create, practice, and present their dances.

- If there's not enough time at the end of the lesson for the groups to present their choreography, ask everyone to record the dance in their journals so they can review, practice, present, and discuss them in their next lesson.

- If there was time to present the dances, reflect on the choreography.

Discussion

Ask each group to explain the most challenging sun word or concept they were inspired by and how they communicated it through movement.

Step 4: What We Know About the Moon

All Grades

1. Compile a list of words describing the moon (the different shapes, the color, its texture), another list containing words that describe how the moon makes you feel when you see it, and a third list containing scientific facts. Your lists may include some of the following words: silver, smiling, cool, gentle, watchful,

face, beams, ever-changing, full, half, crescent, sliver, reflecting, rocky, craters, calm, and orbits.

2. Compare your moon word lists to the word lists for the sun.

3. Some words like *glow* and *beam* may appear in both lists, but the sun and moon beam and glow differently.

One of the challenges to choreographing a Moon dance will be to create a dance that celebrates the differences between the sun and moon.

Step 5: Exploring Moon Words

Recommended Music

Track 7

Instructions

Ask your class to spread throughout the room and explore the words in your moon list.

1. Listen to the music for a moment before calling out the first word.

2. Bring students' attention to the different musical qualities between the sun and moon compositions.

3. The sun music is bright and strong, and the moon music is softer and gentle.

4. The sun generates light, and the moon reflects the sun's light.

5. The moon's shape waxes and wanes in the sky, but the sun's shape doesn't.

6. After you have called out each word from your moon list, continue with step 6.

Step 6: Watch a Moon Dance

Previewing Instructions

Watch the Moon Water by Cloud Gate Dance Theatre of Taiwan video (2:47) from the list of video links in HK*Propel*. This short excerpt is from a longer choreographic work entitled Moon Water. The video contains moments from three sections of the dance. The first and third sections are accompanied by music; the middle section is performed in silence. There are other changes that occur from section to section. Ask your students to keep an eye out for that.

Postvideo discussion:

- "Identify some of the other ways the choreographer was inspired by the movements and qualities of the moon." (The dancers' shapes employed curved arms and torsos and their movements were slow as they rotated on-the-spot; some of the dancers stayed suspended or balanced in crescent-like spaces on the floor.)

- There's something magical about seeing the night's sky reflected in the water. It can feel as if the sky and water are one and the moon is close enough to touch. Ask students if they've ever seen the moon reflected in a lake or other body of water. If they have, how would they describe it?

- "The moon reflects the light of the sun, and it changes from crescent to half-moon to full. Did the spatial relationships between dancers shift from crescent in the first section to full in the final movement?"

- "Did you see anything else that evoked the idea of the night sky?"

Step 7: Create a Moon Dance

Kindergarten Through Grade 3 Variation

Instructions

Ask your class to create a dance inspired by the moon.

1. Remember your movement exploration from step 5.

2. Invite students to show some ideas for showing the phases of the moon: crescent, half, and full.

3. Invite students to show some of their other favorite moon-inspired movements.

4. You can't dance on water to show reflection. Consider other ideas. Could you work in pairs and mirror each other for one section of the dance?

5. Use the wax and wane cycle phases of the moon as a structure for your dance (start small, grow to fullness, finish quietly).

Crescent moon.

Discussion

• Did the Moon dance show the phases of the moon?

• Which other moon qualities did your moon communicate?

If time allows, perform your Sun dance again so you can compare the two dances. Afterward, discuss the ways in which the Sun and Moon dances are different.

Grades 4 Through 6 Variation

Recommended Music

Track 7

Instructions

1. Ask your class to return to their Sun dance groups.

2. Play the music suggestion for the moon for 1 minute.

3. As they did for their Sun dance, each group will create a 24- to 36-beat Moon dance.

4. Identify the words and concepts students discussed after watching the video, including reflection and the phases of crescent, half, and full.

5. Some of the written words for moon and sun are similar, but the movements should be different.

6. After students have created and practiced their moon-inspired dances, invite groups to present their work and discuss.

Discussion

- Ask each group to list the words and concepts they were inspired by and to identify one of the movements they created that they feel successfully communicated the moon.

- If there is time, it's interesting to alternate the Sun and Moon dances. Design a structure for juxtaposing the two dances (if there is an even number of groups try alternating group 1 as sun, 2 as the moon, 3 as the sun, and so on).

Journal Entry for All Grades

"Draw a picture or write a poem or descriptive paragraph about the sun or moon, highlighting one or two qualities that resonate most deeply for you."

EXERCISE 6.5   ECLIPSES

Normally the moon and Earth follow their orbital paths without incident, but occasionally the moon passes between the sun and Earth, and an eclipse occurs. In this exercise, your class will create a dance inspired by an ancient folktale about eclipses. Afterward, they can explore ways to create a dance inspired by our current understanding of eclipses.

Lesson Plan Suggestions

Kindergarten Through Grade 3

First lesson: Steps 1 (video: NASA, 2:35), 2, 3, and 4

Second lesson (optional): If students wish to create a science-based dance or create their own eclipse origin tale, they can do it during this optional lesson

Grades 4 Through 6

First lesson: Steps 1(video: NASA, 2:35), 2, 3, and 4

Second lesson (optional): If students wish to create a science-based dance or create their own eclipse origin tale, they can do it during this optional lesson

Recommended Music: Your choice

Step 1: What Is an Eclipse?

A solar eclipse happens when the moon travels between the sun and Earth and creates a shadow on parts of Earth. The sun, or parts of it, disappears.

Use this NASA educational resource page to watch videos and read information about eclipses. The first video is 2:35 minutes in length and is appropriate for grades 3 and up. Teachers working with younger students may wish to review the text on the page and share it with their students. If your students are very interested in eclipses, share the additional videos of eclipses (but they aren't necessary for this exercise).

After learning about eclipses, ask your students if they've ever viewed an eclipse outdoors. Invite those who have to describe what they saw and how it made them feel. Write their comments on a flip chart.

Step 2: Past Explanations for Eclipses

Ancient Mayan astronomers had a highly advanced understanding of planetary orbits and could predict when lunar and solar eclipses would occur. Ancient Mesopotamian astronomers could also predict eclipses, but for many ancient civilizations, an eclipse was a frightening thing to witness and often considered an omen of bad things to come.

Ask your class this: "If you didn't know how eclipses occurred, how would you explain it so it wouldn't make people fearful?" Write their ideas on a flip chart.

Step 3: An Ancient Folktale

The following is my retelling of a very old Korean folktale that explains how and why eclipses occur. Read this folktale to your class.

The Fire Dogs

"There are many worlds in our universe. The Land of Darkness is one such world. They have no sun to light their days and no moon to brighten their nights. The Land of Darkness is so far away from our world that our sun and moon appear as pale, tiny dots of light in their otherwise perpetually dark sky.

The rulers of the Land of Darkness want to bring light to their people, so they send huge Fire Dogs into the sky to try to steal the sun and moon. These dogs are as dark as midnight and can fly across the sky without being seen. Their mouths are enormous, large enough to swallow the sun whole, but the sun is too hot and the moon too cold for the dogs to keep in their mouths for long.

The Land of Darkness is far, far away, and the Fire Dogs have a long journey between their home and ours, so they don't come here often. But whenever you see the sun or moon covered in an unusual darkness, you'll know a Fire Dog is trying to steal its precious light for those who live in the Land of Darkness."

Source: *Folk Tales from Korea*, edited and translated by Zong In-Sob (New York: Grove Press, 1979), first printed in 1952 by Routledge and Kegan Paul UK. The original and much longer tale from which Zong In-Sob sourced the story was collected from Zong Teg-Ha in Onyang, 1912.

Discussion

- "Does the image of Fire Dogs trying to steal the moon or sun help explain how they disappear during an eclipse?"

- "Is there a 'happy ending' that lets listeners know that everything will be all right?"

- "Can you think of other images or another storyline that could comfort people and explain an eclipse?" Make notes of your students' ideas.

Step 4: Create Dances Inspired by Eclipses

In this step, your students will create an Eclipse dance based on one or more of the following:

- The Fire Dog folktale

- Their scientific understanding of eclipses

- Their own origin tale

Kindergarten Through Grade 3 Variation

- Start with the Fire Dog story. Work with your class and create a list of actions and images inspired by the Fire Dog story, including a land of darkness; the hot, bright sun; the cool, silvery moon (use ideas from the previous exercise); and Fire Dogs that leap, fly, bite, and tear.

- Select a piece of music to use for the exploration.

  · Invite your class to get into readiness position, then call out each idea one by one.

  · Use prompts, such as: "What would the Land of Darkness be like?" "How would the people in the Land of Darkness move?" "What were your favorite Sun dance moves from the previous exercise?" "Can you think of new sun actions?" "What were your favorite Moon dance moves from the previous exercise?" "Can you think of new moon actions?" "Can you create a run and leap combination for the Fire Dogs?" "Would the Fire Dogs

© Janice Pomer

Steal the sun.

return home in sadness without having brought the sun or moon back with them?"

- After exploring elements of the story through movement, organize their ideas into a dance. Not everyone will perform every part. For example, a group can be Fire Dogs racing across the sky, while others perform sun and moon movements that grow larger to show that the Fire Dogs are getting closer (perhaps some of your students who started out as people of the Land of Darkness could join the sun and moon).

- This may be the first time your class will have adapted a story into dance.
  - Ask students: "Would the dance benefit from some lines of text?"
  - If your class likes the idea of using some text, identify where it would be most helpful.
  - Select different people to speak the text and make sure that those who speak are also dancing.

- Create and practice the dance, and if you're unable to divide your class into two groups to watch each other perform, video the dance so your students can enjoy and appreciate their work.

- Afterward, discuss the possibility of creating a dance inspired by their scientific understanding of eclipses. You might want to review the information and/or video from step 1.

- If your class is interested in creating a dance that communicates their scientific knowledge of eclipses, brainstorm ideas with special focus on pathways, such as the following:
  - "How can we show the different orbital paths of Earth and the moon?"
  - "How can we show the different speeds of Earth and the moon?"
  - "What phrases can we use from our Sun and Moon dances?"
  - "What movements should we use for a new phrase to represent Earth?"

- Explore your students' movement suggestions collectively, establish the structure, practice, and video the dance.

Grades 4 Through 6 Variation

- Take a moment to discuss ideas for translating the story of the Fire Dogs into dance.

- Compile a list of essential movement elements, including the following:
  - One or two movement phrases depicting the Land of Darkness
  - A travel phrase for the Fire Dogs racing to the sun and moon (containing runs and leaps) and their journey back to the Land of Darkness (do they change?)
  - Sun and moon movement phrases
- Invite your class to work in groups of six to eight to create a movement piece inspired by the Fire Dogs.
  - There are no beat constraints to the assignment.
  - Before they start working, let your class know when you would like the dances to be ready for viewing so they can plan accordingly.
  - This is the first narrative dance assignment. After everyone has presented, take a moment to reflect on the work.

Discussion

- Identify a unique aspect from each group (the way they interpreted the Land of Darkness, the Fire Dogs' leaping sequence, how they showed the sun and moon getting swallowed).
- "Did the storyline support your choreographic ideas, or did it hamper you?"
- Is the class interested in creating another Eclipse dance inspired by their scientific understanding of eclipses? If most of your students are interested, use an additional lesson to support their work.

Journal Entry for All Grades

"Draw a picture or write a poem or paragraph about being overshadowed. It could be related to the eclipse, or it can be personal." Ask students if they have felt overshadowed. If so, ask them when it happened and how it felt.

EXERCISE 6.6   GRAVITATIONAL FORCES

An exercise on gravity could have been placed in chapter 5, but gravitational force is what keeps Earth and all the other planets safely orbiting around the sun, making it an integral factor to consider when your students create their Planetary dances in exercise 6.7. In this exercise, your students will explore what it might feel like to experience different degrees of gravity.

Lesson Plan Suggestions

Kindergarten Through Grade 3

First lesson: Teach steps 1, 2, and 3 (video: How High Can You Jump on Different Planets?, 8:12), and if time is available, introduce step 4 (follow the grade-appropriate variation)

Second lesson: May not be necessary. Warm up by reviewing steps 1 and 2 and finish step 4

Grades 4 Through 6

First lesson: Teach steps 1, 2, and 3 (video: How High Can You Jump on Different Planets?, 8:12) and start step 4 (follow the grade-appropriate variation)

Second lesson: Warm up by quickly reviewing step 2 and do step 4

Recommended Music: Tracks 6 and 12

Step 1: Traveling

Instructions

1. Create a list of three simple traveling actions (walk, jump, leap, run).
2. Ask your class to spread out arm's-length apart and remind everyone to stay in their own bubbles throughout the exploration.
   1. Call out the first traveling action.
   2. Invite your students to use this action to move throughout the room in different directions and at different times.
   3. After 20 to 30 seconds, call out the next action.
   4. Repeat the process through all the traveling actions.
3. Let your class know that they'd been moving at Earth's gravity and now you'd like them to perform the same movements but to imagine that they are moving in a room with less gravity than they would normally experience on Earth. Less gravity means there's less resistance.
   1. Invite your students to imagine that their bodies feel lighter and to notice how it affects the way they walk, run, jump, or leap.
   2. Go through the same traveling actions with lightened gravitational pull.
4. Repeat the process one more time with even less gravitational pull; perhaps they can imagine they're moving on the moon.

1. Call out prompts, such as: "How high do your feet and legs lift when you try to walk?" "Is it easy to control your jumps?"
2. After 20 to 30 seconds, take a moment to discuss their experiences.

Discussion

- "Did you move differently between the 'normal Earth' gravity and the first reduction of gravity? If yes, explain how."
- "Did the second reduction of gravity make moving easier or harder? Explain why."

Step 2: Gravity and Sports

Instructions

1. Make a list of three actions performed while playing sports: throw, dribble, swinging (a bat or racket).
2. Explore the sports-related actions the same way you explored the traveling actions in step 1.
3. Start with Earth's normal gravity, then reduce it even further.
4. Remind your class to visualize the equipment associated with the sport or activity. If you're dribbling, see the basketball and notice how it reacts to the changes in gravity. If you're swinging a bat, feel the weight of it as you lift and swing it.
5. Try the exploration with increased gravity. How will increased gravitational force affect the basketball you're dribbling, the baseball you're throwing, and the tennis ball you're hitting?
6. After you've explored the sports actions at the different gravities, rest and discuss.

Discussion

- "Did working with sports equipment complicate the exploration?"
- "When were the bats and rackets easier or harder to lift and control?"
- "When did your actions get faster, and when did they become slower?"
- "How was your body affected by the differences in gravity?"
- "Did you ever get frustrated? If yes, when and why?"

Step 3: Experiencing Gravity on Different Planets

Instructions

Watch the How High Can You Jump on Different Planets? video (8:12) from the list of video links in HK*Propel*. This fun, informative video will show your students how high they can jump on different planets, some moons, and asteroids. This video provides information your class will need in exercise 6.7, the culminating dance for this chapter. Afterward, take a moment to review the gravitational facts highlighted in the video.

Discussion

- Which gravities do they think it would be easiest to show through dance, and which would be the hardest?
- Discuss why they think some actions would be more difficult, and brainstorm ideas that may make those movement easier to adapt for different gravities.

Step 4: Dancing With Gravity

Revisit the simple rise and descend pattern from the Paint the Sky dance in exercise 6.3 to highlight and explore different gravitational pulls.

Recommended Music

Track 6 for less gravity and track 12 for more gravity

Kindergarten Through Grade 3 Variation

Instructions

1. Review the Paint the Sky dance your students created for the foundation "rise and descend" warm-up from the exercise.

2. Discuss what they would need to do to adapt their Painting the Sky dance for moon's gravity (or any planet with lighter gravity than Earth).
   - "Will arms lift higher or faster, and will they be easier or harder to control?"
   - "Will you be able to maintain low-level positions?"

3. Explore the movements for a minute or so, then consider how to adapt the movement to communicate a greater gravitational force (perhaps Jupiter's).
   - "Will you be able to lift your arms?"
   - "Will you be able to stand up fully, or will you be stuck in low-level positions?"

4. Combine your students' favorite ideas to create a dance where students' movements fluctuate between light and heavy gravities.

5. Practice it several times, then divide the class into two groups so they can watch each other perform it.

Discussion

- "Which movements were easy to adapt for lesser gravity?"
- "Which movements were easy to adapt for greater gravity?"
- "Was there a movement that was easy to adapt for lesser and greater gravity?"
- "Did the different gravities change the way you felt while you were dancing? If yes, explain."

Grades 4 Through 6 Variation

Instructions

- Invite your class to return to their Paint the Sky dance groups and select a 20- to 24-beat section that can be performed twice in the following manner:
  - The first time, the movements should be performed under reduced gravitational forces.
  - The second time, the movements should be performed under greater gravitational forces.
  - The timing will change between lesser and greater gravity. Though the original dance phrase is 20 to 24 beats, the new versions may be longer or shorter.
  - Levels, shapes, and spatial relationships will all be affected by the changes in gravity—the phrases may look quite different.

- There won't be enough time for your class to complete both the lesser and greater gravity versions in a single lesson.
- Allow time for the groups to record the new choreography in their journals so they can refer to them in the next lesson.
- In the next lesson, warm up quickly with step 1 or 2, then ask your students to return to their groups to finish the choreographic assignment in step 4.
- Invite groups to perform their dances one at a time, then reflect on the experience.

Discussion
- "What did you have to change to make it appear as if you were dancing with less gravity?"
- "While performing the dance with less gravity, did your body feel different? If yes, how?"
- "Did you notice if your breathing changed? Did you notice any other changes? If yes, describe them."
- "What did you have to change to make it appear you were dancing with greater gravity?"
- "While performing the dance with greater gravity, did your body feel different? If yes, how?"
- "Did you notice if your breathing changed? Did you notice any other changes? If yes, describe them."
- "As a viewer, did you find that the gravitational forces communicated different emotions? If yes, describe them."

Journal Entry

"Draw a picture or write about how it might feel to live with less or greater gravitational pull."

EXERCISE 6.7   THE PLANETS

In exercise 6.4, your class created dances inspired by the sun and moon; in exercise 6.5, they created dances inspired by an origin tale that explains eclipses; and in exercise 6.6, your class learned about gravitational force and how it differs from planet to planet. In this culminating exercise for chapter 6, they're going to combine all those experiences to create dances inspired by Mercury, Venus, Mars, Jupiter, Saturn, Uranus, and Neptune.

Lesson Plan Suggestions

Kindergarten Through Grade 3

First lesson: Steps 1, 2 (video: Solar System 101, 4:10), 3, and begin step 4 (selecting the planets to dance; follow the grade-appropriate variations)

Second lesson: Quickly warm up using any of the exploratory exercises from steps 3 and 4. Your class will be creating two planet dances and may require an additional class

Third lesson: If required, you can add a third lesson

Grades 4 Through 6

First lesson: Steps 1, 2 (video: Solar System 101, 4:10), 3, and begin step 4 (selecting the planets to dance; follow the grade-appropriate variations)

Second lesson: Quickly warm up using any of the exploratory exercises from steps 3 and 4

Third lesson (optional): Let your students know before they begin choreographing if there will be a third lesson so they can plan the length of their pieces accordingly

Recommended Music: Tracks 12, 17, 19, and students' choice (depending on the planet)

Step 1: What We Know About the Planets in Our Solar System (Other Than Earth)

Compile a list of words and phrases pertaining to all planets, including orbit (following an elliptical path), rotation, spherical-shaped, gravity, have some type of atmosphere, and appear to us as stars in the sky.

Music: Track 17

1. Ask your class to spread throughout the room and explore the words and concepts as their warm-up exercise.

2. Call out prompts to remind your class to explore different atmospheres: "Are some planets hot, dry, and dusty?" "Are other planets gaseous, cold, and storming?"

3. Call out prompts to remind your class to move at different speeds: "Some planets take years to complete a single orbit around the sun, while others complete their orbit in months."

4. Encourage students to explore isolations for the turning actions: "Can one arm orbit around the other?" "Can your foot trace elliptical pathways on the floor?"

5. Finish the warm-up exploration by returning to parallel position.

6. Ask everyone to close their eyes and visualize planet Earth as viewed from above: the blues and greens and clouds.

7. Invite them to visualize one of the other planets: Mars with its red surface, Saturn with its many rings, or any of the others.

8. Then sit together and watch the video in step 2.

Step 2: Watch the Solar System Video

Watch the Solar System 101 video (4:10) from the list of video links in HK*Propel*. This video will give you and your students a wonderful overview of the planets in our solar system, introducing them to the four terrestrial (or rocky) planets, the two gas giants, and the two ice giants. Students in grades 4 through 6 may benefit from additional research and other videos once they start working on individual planets in their groups, but this video has all the scientific information needed to start their dances.

After watching the video, create a flip chart page for each planet.

1. Use the Elements of Dance to collate information your students know about the individual planets.

2. Divide a flip chart page into five sections horizontally. Create a column on the left and write *Shape*, *Motion*, *Time*, *Space*, and *Energy* in each of the rows.

3. To the right of the column, there should be more than enough space to write in your students' ideas, such as the following:

   • Shape: Include the shape of the orbit and size and texture of the planet's surface (some planets are rocky and dust covered, while gas planets don't have a solid surface)

   • Motion: Include atmospheric movement on and around the planet as well as unique movement characteristics (one planet rotates on its side)

   • Time: Include the speed with which it rotates and orbits

   • Space: Include the spatial relationships with the sun, other planets, and planetary satellites, including moons

   • Energy: Include characteristics associated with the planet (Mars is angry; Saturn is mysterious) and any other planetary features not addressed in the other categories such as surface temperature

One area many students are interested in is the origin of planets' names. In Western astronomy, all planets (other than Earth) are named after Greek and Roman gods. Early astronomers named the planets after gods that shared their unique characteristics. The god Mercury was associated with speed, and Mercury is the fastest planet. The goddess Venus was revered for her beauty, and the planet Venus shines the most brilliantly in the sky. Other cultures have traditional names and stories for the planets. Myths and folktales about the planets can inspire a section of the choreography.

Step 3: Explore the Terrestrial Planets (Other Than Earth)

1. Ask your students to spread out and stand in parallel position.

2. Play either track 12 or 17.

3. Let them know that the first planet they'll explore is Mercury.

4. Begin to call out the words compiled on the Mercury list.

5. Encourage your students to use isolations and full-bodied movements.

6. Repeat the process with Venus and Mars, the other terrestrial planets.

Take a moment to rest after exploring the terrestrial planets and reflect.

Kindergarten Through Grade 3 Variation

Share and discuss movement ideas for the different planets and write down the ideas on the flip chart.

Grades 4 Through 6 Variation

- Ask your students to work in their journals to record (using words or diagrams) one or two movement ideas for each planet.

- Continue Exploring the Other Planets

All Grades

Repeat the process of exploring and record movement ideas for the gas giants (Jupiter and Saturn) and the ice giants (Neptune and Uranus) using track 19.

Step 4: Planet Dances

Kindergarten Through Grade 3 Variation

Instructions

1. Your students' dances for the sun and moon in exercise 6.4 communicated the contrasts between the huge, fiery life-giving sun and the cool, reflective moon. Ask your class which two planets they think will provide similar contrasts for their Planet dances. One of the rocky or terrestrial planets paired with one of the gas or ice giants works best.

2. Review the planet word lists and ask your students what they think are the most important elements to highlight for each planet. For example, the surface of Mars has craters and rocks, and Mars is the dustiest planet in the solar system. If your class selected Mars as one of its planets, you might begin by reviewing the movement explorations for rocks and sand in chapter 5, exercise 5.2.

3. Mercury is the speediest planet in our solar system. If your class is working on Mercury, start exploring ways to travel quickly along an elliptical pathway, and don't forget its speedy day and night rotation. You students don't have to do full-bodied turns to represent fast rotations. Arms circling around each other can illustrate spinning without causing dizziness.

4. When you've selected the planets, start piecing together ideas, and make sure the movements used for one planet are substantially different from the other.

5. That doesn't mean only one planet can show its orbit. Uranus is the farthest planet from the sun and has the longest orbit. A slow, stately traveling pattern would contrast beautifully with quick-footed Mercury.

   1. Create two separate dances, one for each planet.

   2. Connect your students' favorite movement phrases for your terrestrial planet together into one piece of choreography.

   3. Connect your students' favorite movement phrases for your gas or ice giant planet together into a second piece of choreography.

4. Work with your class to practice both dances so everyone is confident performing both Planet dances.

5. Divide the class into two groups, and assign each group one planet to perform for the other.

Afterward, discuss the Planet dances.

Discussion

- "What was your favorite movement phrase to perform from the Terrestrial Planet dance? Explain why."

- "What was your favorite movement phrase to perform from the Gas or Ice Giant Planet dance? Explain why."

Grades 4 Through 6 Variation

Instructions

1. Invite your class to go into six groups (four or five students per group).

2. Write "rocky" on two pieces of paper, "gaseous" on two pieces of paper, and "ice" on two pieces of paper.

3. Place the paper pieces in a bag, box, or hat.

4. Invite a member from each group to select one of the pieces and tell them not to look at it until a representative from every group has drawn a planet.

   - Groups that selected "rocky" may choose Mercury, Venus, or Mars.

   - Groups that selected "gaseous" may choose between Jupiter and Saturn.

   - Groups that selected "ice" may choose between Neptune and Uranus.

All the Planet dances should contain movement phrases inspired by the following elements of their planet:

- Surface

- Atmosphere

- Planetary satellites (rings and moons)

- Orbit and rotational speed

- Additional characteristics, qualities, or mythological connection

Your class has a wealth of choreographic experiences to draw from to create their culminating dance for chapter 6. Before they begin the assignment, let them know if they should aim to have the dance completed and ready for presentation in the second lesson, or if they'll have a third lesson to finalize the pieces, practice them, and present them. Be sure to allow time for students to notate their ideas and choreography in their journals before the end of each class.

Each group may request a musical composition they feel best suits their planet for presentation. Each group may decide to use a costume, prop, and lighting (as was done in exercise 6.3) to enhance their choreography. After all the groups have shared their dances, discuss the process and the choreography.

Discussion

- "What was the most challenging element for your group, and what was the movement phrase you created to communicate it?"

- As viewers identify the most expressive movement phrase from each group, ask them to explain why.

- "Consider ways to combine the dances into an extended choreographic work of the planets."

Journal Entry for All Grades

"Draw a picture or write a poem or descriptive paragraph about one of the planets. It can be from the perspective someone observing the planet from afar, someone visiting the planet, or the voice of the planet itself."

SUMMARY

More responsibility for designing structures and choreographic content was passed on to you and your students in the final exercises of this chapter. In the upcoming chapters, you'll be in charge of everything. You have all the skills you need to guide your students through the next series of exercises; brainstorm ideas and explore them through movement, listen to each other's observations, challenge your students to try new things, and always remember that there are multiple movement possibilities for every theme or concept. If a structure you've established isn't as effective as you'd wanted it to be, don't worry; ask your students for suggestions and together explore new structures. Reworking choreography is something artists do on a regular basis during all stages of their careers.

 Go to HK *Propel* to find audio files, reproducible forms, and a list of video links corresponding to chapter exercises.

© Janice Pomer

CHAPTER 7

People

The exercises in the previous chapters highlighted movement patterns and cycles in the natural world. Humans are part of the natural world, so it's not surprising that those patterns are part of the human experience.

In this chapter, your students will revisit 10 earlier explorations from a human perspective and examine how these movement patterns relate to themselves, their families and communities, and global events. Use exercises from previous chapters as a foundation for new exercises, and with your class investigate ways to apply them to human nature. There are suggestions to help you initiate the brainstorming sessions for each exploration, but go in the direction your students lead you. Remember, there's no correct response or interpretation. Listen to your students' ideas, follow your own creative impulses, and see what happens.

If you've been working pedagogically through the chapters of the book, you're aware of how your students' choreographic skills and confidence has grown. Your skills have grown as well. The exercises in this chapter are the penultimate step to designing your own creative movement exercises from scratch.

For these 10 explorations, your job is to do the following:

1. Review the original exercise with your class.
2. Ask your students to review their journal entries associated with the original exercise.
3. Introduce your class to the suggested ways to interpret the exercise.
4. Select music to support students' movement work.
5. Brainstorm other ideas your students have for interpreting the original exercise so it connects to their lives or the greater human experience.
6. Explore strategies for translating your students' ideas into movement.
7. Discuss the explorations and select which ideas to pursue.
8. Most of the exercise suggestions can be completed in one class, but since you're setting the choreographic structures, the exercises can, if you wish, take longer.
9. For younger grades, you are responsible for facilitating the new choreography with them.
10. After each dance creation and presentation, lead a final discussion reflecting on the process and the choreography that has been performed.
11. Include a question or observation for your students to respond to in their journals.

And if you haven't been keeping your own journal, now is the time to start! Keep a record of the things that worked and the things that didn't; include students' ideas (not just the ones that were explored in the final choreography), and after you finish these exercises, ask your class if they can think of other nature-based movement patterns to explore from a human perspective.

People and Plants

Chapter 2 focused on plants. In the first two exercises in this chapter, your class will re-examine two exercises from chapter 2 from a human perspective. A suggested approach has been provided for the first two exercises in this chapter.

EXERCISE 7.1   REVISITING MAPLE KEYS

Lesson Plan Suggestions

Kindergarten Through Grade 3
First lesson: Revisiting Maple Keys (exercise 2.1)

Grades 4 Through 6
First lesson: Revisiting Maple Keys (exercise 2.1)

Revisiting Maple Keys (exercise 2.1)

In their journal entries, students were asked to imagine how they might feel if they were a maple key, dangling from their parent tree and then falling to the ground. Some students may have compared the experience to children growing up and leaving home or students graduating from elementary school and moving to the next level in their education. This is a movement structure you could use for the school analogy.

Kindergarten Through Grade 3 Variation

Instructions

1. Collectively create a short movement phrase to symbolize each of the following:
   - Learning new things at school
   - Playing together
   - Friendship

2. Establish an order for the phrases and practice them together.

3. Collectively create a short movement phrase to symbolize saying goodbye.

4. Add that phrase to the end of the first three phrases.

5. Independently ask students to perform a short, on-the-spot solo depicting how they might feel after they've left their friends and prepare to go to a new school. It might convey these emotions:
   - Feeling alone
   - Worried
   - Excited
   - Nervous

6. Then finish with a second solo to convey how they feel once they've met new friends and are enjoying their new school. It might convey these emotions:
   - Strong
   - Independent

© Janice Pomer

Fear/nervous.

Strong/brave.

Divide your class into three or four groups and invite your students to perform their solos for each other. Afterward, perform all sections of the dance; the first four phrases depict feelings of community, the first solo phrases depict feelings upon leaving their community, and the second solo phrases show their strength and independence.

Grades 4 Through 6 Variation

Instructions

For this exercise, you can assign groups of students the same structure as the kindergarten through grade 3 variation or create your own structure by inviting your students to review their journal entries for exercise 2.1 and share them with the class. Write their ideas on a flip chart and let them create their own structure for the dance. Whether your class selects a theme and structure of their own or you follow the format for younger grades, make sure you do the following:

1. Clearly outline the required content your students will need to adhere to (ideas for specific movement phrases) and provide a time line (how long the phrases can be and how much time students have to work before presentation).
2. Divide your class into working groups.
3. Select a piece of music.
4. Check in with your students regularly while they work.

Discussion Suggestions

For kindergarten through grade 3 and the other older classes that followed the idea of moving on to a new grade or school, ask these questions:

- "How did you communicate the classroom community in the first section of the dance?"
- "How did the dance change when it was time to say goodbye?"
- "How did you approach creating your solos? Which emotions did you focus on communicating?"

For grades 4 through 6, if your students used other structures and interpretations, create your own discussion questions.

Journal Entry for All Grades

"Draw or write about the commonalities between the way seedlings and humans grow."

EXERCISE 7.2   REVISITING THE THREE SISTERS

Lesson Plan Suggestions

Kindergarten Through Grade 3

First lesson: Revisiting the Three Sisters (exercise 2.5)

Grades 4 Through 6

First lesson: Revisiting the Three Sisters (exercise 2.5)

Revisiting the Three Sisters (exercise 2.5)

Exercise 2.5 was inspired by North American Indigenous People's biodynamic agricultural tradition of planting corn, beans, and squash together in a holistic system where the plants support and nourish each other and the soil. In their journal entries, students were asked to reflect on the ways their friends and family support and nourish each other. Review students' journals before brainstorming ideas.

Kindergarten Through Grade 3

Instructions

- Brainstorm and collectively explore movement ideas based on how families support each other. Then create movement phrases to represent the following:
  - Think about the person or people at the center of the family and the actions he or she performs to support the others (works, pays bills, purchases food, clothing, cooks, listens, hugs, loves, protects).
  - Think about the person or people the central figure(s) directly supports (children and elders). When and why do they require help (food, housing, homework, clothing, medical needs, emotional support), and when and how do the children, family members, and elders reciprocate and help the central figure(s) (listen, respect, stay safe, help at home, thank, and show appreciation).
  - Identify the person or people living with or around the family (aunts, uncles, neighbors, friends, community workers) and indicate what they do (offer assistance, help out when needed, kind words, celebrate occasions together).

Supporting.

© Janice Pomer

- After exploring movement ideas, select three or four movement ideas for each of the three sections: the person at the center of the family, the interactive relationship they have with their dependents, and the support and engagement they receive from the broader community.

- Solidify the movement phrases for each section and then connect the sections together.

- Lead a discussion after the presentations.

- Create a journal entry prompt for your class to respond to.

Grades 4 Through 6 Variation

You can invite your class to follow the suggestion for younger grades or lead a discussion about how the biodynamic Three Sisters system could pertain to local and global issues—for example, human rights leaders speaking out against injustice. The leader identifies and communicates the problem to the greater population, helping the impacted community by bringing attention to their plight which brings support from the greater community. Students have used this template to show how civil rights and suffrage struggles have built public acceptance over the centuries and how the ideas and beliefs of a few seeded change that eventually impacted millions. If your class chooses to work with their own ideas, make sure you do the following:

1. Compile word lists to guide your students' creative explorations.

2. Provide them with a choreographic structure (use those suggested in other chapters or create a new one).

3. Divide your class into groups.

4. Provide them with adequate creation and practice time.

5. After the presentations, create questions to stimulate discussion about the process and the dances.

6. Create a journal entry prompt for your class to respond to.

People and Animals

Chapter 3 focused on animals. In this exercise, your class will re-examine two aspects of animal behavior as they relate to human beings.

EXERCISE 7.3   REVISITING TEAMWORK

Lesson Plan Suggestions

Kindergarten Through Grade 3

First lesson: Revisiting Teamwork

Grades 4 Through 6

First lesson: Revisiting Teamwork

Revisiting Teamwork

All Grades

Teamwork was highlighted in exercises 3.3 (horns, antlers, hooves, and herds) and 3.5 (spiders and insects). Your class may remember the video of the musk ox herd protecting their young from a pack of hungry Arctic wolves. At the conclusion of that exercise, your students were asked to reflect on the importance of teamwork. If you didn't watch the video, go to HK*Propel* and click on the link for chapter 3, exercise 3.3.

Instructions

The length of the dance is up to you.

1. Ask your class to review what they'd written or drawn in their journals at the end of exercise 3.3.
2. Identify what examples of teamwork they highlighted in their journals.
3. Write those ideas down and brainstorm other ideas (including teamwork in sports).
4. Explore your students' teamwork ideas through movement and create dances about teamwork.
5. Kindergarten through grade 3 classes can create their dance collaboratively.
6. Students in grades 4 through 6 should work in groups.

Lead a discussion after the presentations.

Create a journal entry prompt for your class to respond to.

© Janice Pomer

Teamwork.

EXERCISE 7.4   REVISITING HERD MIGRATIONS

Grades 4 Through 6 only

Second lesson: Revisiting Migration and video (Crystal Pike's Flight Pattern, 5:56)

Content Warning: This exercise explores our human refugee crisis and could be upsetting for children who have experienced these tragedies. Revisiting herd migrations is for grades 4 through 6 only.

Large-scale human migrations are triggered by war; oppression; loss of basic resources; and natural disasters, including famine, floods, and earthquakes.

Aftermath of war.

1. Your class watched an excerpt of Crystal Pite's Emergence in chapter 3. Now watch the video of Crystal Pite's Flight Pattern—BBC Interview, her choreographic response to the Syrian refugee crisis (5:56) from the list of video links in HK*Propel*.

2. After watching the video, allow time for your students to process what they've watched.

3. Compile a list of treasured things that refugees leave behind, including their families, friends, homeland, language, jobs, and culture.

4. Compile a list of reasons people become refugees, such as fear of dying, torture, starvation, their children being taken from them, and their homes and land taken or destroyed.

5. Use their words and ideas to stimulate ideas for movement. For example:
   - Running forward—away from bombs
   - Turning back to see the home, family, and friends left behind
   - Carrying belongings, small children, or the elderly
   - Reaching for food, giving assistance, and asking for assistance
   - Slow movements—being tired, hungry, cold, or huddled with others
   - Tug-of-war—caught between the past and present or between two borders
6. Explore movement ideas and design a structure for your students to support a piece of choreography depicting the plight of refugees.
7. Lead a discussion after the presentations.
8. Create a journal entry prompt for your class to respond to.

People and Water

Chapter 4 focused on water. In this exercise, your class will re-examine aspects of water from a human perspective.

EXERCISE 7.5   REVISITING SNOW

Lesson Plan Suggestions

Kindergarten Through Grade 3
First lesson: Revisiting Snow

Grades 4 Through 6
First lesson: Revisiting Snow

Revisiting Snow

All Grades

In exercise 4.3, your students explored the beauty of snowflakes and learned that every snowflake is different. We don't know how many hundreds of trillions of snowflakes fall every year in the world, but the number of snowflakes estimated to fall each year in the United States is 1,000,000,000,000,000,000,000,000. That's septillion snowflakes in one country alone, and half of the United States rarely or never experiences snow!

In 2021, the population of the world was 7.9 billion, and, like snowflakes, each person is unique. Try the following choreographic idea or create one of your own.

- Invite your students to create a short solo to express their uniqueness.
- For kindergarten through grade 3, the recommended length for solos is 8 to 16 beats long.
- For grades 4 through 6, the recommended length for solos is 16 to 24 beats long.
- In the solos, your students can express how they feel—what they like or don't like—movements they feel confident performing, and elements in nature that resonate strongly for them (animals, flowers, storms).

Try the following structure for the presentation, or create your own.

1. Invite your students to share their solos three at a time.
2. Ask three students to find a place in the performance area a safe distance from each other.
3. Double-check to make sure no dancer will be traveling into another's space.
4. Ask the presenters to go into their starting shapes and let them know they can begin when the music starts and hold their finishing shape until the music stops.
5. Because of the variable length of their solo dances, presenters may finish at different times.
6. After everyone has presented in groups of three, see how many people can perform their solos safely at the same time. When the performance area is filled with people, is their uniqueness still apparent, or, like snowflakes, does their individuality get lost in the crowd?
7. Lead a discussion after the presentations.
8. Create a journal entry prompt for your class to respond to.

EXERCISE 7.6   REVISITING THE WATER CYCLE, DROUGHTS, AND FLOODS

Lesson Plan Suggestions

Kindergarten Through Grade 3

First lesson: Revisiting the Water Cycle, Droughts, and Floods

Grades 4 Through 6

First lesson: Revisiting the Water Cycle, Droughts, and Floods

Revisiting the Water Cycle, Droughts, and Floods From a Human Perspective

All Grades

In exercise 4.5, your class explored the Water Cycle. In exercise 4.6, your class explored droughts and may have explored floods. In exercises 4.1 through 4.4, they explored wave action and water in various states and learned that water fluctuates in speed, volume, and form in many different ways. Water isn't the only thing that can fluctuate between extremes. What happens when we are flooded with work or have too little? Some people work more than 60 hours a week just to make ends meet while others are jobless with few employment opportunities. It's important for everyone to have work, but having to work too long and hard or having little or no work isn't healthy for the individual or society.

Help us.

© Janice Pomer

Instructions

Facilitate this exercise by doing the following:

1. Explore this idea from a personal, local, or global perspective.
2. Use any of the choreographic and presentation structures suggested in this or other chapters or create a new one.
3. Younger grades create together, and older grades work in small groups.

4. After presentations, create questions to stimulate discussion about the process and the dances.

5. Create a journal entry prompt for your class to respond to.

People and Earth

Chapter 5 focused on Earth. In this section, your class will re-examine two Earth elements studied in chapter 5 from a human perspective.

EXERCISE 7.7   REVISITING TECTONIC PLATES

Lesson Plan Suggestions

Kindergarten Through Grade 3

First lesson: Revisiting Tectonic Plates with video (Pretty Big Digs, 3:26)

Second Lesson: Revisiting Volcanoes

Grades 4 Through 6

First lesson: Revisiting Tectonic Plates with video (Pretty Big Digs, 3:26)

Second Lesson: Revisiting Volcanoes

Revisiting Tectonic Plates

In exercise 5.4, your class explored tectonic plates and learned how natural forces created mountains and valleys. In exercise 5.5, they investigated how volcanoes can destroy established terrains and create new islands and surfaces. From ancient times to the present, humans have built monuments (Stonehenge), fortifications (the Great Wall of China), large tombs (the Great Pyramids), and aqueducts (Roman) on a massive scale. The fabrication of these monumental projects used to take generations to complete, but 20th- and 21st-century technologies have changed the way we move the earth.

Instructions

1. Watch Pretty Big Dig (3:26) from the list of video links in HK*Propel* to see machines become dancers in this construction site ballet.

2. After watching the video, explore movement ideas inspired by earth-moving machines, including excavators, backhoes, bulldozers, power shovels, drilling rigs, and tractors.

3. Ask your students work in small groups of three to five to create a real or imaginary earth-moving machine.

4. Once they've created their machines, invite them to create a short, repeatable movement phrase for the machine to perform.

5. Brainstorm ideas for a larger piece of choreography, perhaps depicting the before and after showing how the machines have changed the terrain.

6. Lead a discussion about the challenges of creating the individual machines and the longer choreography your class created.

7. Create a journal entry prompt for your class to respond to.

EXERCISE 7.8   REVISITING VOLCANOES

Lesson Plan Suggestions

Kindergarten Through Grade 3

First lesson: Revisiting Volcanoes

Grades 4 Through 6

First lesson: Revisiting Volcanoes

Revisiting Volcanoes

In exercise 5.5, your class created dances inspired by volcanoes. The journal entry prompt for grades 4 through 6 was "Do people ever feel like volcanoes? Write a short paragraph depicting how a person might feel like a volcano: burning up inside and ready to erupt." Use that as a starting point for a discussion about the similarities between people and volcanoes.

Under pressure.

Instructions

The length of the dance is up to you.

1. Kindergarten through grade 3 students should brainstorm ideas together (tell students to remember exploring the volcano when it's calm and when it's angry and ask them what makes them angry and what calms them down).

2. Grades 4 through 6 can brainstorm together and refer to their journals.

3. Use any of the choreographic and presentation structures suggested in this or other chapters or create a new one.

4. Create together or in small groups.

5. After presentations, create questions to stimulate discussion about the process and the dances.

6. Create a journal entry prompt for your class to respond to.

People and Sky

Chapter 6 focused on the Sky. In the following two exercises, your class will re-examine elements studied in chapter 6 from a human perspective.

EXERCISE 7.9   REVISITING THE MOON

Lesson Plan Suggestions

Kindergarten Through Grade 3
First lesson: Revisiting the Phases of the Moon

Grades 4 Through 6
First lesson: Revisiting the Phases of the Moon

Revisiting the Phases of the Moon

In exercise 6.4, your class created dances inspired by the sun and moon. The dances highlighted their unique differences, with the changing faces or phases of the moon being one of the most distinct features. Ask students when and why people show different faces to the world.

1. Humans present different faces at different times (shy, confident, angry, happy) or keep their face neutral, keeping their feelings inside.

2. Kindergarten through grade 3 could combine dramatically expressive tableaus interspersed with movement inspired by those emotions.

3. Grades 4 through grade 6 could explore the idea of hiding feelings and rarely showing their true selves.

4. Or you and your class can brainstorm other ways to explore the concept of showing different faces to the world.

5. Use any of the choreographic and presentation structures suggested in this or other chapters or create a new one.

6. Create together or in small groups.

7. After presentations, create questions to stimulate discussion about the process and the dances.

8. Create a journal entry prompt for your class to respond to.

© Janice Pomer

Puzzled.

EXERCISE 7.10   REVISITING OUR PLANET

Lesson Plan Suggestions

Kindergarten Through Grade 3

First lesson: Our Planet

Grades 4 Through 6

First lesson: Our Planet (this may require an additional lesson if you wish to make this an in-depth choreographic assignment)

Revisiting Our Planet

In exercise 6.7, your class created dances inspired by all the planets in our solar system, except planet Earth. In this exercise, your class will look at Earth from the sky, its surface, and beneath the surface (in water and under it) and explore ways to communicate what Earth means to them. This exercise can do the following:

- Combine any movement ideas and vocabulary from previous chapters
- Reveal how your students feel about the planet: Is our planet something to take for granted, or is it something we must treasure and protect?

The length of the dance and how many lessons you spend on this exercise is up to you.

1. All grades should brainstorm ideas collectively.
2. Kindergarten through grade 3 classes can work collaboratively.
3. Students in grades 4 through 6 should work in groups on individual dances or create sections for a larger piece where all the groups to come together at the end.
4. Use any of the choreographic and presentation structures suggested in this or other chapters or create a new one.
5. After presentations, create questions to stimulate discussion about the process and the dances.
6. Create a journal entry prompt for your class to respond to.

SUMMARY

Congratulations for taking the helm through these 10 exercises! They represent just a few of the exercises in this book that you can revisit. The world revolves and life evolves, and so, too, do the exercises in this book. You and your students can explore more of the earlier exercises from a human perspective. Flip through the text, pick an exercise randomly, and see how many connections you can make between the patterns in nature and human societies and behavior, or invite your students to suggest exercises that they feel resonate with their life experiences. Seeing aspects of oneself in nature deepens our relationship to the world and can provide a source of strength and resilience. We are not alone; we are all connected.

Go to HK *Propel* to find audio files, reproducible forms, and a list of video links corresponding to chapter exercises.

© Janice Pomer

CHAPTER 8

Other Wonders

In chapter 2, your class grew roots and leaves and blossomed flowers. In chapter 3, your students grew paws and claws, horns and hooves, tails, scales, and feathers. In chapter 4, they rippled, swirled, surged, and bubbled. In chapter 5, they pushed and pulled, sculpted mountains, and ignited volcanoes. In chapter 6, your class painted the sky and danced with the planets. In chapter 7, your students explored commonalities between human behavior and the patterns in nature. The world is filled with wonders waiting to be discovered.

As a guest artist working in the schools, I have a finite number of classroom visits before I move on to work with another group of students. On my last classroom visit, I always take a moment to let the teacher and students know that my leaving doesn't mean their dance program has to end. In fact, it's really the beginning because now they have all the tools they need to continue exploring and creating dances inspired by the moving world on their own.

The same is true for you and your students. This chapter contains a short list of other wonders to explore—plants and animals not examined in chapters 2 and 3, water and earth events omitted from chapters 4 and 5, and cosmic occurrences not included in chapter 6—and when you've finished exploring those wonders, you and your students can create your own list of natural wonders to explore.

Here's a helpful overview of the process you've been following throughout the book. Refer to it whenever needed.

1. After you've selected an element in nature for dance inspiration, do the following:
   - Collaboratively compile a list of what students know or imagine about the element.
   - Explore ways of translating their ideas into movement.
   - Invite students to share their discoveries with the class in discussion and by demonstrating.

2. Revisit the list your students compiled.
   - Is there any additional information, or are there more ideas or images to add?
   - Have you addressed all the unique aspects of the subject?
   - Would books or videos provide additional information?

3. Besides considering the individual subject, see if you have also considered the following:
   - Its habitat, terrain, or atmosphere
   - The impact it has on others and others' impact on it (role in the food chain, in an ecosystem, health of the planet, position in the cosmos)
   - Other relationships it has, such as being heliotropic (follows the sun) or part of a symbiotic relationship (oxpecker birds eat the ticks off of rhino and zebra hides)
   - Whether it's adapting to the changing environment

4. Create dances based on the information gathered and students' own imaginings.
   - Kindergarten through grade 3 work collaboratively.
   - Grades 4 through grade 6 work in small groups.

5. Refer to the Elements of Dance Chart (introduced in chapter 1) to remind yourself and your students to create dances using these elements:
   - Shapes at different levels, directions, and qualities
   - Different actions and movements; on-the-spot and traveling patterns
   - A variety of tempos and rhythmic patterns
   - A variety of spatial relationships
   - Dynamic energy and dramatic expression

6. Share the dance creations.
   - Use any of the presentation structures from the book or create your own.

7. Reflect
   - Use in-class discussions.
   - Have students write or draw in their journals.

Let the leadership experience gained in chapter 7 guide you, and if you are ever in doubt, ask your students for suggestions. They're on this journey with you, gaining confidence, developing skills, and deepening their relationship with nature. In the sections that follow, you will find some suggestions for exploring other wonders.

Plants

Cacti and the Desert Environment

There was a short exploration of plants with thorns in chapter 2, exercise 2.2. Use that as a starting point for examining cacti and the role they play in the desert environment.

Carnivorous Plants

Venus fly traps, pitcher plants, and sundews are carnivorous. Flies aren't all they eat. These plants trap and eat spiders, ants, frogs, and small rodents. Explore how their carnivorous diets evolved and how the process of trap, kill, and digest works.

Ferns

Ferns are prehistoric plants. Fossils of ferns date back 383 to 393 million years ago. Start by exploring movement ideas inspired by a fern uncurling from a tight fiddle-head shape and then expanding into a wide, multipronged frond.

Mushrooms and Fungi

Mushrooms are technically not plants. Ask students these questions: "How and where do they grow? How many types of mushrooms are there? Do you know any folktales or legends about mushrooms?"

Animals

Flightless Birds

Penguins can swim long distances and toboggan over ice and snow. Emus and ostriches can run up to 43 miles (70 km) an hour. Ask students these questions: "How and why did these birds develop those skills? Were they ever able to fly?"

Penguins.

© Janice Pomer

The Platypus, Jellyfish, and Other Unique Animals

The platypus is found only in Australia. It's a semiaquatic egg-laying mammal that has a duck bill (snout), a beaver tail, and otter-like feet. Jellyfish as a species are more than 500 million years old, which means they were swimming in Earth's oceans 250 million years before dinosaurs came into existence! Ask students if they can think of other unusual animals to explore (anteater, sloth, armadillo).

Animal Metamorphosis

Butterflies go through the stages of egg, larva, and pupa before turning into a butterfly. Dragonflies transition from egg and nymph (the nymph lives underwater) to dragonfly. What other animals go through metamorphic changes (frogs, beetles, spiders)? Can each student create their own Metamorphic dance?

Animal Architects

Beavers build dams, bees and wasps build hives, weaver birds build communal nests, and termites build tall and complex structures with soil, water, and their own saliva. Ask students if they can use the shapes of animal architecture to inspire choreography.

Water

Tsunamis

These giant, destructive tidal waves are caused by earthquakes and volcanic activity. Tsunami waves can be up to 100 feet (30 m) in height and travel 10 miles (16 km) inland.

© Janice Pomer

Running Waves.

Subterranean Rivers

About 30 percent of Earth's fresh water is found underground. Mexico's Sistema Sac Actun is the longest underground river in the world. Ask students these questions: "How are underground rivers different from rivers on the surface? Do subterrain rivers have their own ecosystems?" Imagine being water that never sees the sky.

Hurricanes and Typhoons

These severe tropical storms are fueled by warm, moist air. Ask students this question: "How does something so simple (warm, moist air) transform into a deadly storm with gale-force winds, high tides, and pounding rain capable of destroying coastal communities and island nations?"

Icebergs

Icebergs are pieces of ice that have broken off glaciers or an ice shelf. The act of breaking away from the glacier is called *calving*. These majestic shapes float in the ocean and move with the currents. Only a small portion of an iceberg is above water—90 percent of an iceberg is underwater. Ask students if they knew that all glaciers and icebergs are freshwater.

Earth

The Carbon Cycle

One of the most important natural cycles on Earth is the carbon cycle, an ongoing process where carbon atoms travel from the atmosphere to Earth and then back into the atmosphere. Explore movement ideas for the individual stages of the cycle and connect them to create a Carbon Cycle dance. Ask students, "What happens when the natural balance of the carbon cycle is disrupted?"

Earth's Core

There's so much movement beneath the earth's surface. The earth's crust and tectonic plates were examined in chapter 5; now dig deeper and explore earth's outer and inner core. Ask students this question: "Did you know that the earth's cores spin in different directions and that the cores are responsible for the magnetic field that protects the planet?"

Gemstones

Many of us have collected stones—smooth, round stones; oddly shaped stones; skipping stones; or a stone to remember a favorite place—but imagine a stone the size of your smallest fingernail being worth a fortune. Explore why gemstones are so valuable. Ask students this question: "What Earth energy caused the formation of diamonds, rubies, and emeralds? Why are they different colors and densities?"

Fossil Sites and Tar Pits

We think of tar and asphalt as synthetic products, but the earth has deposits of naturally occurring tar and asphalt, and unlucky prehistoric animals that entered the pits became stuck and died, so their remains are preserved in the tar. Sedimentary rock is another way Earth's top layer preserves the past; fossils of dinosaurs and cellular life forms are entombed in rock.

Sky

Comets

Comets are comprised of frozen water, gases, rock, and stardust. Think of a giant snowball hurtling through space. They orbit elliptically around the sun just like planets. When the heat of the sun warms the comet, gases are released, and that's what makes their fiery tails.

Constellations

The constellations of the northern and southern hemisphere have many names and various origin tales. Select a constellation and use one of its origin stories as an inspiration for dance.

Supernovas

In the final moment of a star's life, it becomes a supernova, a massive, luminous explosion. In approximately 5 billion years from now, our sun will become unstable and explode. Revisit your Sun dance and add a supernova ending.

Our Galaxy

Our solar system exists in the Milky Way Galaxy. Ask students, "What does our galaxy look like? How was it formed?" Use images from the Hubble telescope to inspire your students' dances.

CLOSING THOUGHTS

You will never see the same cloud twice. The world is filled with wonders waiting to be discovered. Take your class on wonder walks through their community and create dances inspired by all the wonders they see—a plant growing in cracked pavement, bubbles trapped under thin sheets of ice, a murmuration of starlings swooping overhead, or an abandoned wasp's nest suspended from a tree branch. The wonders never end. Through these nature-based movement exercises, your students have learned about themselves and the world. In nature, there is beauty, strength, conflict, and fragility, and those qualities exist within each of us, our families, and our communities.

I have always been fascinated by nature's micro- and macrocosms, the cellular worlds in our bodies, and the interconnectivity of the universe. In this book, I've shared my curiosity and passion for nature with you and your students in the hopes that these dance experiences deepen your relationship to the moving world we live in.

 Go to HK *Propel* to find audio files, reproducible forms, and a list of video links corresponding to chapter exercises.

About the Author and Composer

© Barry Prophet

Janice Pomer has been teaching, performing, and creating in the fields of dance, music, and theatre in Canada since 1976. Based in Toronto (Tkaronto), Ontario, Janice offers dance and creative movement experiences for learners of all ages and abilities in urban, rural, northern, and First Nations communities by visiting schools, postsecondary institutes, dance studios, and cultural centers.

Pomer is the author of two previous Human Kinetics titles: *Perpetual Motion: Creative Movement Exercises for Dance & Dramatic Arts* (2002) and *Dance Composition: An Interrelated Arts Approach* (2009). She creates study guides for boards of education, provides dance resources for dance companies and festivals, and designs interactive school tours and programs for art galleries and museums that incorporate creative movement as the catalyst for deepening students' understanding and appreciation of the exhibits.

For more information about Janice's work, visit https://janicepomer.ca.

Barry Prophet is a composer, sound artist, installation artist, sculptor, and educator whose music has appeared in galleries and theatres in Canada, the United States, and Europe. Creating unique sounds since 1979, he has been praised for his innovativeness: "Prophet gently blows the doors off our settled notions of timbre and tonality" (Robert Everett-Green in *Globe and Mail*). He performs traditional and experimental percussion (including his microtonally tuned glass percussion performance sculptures), electro-acoustic compositions, and environmental sound art.

© Barry Prophet

Barry's outdoor interactive sound sculptures include "Synthecycletron," commissioned by New Adventures in Sound Art as a seasonally permanent attraction on Toronto Island (2007-2018), and "Sound Booth," which was part of W.K.P. Kennedy Gallery's Ice Follies 2010 exhibition and was later featured in the book *Mobitecture: Architecture on the Move* (Phaidon, 2017).

Books

Ebooks

Continuing Education

Journals ...and more!

US.HumanKinetics.com
Canada.HumanKinetics.com